TEXTILE PRINT DESIGN

TEXTILE PRINT DESIGN

A how-to-do-it book of surface design

Richard Fisher
Adjunct Assistant Professor

Dorothy Wolfthal
Assistant Professor

Textile / Surface Design Department
FASHION INSTITUTE OF TECHNOLOGY

FAIRCHILD PUBLICATIONS

Victoria Arthur, Designer

Standard Book Number: 87005-513-5
Library of Congress Catalog Card Number: 86:80236

Printed in the United States of America

F.I.T.
COLLECTION

🪷 Preface

This is a how-to-do-it book. Its purpose is to guide the beginner into a career in textile print design. Step by step it outlines the process of creating original designs for commercial use. It is primarily aimed at students and teachers as well as people in other visual arts fields who are interested in designing for the textile industry.

Textile *print* design is the process of creating original artwork for the purpose of printing on fabric. We begin with research of the immediate needs of the marketplace. With paint, brushes and paper, designs are created for commercial uses.

The sequence of chapters reflects the unfolding progression of the design process. Beginning with a review of the products requiring design, we discuss the importance of research, the tools and supplies needed, the elements of design the artist is continually involved with, and then a description of how to proceed. The chapter on techniques is large since the ways of working are many. In fact a variety of techniques is found throughout the book.

Having developed a group of designs, it is part of the plan to present them and to sell them in a professional manner. Portfolios are discussed in Chapter 7. It is necessary for the professional designer to have a working knowledge of the production methods used in printing the patterns. Repeats and color combinations are central to this process. The last chapter discusses business practices, invoicing, copyright, agents, as well as the jobs and careers possible in this field.

The discipline of textile print design deals primarily with the apparel and home fashion industries. But the professional designer is not limited to these alone. Designing for many other products requires the same skills and procedures described in these pages. Wallcovering, advertising design, package design, paper products, greeting cards, housewares, printed rugs, and domestics, are some possibilities. Shifting from one industry to another and from one product to another is more easily accomplished by the trained artist. We want to stress the value of the textile design discipline as a training for many other visual arts. Craftsmanship and artistic skills, marketplace and production know-how, color sensitivity and understanding, business and sales procedures, are common to all the industrial arts.

There is an important area of textile design which deals with *woven* design. As the title implies, we are concerned here with *printed* surface design. However, exciting designs and textures can be printed which are derived from woven fabrics.

What is textile print design? "*Design* is the organization of parts into a coherent whole. Although it is considered to be a human expression, design is in reality the underlying process by which the universe was formed through orderly procedures of *selection* and *evolution*." So says Marjorie E. Bevlin in *Design Through Discovery*.

And so it is with textile design—we are involved with *selecting* the colors, motifs, techniques, etc., the elements of design that we wish to use. Through an *evolving* process, we integrate these various elements into a unified whole. Textile *print* design is the process of creating original artwork for the purpose of printing on fabric. We begin with research of the immediate needs of the marketplace. With paint and brushes, designs are created for commercial uses. Industry production methods impose limitations on the design in order that the artwork can be printed.

Many millions of yards of apparel fabric are printed each year in the United States. The textile apparel industry is one of the largest employers in the country. Many additional millions of yards are printed for the home fashion industries, and the demand for new and original designs is large.

Printing patterns on cloth is an ancient art and the history of textile print design is a fascinating study. Egypt 4000 years ago, China, Greece, Oceanic cultures, Peru and Mexico, France and England from the 12th century on, Scandinavia, Africa, all are inspiration for the designer. Every culture and every country has a textile design tradition and from these rich sources many works today are created.

Textile print design is a *graphic* art. We use the word *graphic* here to mean for the purposes of printing—using some form of reproduction such as a printing press or a silk-screen frame. The word *pattern* is used to mean the continuous repetition of the design as it prints along the length of the yard goods, dress or drapery material, as well as wallcovering material. This is one of the most basic aspects of textile design.

Most of us tend to use the word *fashion* when referring to clothing and the apparel market. The "world of fashion" is glamourous and exciting and like a barometer it reflects our cultural trends and tastes. In a larger sense the word *fashion* is used to mean the marketplace: what people are buying, what is the latest "in" look or direction a particular product is taking. And this idea can apply to many products other than clothing. This is more apparent when you think of automobiles and the industrial product design field in general, or perhaps the style of houses that is currently popular, or more dramatically the latest rock group. Fashion goes hand in hand with merchandising.

In many ways the textile print designer and the fine artist have much in common: both are creative, both have a love of craftsmanship and continually strive to refine similar skills. Both explore the possibilities and limitations of whichever media they choose, from photography, oil painting, printing inks to gouache, pencil, etc. Both are committed to their work. Both are deeply involved with the visual arts. Essentially the textile designer is an artist. In fact many fine artists also practice textile design.

But there is one important area in which the professional designer differs from the fine artist. The artist when working in the fine arts field responds to an inner voice when it involves the integrity of his work, and is not primarily concerned with what others think. *The professional designer* responds to the marketplace, to the requirements of industry, to the needs of the manufacturer and sales personnel, and to the demands of the consumer.

Professionalism means being flexible, adaptable, and willing to vary techniques, color, and designwork to suit the needs of industry. Designers respond to trends, cultural changes, marketplace demands, production limitations, and sales pressures. And to all of this they bring artistic skills and sensitivity.

What is creativity? Creativity is an essential ingredient in every human being. Some of us have talents in specific areas, such as music, writing, sculpture, painting; or in organizing a business, planning a party, assembling a machine. Creativity is present in each of these pursuits, although many people have convinced themselves that they are not creative, as if it were an absolute fact. But they can begin, with hard work (and many mistakes) to unfold their dormant creative potential.

In general the creative process involves an initial stage of searching and struggling with tentative solutions. Then there may be a period when we "put it aside," intentionally forget about it, see a movie, read a book or go to bed. Later a solution can "pop up" unexpectedly. Or, possibly when we sit down to work again a new direction will come forth. It seems that the unconscious mind needed the time to scan the various options.

It is conceivable that the artist is completely unaware of this chain of events. Awareness may not be necessary. The spontaneity and freedom of artistic expression can come by receptivity to the creative process.

1987   *Richard Fisher*
Dorothy Wolfthal

Acknowledgments

In appreciation for their support and help we wish to thank:

- ❦ The Fashion Institute of Technology for the opportunity to teach and bring art and textile design to new generations of designers.

- ❦ To our students over the years, whom we have taught and from whom we have learned—and whose work appears on these pages.

- ❦ To our colleagues in the Textile/Surface Design Department for the constant interchange and sharing of ideas and information.

- ❦ To FIT's Edward C. Blum Design Laboratory ("the Design Lab") in the Shirley Goodman Resource Center, for making their priceless textile collection available to us in our research.

- ❦ To Jack Prince for his intelligence, wit and generosity to textile designers for more than a quarter of a century.

- ❦ To Peter Capo of Fresh Paint Studio for his assistance, trust, and friendship.

- ❦ Among those individuals and firms who graciously shared their professional experience and allowed us to use their works: Albert Zellers, Greeff Fabrics; Jerome Rossman, Fisher and Gentile; Geeta Manansingh, The Sublistatic Corporation; Gerry Robins, Cranston Print Works; Sonny Baron, Riverside Printers; M. Lowenstein; Joel Tro, Golding Industries; Erica Fineberg; American Printed Fabrics Council; the American Textile Manufacturers Institute; Philip Salaff, technical expert and friend; Anne Marie de Samarjay; Dorothy Tricarico; the Textile Designer's Guild for their informational material and for their unique role in conferring strength and aid to the profession.

- ❦ To Edward Newman, Ann Evans, Albert Strausman, Edward Seltzer and John Dowling for their encouragement and for generously giving their time and help.

- ❦ To our editor, Olga Kontzias who with patience, intelligence, professionalism and humor, helped us pull it all together.

- ❦ To David Wolfthal and Polly Fisher for their endurance.

To all these and to any others who may see their influence in this book, we wish to extend our thanks.

Are you in earnest?
Seize this very minute!

What you would do and dream,
You can begin it.

Boldness has genius, power
And magic in it.

Only engage,
And the mind grows heated.

Begin, and soon the work
Will be completed!

Goethe

❧ Contents

PRODUCTS & THE MARKET

Try to recall the many places where you have seen printed designs: on all types of clothing, for all seasons; in every room in the house, on such utilitarian items as dishtowels, cookware and paper napkins, as well as wall coverings, draperies, bedding and bath mats; practically everything in the nursery; in countless public places—offices, stores, hotels, motels, and restaurants; on all types of materials—paper, vinyl, laminates, leather, linoleum, and of course most especially on every type of fabric.

When you consider a career in print design, you can begin to see that there are infinite outlets for your efforts. These outlets—markets—can be separated into several major groups, plus a number of additional very interesting and sometimes esoteric categories.

The two major areas for design are the *apparel* and the *home fashion* markets. Both are extremely large and varied.

In addition, there are many perhaps less obvious outlets for the skills of the textile designer. A partial list of examples would include: *housewares and other home products,* such as dinnerware, china, pottery, mugs and glassware, cookware, kitchen appliances, and giftware. *Paper products,* such as gift wrappings, party products, playing cards, greeting cards, and various types of packaging encompass many more outlets for design skills. As a professional textile designer, you are concerned primarily with industry-oriented, mass-production products rather than handicrafts. However, there may also be occasional custom designing, the one-of-a-kind product for evening wear, wall hangings, screens, and other special purposes.

APPAREL MARKET

Clearly, the greatest number of designs sold for printed fabrics is in the field of apparel. In any given season one can see literally hundreds of different designs in the clothing sections of department stores and specialty shops, as well as in the catalogues, both large and small, that serve as the "stores" and "shops" for a good portion of the public. This apparel market probably represents the greatest amount of actual yardage of printed fabrics: the ready-to-wear clothing that most people buy.

Women's Wear Fashions are constantly changing, and possibly nowhere faster than in women's clothing. If you are going to design prints for

A journey of a 1000 miles must begin with a single step.

Lao-Tzu

Two major product areas for the designer are apparel and home fashion. Both are extremely large and varied.

women's apparel, you will become aware of fashion trends and influences, the changing directions of color and style with the passage of the seasons. The women's apparel field of textile design is extremely broad and varied, ranging from high-style couturier fashion to moderate-priced, mass market, and economy fashion. Women's clothing may include: blouses, dresses, sportswear, swimwear, lingerie, rainwear, outerwear, and formal wear for evening, bridal and special occasion gowns.

Women's *scarves* provide a large outlet for your designing skills. They may range from small casual kerchiefs through the distinctive "signature" scarves attributed to prominent fashion designers, to large, dramatic shawls. Scarves are sometimes manufactured from allover printed yard goods, but more characteristically, scarves fall under the category of *engineered* designs, (see **Chapter 4**), which are designed for their specific purpose and shape.

If you enjoy the ever-changing fashion world—fashion shows, high-style magazines, latest clothing trends—then you may find a stimulating, exciting career in designing printed fabrics for women's apparel.

Men's Wear Another segment of the apparel market for textile designers to explore is in *men's wear*. Fashion changes take place in men's wear too, although perhaps not as dramatically as in women's fashions. Still, designers remember the Nehru shirt, the leisure suits, the period of boldly printed shirts for men, the shifts from narrow to broad to narrow (and sometimes to zero) in lapel widths, pants, collars, neckwear, and shoulders. As new seasons come and go, fashions in men's wear are making more and more drastic changes. Men's fashion designers are always seeking new looks for the printed fabrics to be used in their collections.

Traditionally, prints are most likely to be used in men's wear in the following products: shirts, sportswear, sleepwear, loungewear, neckwear, beachwear, linings for coats, jackets and accessories. In some areas of men's fashions, conventions are hard to change; however, in recent years new designers are breaking away from tradition in men's wear, and with these changes we will also find new approaches to textile design for the men's wear market.

Children's Wear This is an area that falls into several groupings: infants' and toddlers' wear, girls' wear and boys' wear. Older children's apparel (that is for teenagers) is for the most part really at the young end of the adult market (juniors and young men).

For *infants'* and *toddlers' wear* over many generations the formula has been "pink for a girl, blue for a boy" with diminutive prints in delicate florals, and a gentle, babes-in-toyland look. In recent years, however, colors have been fresher and stronger and design ideas more varied creating a fashion world of its own. In the toddlers' market (ages approximately one to three) the designs on fabric begin to reflect the world and the times. Along with the flowers, ribbons, birds, and baby animals, we see comic-strip, TV and movie influences, current story lines and themes.

Practically everything infants and toddlers wear can be and often is made of printed material, even disposable diapers. The garments for this market may not require much yardage per item but this is compensated for by two important factors: first, some printed products for infants, notably diapers and bibs, are disposable and constantly replaced; second, there has always been an ongoing supply of new consumers!

Print fabrics would be used for such clothing as: shirts, sleepwear, overalls, outerwear, dresses, beach and playwear. A closely related design area includes the many accessories and furnishings associated with the nursery: blankets, carriers, strollers, playpens, swings, high chairs, mattresses. If you have a "hand" for whimsy, if you enjoy drawing figures and animals, if you have a knack for cartooning and illustrating, if you can paint delicate flowers, you may find the field of textile design for infants' and toddlers' wear inviting and rewarding.

Girls' and *boys' clothing* presents a distinct market with its own requirements. Pre-school and school-age children are interested in their clothes and children's wear can be whimsical, utilitarian, trendy—very

Prints are used on many products: blouses, dresses, swimwear, lingerie, men's shirts and sleepwear, and more.

often a reflection of the world and the times. (Rock music stars and groups appeal to children of all ages.)

A partial listing of children's apparel for which printed design fabrics are used includes: *for girls,* blouses, T-shirts, sweatshirts, dresses, skirts, swimwear, long and short pants and overalls, sleepwear and loungewear, underthings, outerwear and rainwear (including linings), accessories such as scarves, socks, umbrellas, and boots. *For boys:* shirts, T-shirts, sweatshirts, sleepwear, underwear, footwear, some outerwear, shorts, and swimwear.

Design & Market Considerations in Textiles for Apparel

Seasonal   The season for which a design is intended will have a strong influence on the look of the design. By far the greatest number of new textile designs appears in stores and on magazine pages in the spring. This is the season when there is an exciting burst of color and design. People are most receptive to a freshening of mood; usually the colors shown are brighter and lighter, new designs are introduced, and new trends in fashion and in textile designs make their appearance in the spring openings.

This mood extends into summer, and the designs continue to reflect the less formal life of the season. Colors are light and bright; cooler, lighter-weight fabrics are used for city as well as for beach, sport and vacation wear. Prints are in evidence everywhere and at all times, day and evening.

Toward the end of summer, the fashion world reflects a more serious feeling. Stores are featuring warmer fabrics and usually darker, richer colors, reflecting the approach of *fall.* In the course of a year, there are two periods when the fashion world watches for new currents and indications of changes. One is at the beginning of spring, which brings a lighter, more relaxed, less formal approach to fashion. The other is at the end of summer, when the fashions for fall are presented, and often the new looks are launched. Trends change from year to year, but as a rule, textile designs are less playful, more formal and richer as fall arrives.

Winter is a mixed picture, partly geared to the cold weather, partly to party clothes and accessories for the big holiday market, and partly to cruise and vacation wear. As a rule, cosmopolitan city winter fashions follow the fall indications: deeper colors, often including black; fewer florals; more small geometrics, paisleys, foulards, stripes, and plaids, all in a more somber spectrum. And then there is the *transitional* look, appearing at the time when winter fashions begin to look tired. This is a changing time, a little more colorful, with a somewhat lighter touch, but not yet spring-like.

Many of the fashion centers of the world are cities where there are changing seasons—New York, Paris, London. These are the places where most fashions originate. In the United States there are fashionable cities in the so-called Sun Belt, including Texas and California, where there are not such marked seasonal changes, and the fashion looks are adapted to the local climate.

Timing   New looks, designs and trends do not appear overnight in the stores, shops, and catalogues. Apparel textile designs are usually conceived and executed approximately a year before they are seen in the marketplace. It takes that long for the many steps along the way.

• *Step 1.* First an *idea* is conceived and brainstormed in discussions among stylists, color stylists, salespeople (who bring feedback from their clients), and designers. Some *preliminary sketches* are made, and from the rough sketches a design is worked up into a *finished croquis.*

• *Step 2.* If the croquis sells—if a garment manufacturer decides to use it, let us say, for the spring line—the croquis is then *put into repeat,* usually by a repeat artist, but sometimes by the originator of the croquis, the designer (see **Chapter 8**). At the same time a *reference piece* is made and retained for use in making color combinations as well as for other purposes.

• *Step 3.* The finished repeat is then sent to be printed by one of several printing methods (see **Chapter 8**). The entire process may take six weeks or more.

Designs for children's wear can be traditional, or can reflect current fashion trends.

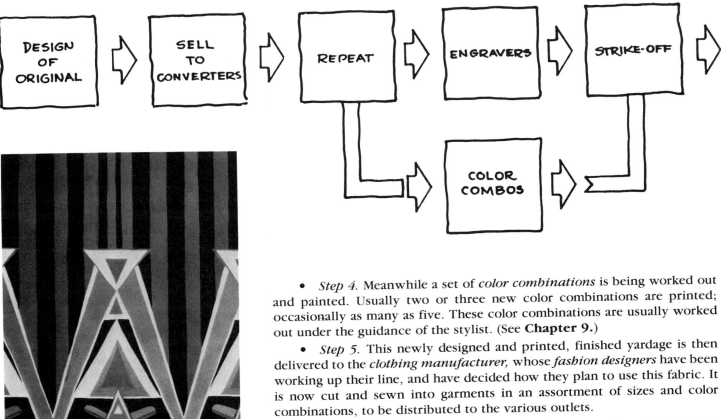

| DESIGN OF ORIGINAL | → | SELL TO CONVERTERS | → | REPEAT | → | ENGRAVERS | → | STRIKE-OFF | → |

REPEAT → COLOR COMBOS →

- *Step 4.* Meanwhile a set of *color combinations* is being worked out and painted. Usually two or three new color combinations are printed; occasionally as many as five. These color combinations are usually worked out under the guidance of the stylist. (See **Chapter 9.**)

- *Step 5.* This newly designed and printed, finished yardage is then delivered to the *clothing manufacturer,* whose *fashion designers* have been working up their line, and have decided how they plan to use this fabric. It is now cut and sewn into garments in an assortment of sizes and color combinations, to be distributed to the various outlets.

- *Step 6.* The finished products—the dresses or blouses, gowns or swimsuits—are shipped to their final outlets, the retail merchants. Store and window displays, sales catalogues, and brochures are prepared. Advertising and publicity are called into play, sometimes locally, sometimes nation- or even world-wide. The last step, for which all the other steps have been taken, is that a consumer buys the garment and wears it. One of the satisfactions in the career of a textile designer, whether a beginner or an experienced hand, is to see the design which started as a rough sketch on a drawing board, displayed in a store window, featured in a fashion magazine, or being worn in public. However, by the time this happens, ten months to a year have elapsed and the designer has sent off into this same process a good many additional designs.

Trends and Changes If you are working as a textile designer for a studio, a converter or a fabric company, you will probably receive your instructions from a stylist, and it is up to you to translate these directions into textile designs. The stylist's responsibility in this regard is to seek out through various sources the ideas which eventually result in the firm's line for a particular season.

However, possibly you are free-lancing, or would like to be a stylist, or have plans to start your own studio. Or you simply would like to understand and become more knowledgeable about fashions in textile design. For any number of reasons it is extremely important to learn to sense trends and changes, to become aware of currents in the marketplace.

In general, textile designs for apparel may have a dated look after a year or less, because the "in" color of last spring is out this year, or the big, abstract dramatic look has been replaced by the small realistic floral. Sometimes you can give a design a new, current look by re-doing it in this year's colors. Converters and manufacturers sometimes use this procedure. The design is already their property, the screens already exist and they want to try to get further mileage out of the pattern. In this case they will usually have a new set of color combinations made up in a more current look. Occasionally this is enough to give life to a design for another season.

There are some looks in fashion, however, that are so distinctive, so recognizable, that in a year or so it becomes evident that the designs belonged to some particular period and are simply out of date, no longer in fashion. The reader may remember the "funky" look of the early seventies,

Cultural events influence the look of designs such as this adaptation from an Egyptian museum exhibit.

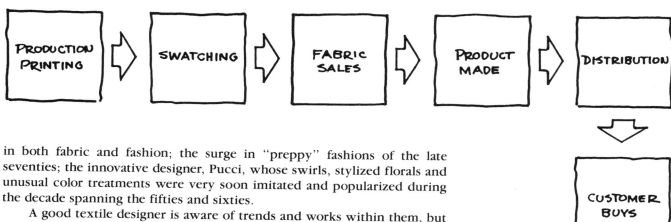

PRODUCTION PRINTING ⇨ **SWATCHING** ⇨ **FABRIC SALES** ⇨ **PRODUCT MADE** ⇨ **DISTRIBUTION** ⇨ **CUSTOMER BUYS**

in both fabric and fashion; the surge in "preppy" fashions of the late seventies; the innovative designer, Pucci, whose swirls, stylized florals and unusual color treatments were very soon imitated and popularized during the decade spanning the fifties and sixties.

A good textile designer is aware of trends and works within them, but avoids slavish imitation without originality. Sometimes the initial ideas come from the stylist, a salesperson, or a manufacturer. But there are times when new and influential directions have their start in the textile designer's studio—when a creative designer has read *Women's Wear Daily,* studied the latest issues of French or Italian *Vogue,* done his or her homework, and then decided that there are still some other ideas that could be developed. The artist may have a special style, a unique "hand" as distinctive as a signature (indeed an actual signature may eventually be used!). Often the artist has a quiet intuition or a sudden inspiration. These new ideas take shape on the drawing board and may capture the interest of an imaginative client; it is possible that the artist can influence the market, and a new look is born.

Fabric Surfaces An important factor the textile designer considers is the material on which designs are printed. In addition to changes in types of fabrics—warm or cool, light or heavy—the public's taste in fabrics is changeable from year to year. There was a time when the practicality of wash-and-wear, drip-dry synthetics, was most important to the consumer. The public, perhaps partially in response to ecology problems, began to desire the "natural" in many aspects of life, including clothing, and the natural fibers once again became popular. Pure cottons, silks, wools, and linens were in demand. However, the convenience and ease of synthetics were too appealing and various blends became popular: cotton/polyester, wool/nylon, etc. A large variety of *textures* on which designs are printed is used for apparel as well: knitted and woven fabrics; smooth, pebbly or rough; velvets, corduroys and velour to name a few.

For the textile print designer the factor of variety and change of trends in fabrics is important. You will learn that the nature of the designs that you create will be determined to a considerable extent by the type of material as well as the type of garment for which your design is intended. It will also be affected by the ever-growing technology, the state of the art.

We have observed the influences of the marketplace—fashion trends and seasonal changes. Even political, social and cultural events will influence what you design from week to week. A cultural event was the King Tut exhibit of a few years ago which traveled across the country and prompted a wave of Egyptian designs. A political event, such as the recognition of mainland China by the U.S. and the easing of trade restrictions, brought about the appearance of a whole range of designs and patterns with a Chinese look. Still another and very strong influence on the fashion world has been the vogue for science fiction. Futuristic films, TV programs, computer games, great strides in technology—these are reflected in print fashions across the board, including infants' and children's wear, women's and men's apparel, accessories, and evening wear.

In order to design successfully you will want to become attuned to all the influences and considerations of the market. Timing is important. Seasonal variations and fashion trends from abroad will be studied and adapted or rejected. Trade publications are helpful in sensing the pulse of the market. *Women's Wear Daily,* the newspaper of the fashion industry, is considered the standard, and is read by designers, stylists and others in the creative as well as in the business sector of fashion.

It may take six months to a year from artist's original design to use of final product by consumer.

Specialization

A versatile designer can work the entire apparel field of women's, men's and children's wear, from top-of-the-line to economy clothing; or as sometimes happens, you may find one of these areas the most interesting and decide to specialize, perhaps creating printed designs for lingerie, or children's wear, or men's ties and neckwear.

Another type of specialization may occur cutting across the various markets. In this case, the designer may become expert, for example, at creating beautiful, lush florals, which might apply equally to blouses, lingerie and some girls' wear. (This also applies as well to the design field of home fashions and related products.) Another designer may have a very good "tight" hand for paisleys, foulards, etc., suitable to men's, boys' and some women's wear. Or perhaps the designer is clever at creating novel *conversationals* (see **Chapter** 4) which could be printed for infants', children's and some adult clothing, as well as for the home furnishings and paper products fields.

Designers can specialize in paisleys and other types requiring a "tight hand", in beautifully rendered lush florals, or novel conversationals. A versatile designer might work the entire range. (Facing page, © FISHER & GENTILE; this page: left, Design Lab, FIT; right, © DOROTHY WOLFTHAL.)

HOME FASHION MARKET

Home furnishings * materials are used in homes and commercial interiors, and include drapery, upholstery, and rugs. *Wallcoverings* are another home fashions product. *Domestics* refers to sheets, pillowcases, bedspreads, towels, facecloths, and other bath products. In addition there are also tablecloths, dishtowels as well as other kitchen and dining products. Terminology varies among studios, retailers, interior designers, engravers and printers and this can lead to difficulty in communication. However, in the language of the studio and of textile designers the term *decorative design* usually refers to artwork created for all these products.

Home fashions can be divided roughly into two categories, *high style* and *mass market*. High style would include the elegant, conservative look associated with classic decorating as well as the more advanced, experimental, daring concepts generally regarded as urbane, cosmopolitan, sophisticated which are also used for commercial interiors such as offices, some restaurants, and hotels. Fabrics and wallcoverings in the high-style market are frequently sold through interior designers and decorators.

Mass-market designs, naturally, are those with more popular appeal. These are the designs that appear in department stores, catalogues, and

*Another term used for *home fashions* is *home furnishings*. *Decorative design* is a term which includes all design work that is not apparel.

home-supply stores. Clearly, the high-style market has a lower number of sales, with the greater number of designs sold to mass-market manufacturers. Obviously, as a designer, you would be wise to aim for the mass market if quantity of sales is your goal. Although the latest fashions may be less likely to start here, the level of aesthetic content, nevertheless, can remain high.

As time goes on, the difference between the two is becoming less. Lifestyles, the influences of TV, cultural changes, and catalogue buying have made most products available nationwide and differences of style have become less pronounced.

Wallcoverings are frequently designed to work with drapery and upholstery fabrics. However, wallcoverings are a separate category. The demand for new designs each year is large, and many designers work up new directions aimed primarily at the wallcovering market. The sale of wallcovering designs exceeds the sale of designs for other home fashion products. To walk into a retail shop selling wallcoverings is like walking into an art gallery. There are so many books, so many manufacturers, and so many patterns and ideas, it is a feast for the eyes and the mind.

Wallcovering books are not only fascinating art collections but they are valuable tools for selling. Often, fabric swatches are included. Fabrics are often printed with the same pattern as the wallcoverings and are used for draperies or bedspreads. Photos of rooms using the same patterns are also included in these books and it is often quite dramatic how different from the sample the patterns appear in their photographed settings. Light and quantity of pattern and relationship with other colors and objects in the room all influence the look of the design. It helps the consumer as well as the professional decorator to visualize the effect of a design in context. It is a difficult feat and requires some experience to feel comfortable relating the scale of the pattern to the amount of wall space to be covered and to the size of the room.

The range of subjects found on wallcoverings is extensive including

almost any type of design imaginable. Flowers are popular; animals, objects of all kinds, textures, and scenics abound. Some wallcovering books specialize in kitchen-type designs, some in designs for nursery or children's rooms; and there are many selections for living rooms, bedrooms, restaurants, and offices. Just about any type of design can be found. Scenic murals and single panel designs are also available. This is an unusual area for design ideas which can cover the width of five and even more rolls of wallcovering.

Materials used for printing wallcoverings are paper, natural materials such as grasses and other fibers, fabrics, and vinyl (polyvinyl chloride, or PVC). Vinyl film is used extensively in the industry for its permanence and washability. It also presents no problem whenever it is necessary to strip it from the wall. The vinyl film is usually laminated to fabric or paper. This backing gives it the dimensional stability necessary for printing, registering, and hanging. Without this backing the film is like a sheet of rubber and stretches when printed, distorting the design. When paper, instead of vinyl film is used for printing, it is often coated with a clear vinyl liquid (similar to a varnish) for greater durability.

There are certain considerations that are unique to *drapery* design. Since draperies usually hang in folds, a single object or scene is broken up or truncated and the remaining forms and colors create an allover pattern. Like wallcovering the motifs are usually one way (right side up), but unlike wallcovering, borders are often found running the length of the goods. This is in consideration of the window applications of the drapery. The valance may also use the border motif. The scale of motifs for drapery may range from small to large and the fabric is usually 48 or 54 inches wide.

The same fabrics and designs used for draperies may also be used for *upholstery*. But with upholstery an allover tossed layout can be used as well, since the motifs need not be limited to a one-way direction. A special layout found in upholstery design is a *four point* or *star* layout as it is sometimes called. A single motif (a bouquet of flowers for instance) may make up the entire design. It is intended to be centered on a cushion or pillow. The

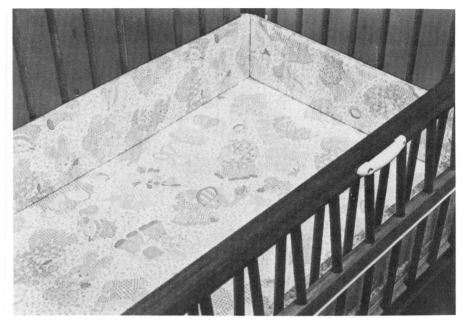

Infants' and toddlers' furniture uses vinyl film "fabric" with friendly, cheerful patterns. The products are designed to appeal to grandparents as well as parents.

bouquet then begins to reappear in the four corners of the cushion and if you look at the uncut fabric you will see the bouquet printed in a star type of layout.

Children's furniture uses a vinyl film product for high chairs, playpens, swings, crib mattresses, and other related items. The "fabric" as it is called in this industry is a laminate of vinyl film and a knitted cloth fabric (for stretchability). The vinyl is readily washable and is printed and embossed and finished for aesthetic and fashion purposes. The designs must sell the product and appeal not only to parents but grandparents. And changes of fashion are found in this market as well. Colors are friendly and the motifs can range from toys and stuffed animals to patterns of flowers and more sophisticated textures.

Outdoor furniture, including umbrellas, frequently uses large, splashy designs with bright, sun-drenched colors. Here too the upholstery material is often vinyl film.

Drapery and upholstery fabrics are especially exciting for the designer since the range of colors is large. Six colors are quite common; eight and even up to twelve colors are possible. Of course the production costs of the product increase in direct proportion to the number of colors used. Fewer colors are also found on upholstery as well. Wallcoverings can be printed in one to five colors, but here we can use *percentones* to extend the color effects (see **Chapter 9**).

Domestics is a general term that refers to sheets, pillowcases, quilts, comforters, towels and facecloths, bath mats and shower curtains, etc. Another term for this category is *bed-and-bath*.

It is not unusual to design bath products to relate to bedroom products in color, theme and pattern. Entire merchandising and selling programs are often developed in order to present these products to the consumer.

Bed-and-bath products differ from wallcoverings, draperies and other decorative materials in a most important way: they are not permanently installed, their cost is lower, and the consumer can readily change them to create a new look. As a result the designer of these products, somewhat like the apparel textile designer, must be more attuned to frequent changes in fashion and the current trends, and it follows, of course, that the number of designs sold is greater.

Shower curtains are another product with special design considerations. Rather than an allover pattern, we often find scenics or a single large motif filling the six-foot square curtain. The materials are vinyl film or water-resistant fabrics. Motifs are one way and range from seashells and seashore subjects to a Victorian "stained glass" look, pop-music themes, and

many more. Whatever is innovated as a new direction for any product, it must be timely and relate to current cultural interests if it is to sell.

A close relative to bath towels is beach towels sometimes called *beach sheets* since they are much larger than the standard bath towel. Printing on terry cloth eliminates fine line detail and the challenge is to invent motifs and techniques which are bold enough to be printed and legible on the textured terry cloth surface.

The specifications and sizes for home furnishings products such as towels and pillowcases can be measured at home, but the final specifications must be industry standards which are best obtained from the manufacturer. The designer should consult with his/her customer and clarify the design limitations and requirements before design work begins.

COLLECTIONS

A *collection* is a group of designs that *relate to each other* by having *a common denominator*—a theme that underlies each croquis. Each design is a separate and independent work, but there is a unifying factor that ties them together into a collection.

How Collections are Generated

Say, for instance, you are inspired to do a series of designs based on Chinese water motifs or oriental wave patterns. As you research such a theme, gathering visual materials from books, museums and picture collections (see **Chapter 2** about reference and research), many ideas will come to you and it will be possible to execute several designs that look different from each other but relate in subject matter. Scale can change as well as color; some sketches will introduce new motifs; one might emphasize a floral, another might emphasize a textural pattern.

If you are working in a textile design studio, the usual procedure will be something like this: the studio head, or stylist will have arrived at some decisions as to what the new designs—the line—should look like. The designer (you) will be given a description of what is required. Perhaps you will be shown some rough sketches, some color swatches and clippings from magazines and design services. You may be asked to develop a *group* of ideas of a particular type, not just one or two. You will probably work up a few rough, preliminary ideas, some *thumbnail sketches* or maybe *start a corner* of a few croquis (see **Chapter 5**).

There is good reason for this manner of working. First, as a designer

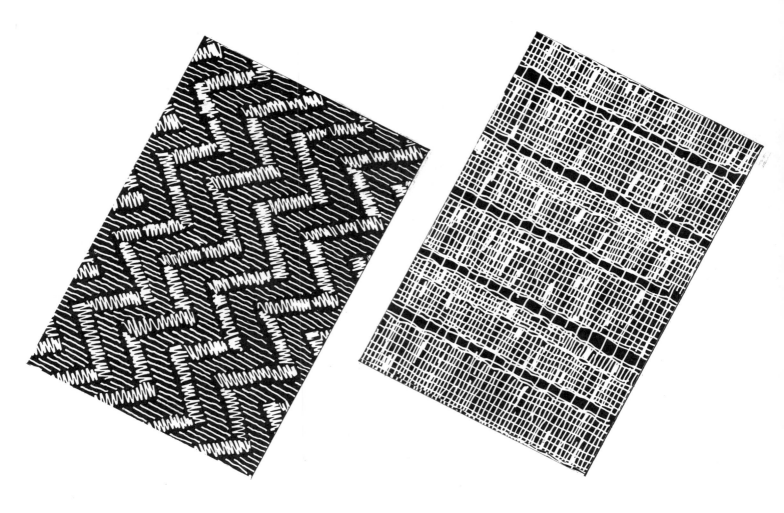

The unifying factor of this Print-a-Weave collection (top) *is the graphic interpretation of different woven effects. (See Chapter 3 for description of technique.)* © *RICHARD FISHER. This collection of designs (*facing page, bottom*), which is appropriate for apparel, is unified by a sports theme.*

starts to work, one idea leads to another, the creative juices flow, and several promising directions spring from this process. It's like a snowball effect. Each new idea produces still others and soon there is a swarming of possibilities. Secondly, you do not use your time painting a finished croquis until you have had the opportunity to select and reject among the ideas that have been conceived, and to make corrections and changes before going on to the finished artwork.

In this manner a *group* or *collection* is generated having some central theme or idea in common. It might be a group of designs based on a common historical documentary source; a group of florals with similar color treatment or technique; several designs following a particularly timely trend.

If you are an independent designer (a free-lancer) you would be wise to follow a similar procedure. You will surely be keeping current through the many research sources available to you. You will probably receive some direction from your contacts in the industry, including ongoing and potential clients. Based upon these sources as well as your own skills and instincts, you will develop a portfolio of designs with an integrated look, designs that go well together, based on a common theme and presented in groups of related types. When these are presented together as a collection, they assume more importance; they are more convincing to the potential buyer than a larger number of unrelated designs would be. They reinforce each other, have a greater impact and lead to more sales.

Collections for Home Fashions

Frequently, home fashion designs follow a *theme,* with documentaries and conversationals playing an important role. Here, research is especially critical. Several designs will be put together in a *group* or *collection* based on a particular theme.

There are special themes for commercial, institutional and public areas. In the home there are also special areas such as nursery, juvenile, kitchen,

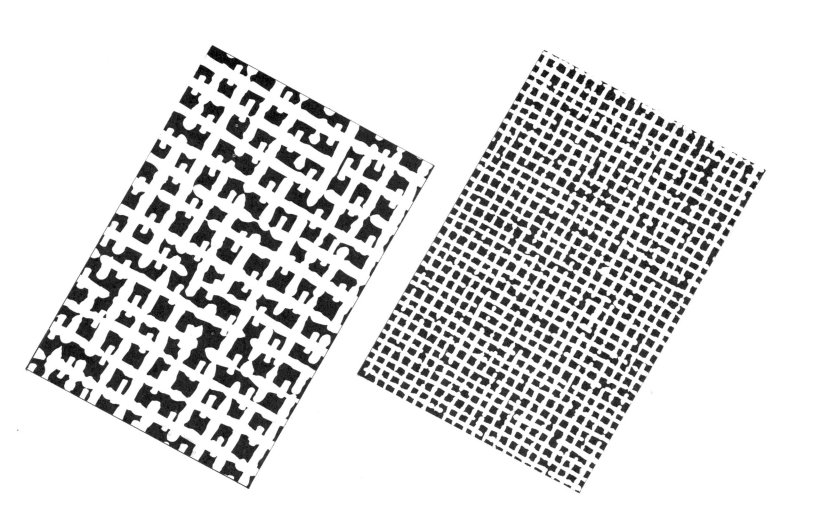

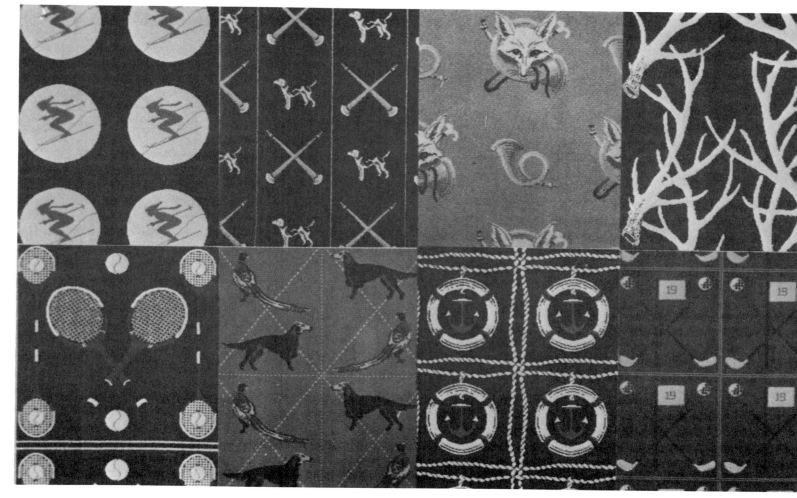

bed-and-bath, as well as general living areas. Some theme examples are: for the *nursery:* baby animals, stuffed toys, ribbons and bows, nursery rhyme characters; for the *juvenile* areas: clowns and circus, sports (football, baseball, tennis, etc.), outer space, Early American toys, and dolls; for the *kitchen:* botanicals, herbs and spices, cooking implements from other times and places, recipes, fruits, vegetables and other foods; for the *bath:* almost anything relating to water, such as sailboats, beach scenes, ducks, and swans, fish, waves, and clouds.

Other themes underlying collections are holidays, such as Thanksgiving, Christmas, or July 4th, and special occasions such as weddings and bar mitzvahs.

Themes for collections are often given commercially appealing titles such as "New York, New York" or "Living Desert", "Great Barrier Reef" or "Computer World." It is helpful to refer to the trade publications to see what names are currently being used. Trade publications also suggest reference sources (such as Henry Ford Museum in Dearborn, Michigan). Even though a theme has been promoted by a manufacturer in the past, it is still possible to originate a new look bringing in new colors and combinations of color, a new twist, your own unique way of seeing the subject.

"New Country Gear" was an example of an innovative manufacturing/ merchandising method. Many products were coordinated to each other, ranging from shower curtains, quilts, comforters, wallcoverings, and rugs, to ceramic dinnerware, related napkins and tablecloths, candlesticks, etc. What has united all these diverse products is the theme of American Country, and the colors derived from the American farm landscape.

The Jack Prince collection of "Aerobics" is another example of strong, vital merchandising acumen, coordinating many products into an integrated *unity* and using beautiful, contemporary design and color. In this case the vision of one artist has remained whole and intact.

Planning and researching a theme is very exciting and the development of the collection most rewarding. Another plus in designing a collection is the possible sale of more than one design. If a stylist likes the theme idea, he/she will probably buy many of the designs you are offering. Remember that each design must be unique and individual and stand on its own merits, separate from the others. Designs in a collection are always major works and can be sold individually or as part of a group.

COORDINATES

Two or more designs *made to be used together* are called *coordinates.* Some coordinates may be very simple allover textures lifted from a section of the original. Or the coordinate may be a secondary flower that is repeated in a set layout. These other designs that relate to the main design are often added to help individual customers as well as interior designers and decorators to integrate the room decor. Probably the most familiar group in which coordinates are used is the so-called *bed-and-bath* area. A bottom sheet can have one design; the top sheet may have the same or a similar design with a border (turn-back) using related motifs; pillowcases may be an *engineered* design made to fit the specified dimensions and using some elements from the border as well as from the sheets. The scale could change, the motifs take on a picture quality or possibly a frame-like border. Other variations of the motifs and colors could be used on a comforter and even a contrasting look (such as an allover texture) is possible provided it complements the original design. As for the bath: towels, shower curtains, and bath mats would all use variations of the original theme.

This principle of theme and variations is used throughout the home fashion field. Wallcoverings, draperies, and upholstery are often coordinated; in the kitchen, not only wallcoverings, curtains and towels, but also products such as cups and mugs, kitchen appliances, tiles, aprons, and oven mitts all may be coordinated in design, theme, and color feeling. Look through some wallcovering sample books to see the photographs of room

Bath towels in a contemporary style from the "Aerobics" collection by designer Jack Prince.

The unifying factors of these apparel designs are color, motif and technique. © *DOROTHY WOLFTHAL.*

settings using coordinated designs on walls as well as drapery, pillows, and furniture.

The principle of coordination is also frequently used in designing for *apparel fabrics.* The blouse, skirt, jacket or vest may be in coordinated designs, the skirt having a border, the blouse having some elements of the border in an allover pattern on a smaller scale, and the vest in a solid color, perhaps lined in the blouse pattern. Swimwear is often combined with a caftan or other beach cover-up in coordinated prints. In apparel, of course, these parts may be worn separately, combined with other patterns or with solids. However, the key to coordinates is that they look as though they are designed to be used together.

Examples of Coordinates

1. *Multi-floral with foliage*
    - One flower from above, using:
        a) Set layout
        b) Change of scale (larger or smaller than in original)
        c) More covered or more open, tossed layout
    - Foliage alone

2. *Floral with geometric design element as background*
    - Floral alone
    - Geometric element alone
    - Negative treatment of geometric element (light on dark or vice-versa)
    - Change in scale of floral

3. *Patchwork design*
    - Single element or motif from patchwork as allover design
    - Stripe or border incorporating some elements from patchwork design

4. *Conversational motif on textured background*
    - Texture alone
    - Conversational motif alone, using:
        a) Same size and layout as original
        b) Same motif in different scale (smaller, larger)
        c) Different coverage (more widely spaced, more covered)
        d) Texture in combination with solid color and conversational motif to create stripe, border or engineered design

5. *Multi-color abstract design, set layout*
    - Smaller allover pattern, using one element of original and only two of the colors
    - Stripe formed from one or two of the elements in the original design, using:
        a) All the colors of the original
        b) One or two of the colors of the original

6. *Negative-positive value or color treatment,* i.e. light-on-dark, and the same design dark-on-light

These suggestions are merely an indication of the many possibilities for developing groups of coordinates. You can also:

- Drop the blotch on an existing design and show the motifs on a white ground.
- When your design has an interesting outline treatment, try using for a coordinate, only the outline, possibly on a ground tinted in one of the colors of the original.
- Change the scale and/or coverage of the original design.

Coordinated designs are used in many product areas.

THE DIFFERENCE BETWEEN
COLLECTIONS & COORDINATES

Collections are groups of designs that have been developed around a theme or concept. They are not meant to be used together, but instead *have some central idea in common.* It may be the subject matter (Chinese water theme, outer space, circus, etc.), a re-interpretation of some currently popular idea (William Morris, Art Deco, Greek Revival, Art Nouveau, etc.), a special technique (ikat, batik, etc.), or the color look (muted pastels, stained glass, etc.).

Coordinates are sets of designs that are *meant to be used together* in the same costume or in the same room. They can consist of as few as two or as many as five or six or more designs all having some *design elements* and *colors* in common.

It must be emphasized that in creating a group of coordinates, *color is one of the most important unifying visual elements.* It is not necessary to use all the colors in all the coordinates, but they *almost always* have some colors in common. However, the ultimate criterion of a successful coordinate is that it complements the original design and works well with it.

ENGINEERED DESIGNS

Most textile designs are created for repeating, continuous patterns. An exception to this is in the field of domestics. Here, many products require *engineered designs,* created to be contained within a particular size and shape. Some of these products are pillowcases, bath mats, and shower curtains. For such products the textile designer creates a design to fit the specified dimensions much as an artist paints a picture to fit its canvas. The engineered designs (the ''pictures'') are then printed repeatedly on the yardage, cut apart, and manufactured into the finished products.

Another group closely related in the manner in which they are designed are the kitchen/dining products. Tablecloths and napkins, placemats, and kitchen towels frequently are produced using engineered designs.

In apparel, we also find engineered designs used, such as on scarves. A design can be made to fit the front panel of a vest, the back panel or possibly a sleeve running from shoulder to wrist. Skirts, too, may be engineered and even an entire garment (a dress from the neck to the hemline) can be one complete design without a repeating, patterned aspect.

COMPARISON OF HOME FASHIONS &
APPAREL TEXTILE MARKETS

Number of Designs

Many more designs are sold for the apparel market than for the decorative trade each year. It is to be expected that wallcoverings, upholstery, and drapery will be selected by the consumer with the intention that they will remain in place for a number of years. Generally speaking, this means a slower rate of change or fluctuation of fashion. It also means that fewer designs are created and sold in the field of decorative design.

When you walk through the blouse or dress department of a large department store you will see a great many patterns—large and small, engineered, coordinated. Visit the same department a few months later; the stock will probably be entirely different, with possibly a marked-down rack of the few remaining garments that you saw previously.

Do the same in the upholstery fabric department and you may find quite a different picture. There will be a large number of designs to choose from in a broad price range. But several months later you may find the selection essentially unchanged. Even a year or more later you will continue to be able to find a good number of the same patterns, which may in fact be on their way to becoming classics.

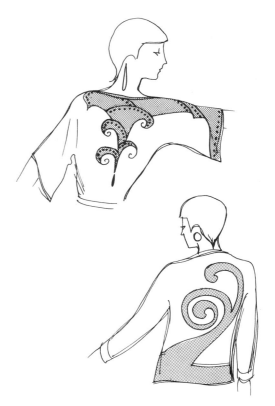

Engineered designs are created to fit within a particular size and shape. This applies to home products as well as apparel.

The skills and crafts used in designing for fabric can be used for surface design on many other products. They include dinnerware, cookware, and giftware. Party favors, cups, plates and napkins may coordinate around the same design idea. Greeting cards are another area utilizing design skills.

Timing

As previously discussed, apparel designs are usually executed about a year before they appear on the market (see **page 3**). This type of timing does not necessarily apply to decorative designing.

Duration of Selling Probability Apparel designs are sold during the season they are executed—the first year, with some chance that they will sell for the same season a year later.

This transience in the fashion field does not exist to the same extent in the world of textile design for the decorative field where an artist's design has a longer period of saleability. Unlike an apparel design which must be sold in the season for which it is created, a decorative design may be saleable many years from the date of its creation. The designs do not age rapidly as they do in the apparel field where a current look or vogue can change overnight and a new wave of fresh and exciting fashions takes the limelight.

Designs for the decorative market may sell even five to seven years after they are originated, or perhaps still longer. To be sure, there are fads and fashions in this field too; in recent years there has been High Tech, revivals of Art Deco and nostalgia designs recalling the thirties, the forties, or later. These become dated and are soon replaced by another fad. They account for no more than a modest percentage of the yardage sold in the decorative field, and a croquis for the decorative market is generally of more lasting sales value, as traditional types are less vulnerable to fashion trends.

Seasonal Changes In designs for apparel, the look definitely changes for the seasons of the year: spring, fall, holiday and cruise, transitional, all have recognizable characteristics.

There are some seasonal changes in the decorative field as well. The color look is lighter and fresher for spring and summer, with some designs showing an informal, playful, lighthearted approach. Vacation and beach houses are opened; outdoor furniture is in use. The same casual, relaxed feeling is reflected in city houses and apartments. For fall and winter the feeling is more formal, warmer; colors are richer and deeper. Still, the seasons do not play as important a role in the decorative market as they do in the apparel market.

Scale

Traditionally, floral as well as abstract and conversational motifs are larger for the home fashion designs than for apparel. But it is always possible to find exceptions, and you may see small floral prints on walls and drapery, and large upholstery-type designs on skirts and gowns.

Number of Color Combinations/Colorways

For the decorative field we find colorways vary in number from none (the juvenile furniture market considers a new color combination as a new pattern which competes with the original) to one or two for a limited market through as many as twelve to fifteen. However, it is costly to offer a large selection of color variations. Two or three colorways are most common, and we often see as many as five or six. In apparel, usually no more than three or four color combinations are printed for a single design for a single season.

Incidentally, the term *colorways* is heard most frequently in referring to decorative design, and *color combinations* is used more often in the apparel field. (Painting of color combinations is discussed in **Chapter 9.**)

OTHER PRODUCTS/OTHER DESIGN AREAS

A very exciting aspect of this textile design discipline is the possibility of designing for products other than those already discussed in this chapter. The skills and experience acquired in designing for apparel and home fashions can be used for other surface design, for instance, dinnerware, glassware, ceramic products, kitchenware, decorative packaging, wrapping paper, playing cards, greeting cards, printed rugs and carpets—in fact, any surface needing decoration and using a printing process has a direct connection to textile print design. The practices of market research, use of reference materials, execution of design ideas, customer relations, the translation of artwork to the printed product—all have common ground with the art of textile design.

Paper products including wrapping paper, is an extensive market with patterns closely allied to those of apparel fabric. Party products in which paper plates, cups, napkins, favors, etc., coordinate with the same design or under one theme idea (here the possibilities for design are extensive). Playing cards with score pads, coasters and napkins sold in sets; shopping bags for department stores, museums and other institutions have decorative design for promotional purposes; tissue boxes and many supermarket products need design ideas and skills.

Greeting cards are another category. They are often illustrational in nature since a message or story is intended. The textile designer finds him/herself quite capable of designing for this product as well.

Pantryware including electrical appliances, cookware, canisters and tins, are more products that constantly require new designs; *dinnerware* including porcelain china which has a high-style look, ironware and stoneware a more earthy look, and plastic tableware a bolder, brighter look.

There are many trade shows each year all around the country where the designer can research the markets and learn what has been and is currently selling. There is also the possibility of contacting the manufacturers in order to open new avenues for work. Chicago, Dallas, and New York—to mention a few—all have annual and semi-annual trade shows for distribution of products. In addition, many markets have permanent showrooms; an example is 225 Fifth Avenue, New York, which houses many housewares and giftware companies.

It is good to know that the skills and experience gained as a textile print designer can be readily adapted to the products mentioned above. There are still others unnamed here and with research into industry needs, design opportunities will readily present themselves.

WHAT TO DESIGN

The beginning designer is full of ideas, energy, ambition—can't wait to start putting brush to paper. However, no one, even the experienced designer, can create successfully in a vacuum. You are hoping to work for an industry that has specific needs and requirements in many product areas, constantly changing and developing as the seasons pass and as technology progresses. Contact is needed with the field for which you want to produce; inspiration and information from the larger world of the arts must be sought to feed your creative imagination. To be able to design successfully it is necessary to find answers to some basic questions.

- What products will you design for?
- How will you find the marketing and manufacturing requirements for these products?
- Where will you get the ideas for your designs?

It soon becomes clear that something more than talent and energy are necessary. You will have to develop habits of *research* that will stay with you throughout your career.

RESEARCH OF THE MARKET

Research means inquiry, examination, investigation. It's a form of detective work, seeking out answers, to get an understanding of which way to go, which choices to make. Even if you think you know what segment of the industry you want to aim for, take the necessary steps to be able to set realistic goals, and yet not close the door to possible options.

You could choose women's wear—top, middle, and mass-market. And women's wear can be further broken down into sportswear, evening and formal wear, lingerie, blouse, dress, swimwear, and more.

Children's wear also has a number of categories. How about the men's wear field? Or maybe not apparel at all, but rather the home fashions field would be more interesting. Should it be drapery, upholstery, wallcoverings, or products for the bed-and-bath area; or perhaps kitchen/dining, including the interesting accessories, such as napkins, placemats, pot holders, aprons, towels? Maybe one-of-a kind items?

In order to avoid total chaos and confusion, not to mention a great deal

For inspiration and excitement, research past periods and current trends.

An early American quilt is the inspiration for a GREEFF fabric. Border as well as motifs are faithfully reproduced in this documentary design.

A design for infants' furniture was inspired by toy animals. The product for which you design will suggest motif, color and technique.

of wasted time and energy, some limits must be set, some tentative goals determined.

Which Products?

To help you decide what product to design for, you must first find the need. What do the manufacturers need? What is selling? What do consumers want or better still, what will they want next season? How can a beginner seek out—research—the answers?

1. *Study the publications*—fashion and interior design magazines, trade magazines. Most libraries have complete listings of periodicals in all categories, as well as collections on their shelves. Some can be borrowed, others studied in the libraries. Become familiar with the leading ones. This does not necessarily mean subscribing to them. In general, this is too costly, although occasionally you may wish to buy a particular issue which is especially rich in ideas.

2. *Get out into the stores.* Spend a day or two searching the department stores, shops, and boutiques. Look at the window displays, the textile designs being featured at various price levels. Look at what has been marked down. Try to figure out why the marked-down items haven't sold. Go into the children's wear department, the men's wear; look at sheets, towels, upholstered furniture. Study the model rooms. Are there lots of prints being shown? Keep a sketchbook and make notations that you can refer to later. Remember, at this point you're trying to acquire information to help you make some basic decisions.

3. *Talk to salespeople.* Retail salespeople have regular contact with the buying public, and can be a valuable source of market and career information. Salespeople connected with textile studios and converters work with artists, buyers, fashion designers, and manufacturers. They can give you a good picture of the business from their particular point of view.

4. *Visit studios.* A chance to talk with artists and stylists, to observe the way a studio works, would be an invaluable aid in guiding the beginner in the direction to go. However, a textile design studio is a busy place where time and space are limited and valuable. To arrange a visit you must call or write in advance; explain your purpose, ask for an appointment, perhaps with an opportunity to show any work you may have done. You may strike a sympathetic chord with someone who is interested in guiding a beginner and answering your questions.

There are large manufacturers and converters who maintain their own studios. Some of these occasionally open their doors to groups, usually art classes, and give tours and explanations of their operations. They might also be receptive to an inquiry by a serious, interested individual.

5. *Visit engravers and printers.* A very valuable source of information is the supplier: the engravers and printers who have contact with many companies and market trends. New fabrics and designs can be seen while they are being produced. One example, Riverside Printers in Buchanan, New York, is a hand-print (silk-screen) plant actively engaged in the wallcovering market. Designs are contemporary, and Riverside offers an innovative custom service. A visit to this supplier is an education in what types of designs to create, the customers who will buy them, how to distribute the samples and how this customized color system responds to the preferences of decorators and customers.

6. *Collect catalogues.* In recent years *catalogues* (*e.g.* Sears and Spiegel) have grown to be a more important merchandising tool. Some catalogues aim at people who have become more affluent but do not have as much time in their busy work schedules to shop in stores as in the past. The products sold in these catalogues are generally of high quality and the convenience of catalogue merchandising is obvious.

Sales brochures inserted as newspaper supplements as well as those mailed out by leading department stores can help you understand the market for many products: the current trends, the price levels, color preferences, the actual size requirements of various products, how they are presented, and how merchandizing needs affect the designs.

7. *Talk to manufacturers.* A valuable source of information about any product is the manufacturer himself. He has his fingers on the pulse of the market for his products and is keenly aware of the competition as well as the market trends. Talk with their stylists, visit trade shows, ask their salespeople about trends, colors, and general directions of their products. Information is gladly given if they realize you are a designer and will contribute to the flow of new work for their products.

You have been trying to determine the needs of manufacturers, salespeople, and consumers. This preliminary research has been an effort to help you set limits, to define your endeavors.

Now further research is called for, this time into specific products. For home fashions—upholstery? drapery? what room? What should be the mood? Begin to acquire photographs of interiors. They can be found in countless magazines, newspapers, brochures. Visit shops, interview interior designers and decorators as well as wallcovering shopkeepers and sales personnel, this time to learn the particular requirements. What's the difference in the types of designs for the "uptown market" and the "mass market."

In the field of wallcoverings, so closely related to upholstery and drapery, there are hundreds of manufacturers, thousands of wallpaper books in shops in every town. Each shop is an art gallery in itself. The books are fascinating to leaf through, and they can give you a clearer understanding of trends, specific markets, merchandising techniques, and targets where manufacturers hope to sell their products.

For *apparel,* the most readily available resources of market trends are department stores and boutiques. Really study how a printed fabric looks as a dress, as a swimsuit, as a blouse. How do these differ in the various price categories? How do these prints compare with the ones used for lingerie, or for evening wear? Is there a difference between the prints for junior wear and clothing for a more mature market? Look at babies', toddlers' and children's wear. Do these prints have a distinctly different look in scale, coloring, subject matter? How are prints used in men's wear?

Your sketchbook by now is probably filling up with the results of your observations. We have considered the *markets* for textile designers to research; what products to design for, where the needs are. Further research into the needs of these various markets was suggested, and how they differ from one another.

The different products, however, do not stay the same from season to season. Whether you're interested in the apparel field or in home furnishings, wallcoverings, domestics—there is a factor that exerts a constant, dynamic influence: the ever changing tides of *fashion*. A great deal of study has been made of the subject of fashion: how it has influenced people, how it is manipulated; how it is a reflection of political and sociological developments throughout human history. It is a fascinating subject, with many levels of meaning: custom, style, trends, manners, and is understood differently in different cultures. As an integral part of the textile designer's career, the currents of fashion must be under continual examination.

Fashion has two broad meanings: for the clothing industry it is specifically the trends and innovations of the fashion world, high style and next year's look in clothes. In a larger sense fashion means the marketplace: what is marketable, what will people buy. This applies to any and all products: automobiles, houses and furniture, the latest in television and electronic gadgetry and entertainment, etc.

There is a guiding principle that can give you a broader point of view, an understanding of which way to go and what kinds of designs are likely to be well received in the near future:

First Steep yourself in the history and traditions of textile design and visual arts of the past—China, Japan, India, Egypt, Europe, the Americas; past eras, ancient and recent history throughout all areas of the world. Your resources are many, readily available and not necessarily expensive. Most cities have museums and galleries, and historical societies, often with gift and book shops where you can get cards, reproductions, catalogues of exhibitions, prints, and books. Special events in the art world such as museum exhibits focusing on particular art periods, collections, or artists' retrospectives are very rich sources of design material. They often have a strong, immediate impact on the entire fashion and decorative world.

Many colleges and universities maintain well-stocked libraries and have permanent collections in their own museums and galleries. In addition they often host temporary collections and exhibitions. These are usually available to artists and designers for research. Most libraries have sizeable collections of historical art as well as picture collections from which you may borrow. In New York, the Public Library at 41st Street has an invaluable picture collection which has been a rich source of ideas to textile designers for years. The Donnell Library, in New York, specializes in art books and periodicals. At the Fashion Institute of Technology, in New York, the Design Laboratory is an elegant resource for research and inspiration. The collections of fabric swatches and fashion accessories are extensive. The Textile Museum in Washington, D.C. is another exciting source for the designer. For additional resources see **Appendix.**

Certain periodicals, such as *National Geographic, Smithsonian,* and *Connoisseur* are useful sources for research into the history and traditions of design of people, places and periods. See **Bibliography** for a more complete listing.

In addition to learning about other lands and peoples, it is important to learn about the trends and fashion looks of the *immediate past*. What was last year's major theme? What did consumers buy in wallcovering and upholstery designs? What types of prints were used in women's wear (blouses, dresses, etc.) for the past three spring and summer seasons? This is the first stepping stone to knowing—with confidence—the new look.

Second Become thoroughly familiar with what is being done *now*—what is in the department stores, in fashion and trade magazines; what is

A photo of an antique vase in a magazine was the inspiration for a new design.

Learn about the visual art of the past from libraries and museums. Get to know the look of today's products

current in the manufacturers' showrooms. In other words, what is *today's* marketplace. Talk with your fellow designers. Read the newspapers. The metropolitan press reports regularly on fashions in home furnishings and apparel, as well as on art and design trends. Newly arrived designers and artists may be the subjects of feature articles full of useful information if you learn to seek it out.

As mentioned elsewhere, *Women's Wear Daily* is *the* daily source of information in the apparel market. *Home Furnishings Daily (HFD)* offers the same kind of trade information in the decorative field.

By knowing what happened in history, what was "in" five years ago and what was last year's look, as well as what is current *right now* in the fashion world, we begin to sense trends and anticipate directions. The formula: PAST + PRESENT leads to FUTURE (the next step).

Third It is essential, then, to take *the next step:* not what might be *great* in five years, "way out," but what follows from the past and the immediate present. This way a designer or stylist may be able to turn the fashion trend in a new direction and create a new look.

So far the process sounds very intellectual. Although an analytical understanding of trends is helpful, in the long run professionalism is also a matter of feelings, of your artistic instincts. Feelings are essential to this guiding process and intuition is all-important. Ultimately, an artist responds to his/her inner voices. The professionals who are on top of it all, who are the leaders, know the market *and* honor their intuition as well.

Professionalism, then, is the result of a number of factors; a thorough grounding in the *past* and *present,* and continuous research in the marketplace, into *what is.* Fashion influences and is influenced by what is going on in the world, from Iran to China, from Paris to Buenos Aires, from London to Dallas to New York. And it includes your immediate world: the city, the seasons, TV, the latest rock-group message, the merchandising world (what is currently happening with products for which you wish to design).

To paraphrase a statement of Robert L. Green, a noted analyst and raconteur of the fashion world—listen to the lyrics of the newest music and you'll find the latest cultural trends coloring the teenage markets—and these markets are highly influential on much of the clothing industry. As a professional designer you will also learn to listen and respond to the many voices of the marketplace.

There is great pleasure to be found in research discoveries. Searching out a subject in depth, finding all there is to know about it, exploring the various facets and aspects of it, learning of other cultures and peoples of different lands and other times—these are all part of a career in textile design. Your research can broaden your personal horizons and understanding of art, and is a continuing source of inner satisfaction.

REFERENCE MATERIALS

Start to build your own reference collection. In fact it will be hard to avoid accumulating all types of visuals. The cards and catalogues that you acquire on your visits to museums and galleries may be a start. Soon you will add clippings from magazines and newspapers; art calendars, which are often beautifully printed, provide reproductions of artwork, nature prints, animal pictures, and more. In fabric and department stores you can buy small swatches of fabric that have some particular appeal to you. Remnant stores, thrift shops and flea markets are additional sources of fabric samples from earlier decades. Your choice of these collections reflects your own highly personal tastes and preferences. They are a good barometer of who you are and what you like, a process of self-discovery.

Very carefully and selectively start collecting reference books. On your visits to libraries, make notes of the books that you feel might be valuable design sources. Museum shops have many exciting books for sale. Be on the

lookout for reprints, book sales and used copies. See **Bibliography** for a listing of some valuable design reference books. You will gradually build your own reference library which will be a ready source of inspiration and information.

Another source of material for your reference file is yourself! As an artist, you are continually sketching, drawing, making visual notes of what you see around you—on city streets, in your travels, in and around your home. Once you start really observing with an open, receptive approach, there isn't a place you look that doesn't offer something of aesthetic value. It could be the angles and shadows of the buildings across the street, the texture of a dog's fur, a newly opened leaf on a house plant, the look of falling rain. Draw them as you see them—make variations, decorative shapes and patterns of them. The sketchbooks that you fill with both drawn and written notations will become a valuable source of reference and inspiration. And these notations have an additional advantage—they are unique, original, strictly your own.

Your camera is a valuable research tool that will provide reference material reflecting your own responses to the world. Be alert to possibilities. With the camera you can retain fleeting images—a line of icicles at the roof's edge, autumn leaves on a pathway, a child's toy pinwheel, the lights of traffic at night.

Soon you will have enough reference materials to begin to classify and catalog them. Develop your own system. You may choose to paste your clippings into pages of a looseleaf notebook. You may collect them in labelled manila envelopes. Legal-size hanging-type files are convenient since they are flexible and easily expandable. Sort them into categories that make sense to you: documentaries, realistic florals, stylized florals, paisleys, conversationals. Group them according to subject matter: historical periods such as 17th-century French, Early American, Art Deco, Byzantine; sets of coordinates; color inspiration material; toys and juvenile ideas, pictures of interesting objects (good for conversationals).

It is important to collect all kinds of reference materials for design ideas. From a watercolor study by Emil Nolde (facing page, bottom). *Fine arts are an important source of inspiration.*

Enlarging Visual Vocabulary

When starting out, the tendency may be to design your "favorite" things. If you love certain types of flowers (or find that you can draw them easily) or if you prefer certain colors or combinations of colors, or if your own preference runs to certain particular fashion effects, you are apt to get "stuck" on these personal tastes and continue designing versions of the same few ideas.

Competent, versatile professionals, while still retaining their personal preferences, can nevertheless design in many styles. They are not reluctant to use all types of reference materials, adapting, combining and re-organizing, using their talents and skills to create new and exciting designs. Starting a flow of ideas is a very exciting experience. One idea generates another and soon many ideas start to surface, and new directions open up. The use and study of reference material will broaden your tastes and greatly expand your artistic potential.

The Purpose of Reference Materials

Students are frequently reluctant to use reference material of any kind. They tend to idealize "creativity" and feel that it's dishonest to copy and not to be original. This is a commendable reaction, but in truth nothing is totally original. Everything we design is the product of mental notations and observations, ideas we have subconsciously recorded from the world around us and which we draw upon when we need them. And this is equally true for beginners, students, and seasoned designers.

As a matter of honesty and integrity, it goes without saying that we do not literally copy something and then claim it as our own. The purpose of reference materials is for inspiration, for education, for enlarging our visual vocabulary.

Shakespeare, a great original playwright, used existing plots, borrowed ideas from Christopher Marlowe and other poets who had preceded him and enlarged these ideas into new relationships, clarified the elements of playwriting with his own insights and artistic capabilities. The airplane was "created" simultaneously all over the world within a period of ten years. The internal combustion engine was already being used, the principles of aerodynamics were being studied and all the various separate elements of *aeroplanes* were waiting to be assembled, brought together into a new relationship by the Wright brothers.

Studying the development of many painters reveals an early phase of their artistic growth in which other artists influenced and inspired the beginners. And to these early influences were added the beginner's own unique perceptions as he/she developed.

Outside inspiration and influence have an important place in the creative process as long as it is *a starting place* and *a stepping stone* to one's own personal expression, and as long as the beginner does not become stuck on *copying only.*

Imagine that you are working on a collection of Victorian designs for wallcoverings and upholstery. In order to have your patterns look authentic in style, color and subject matter, you will want to refer to genuine Victorian designs. If your intention is to be faithful to the original, then you would interpret the documents closely. However, you may decide to adapt these design ideas to a current trend in the marketplace. You could start with a bouquet, or a figure, and combine it with other motifs, arrange and re-arrange design elements, simplify the treatment for the modern eye. Your source material might be actual swatches of fabric, photographs of historical scenes, or pictures that you have accumulated in your files or found in books on home decoration. But by the time you have modified these images, combined them into new relationships, and put this material together into your designs, you will have created something new, original, and with your own "signature."

Whenever you need to refer to seed catalogues, pictures of animals, primitive motifs, Art Deco forms and colors, or any number of subjects and sources, you are simply recognizing that no one can possibly know what everything looks like! A basic use of your research then is for information. In

A documentary design often is an authentic interpretation of historic reference materials. An old serving platter was the inspiration for the drapery design.

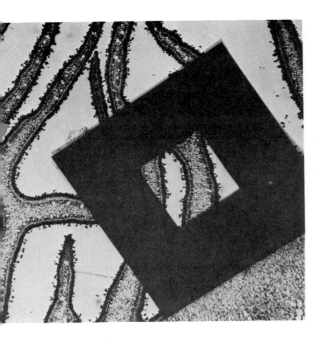

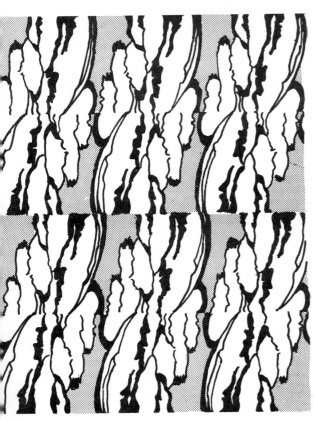

time you may find that you have absorbed these images and that they have become part of your storehouse of ideas. You will be able to recall information without the immediate presence of specific reference. But in general it is best to review your material each time there is a need. There is an ancient Chinese saying that "a picture is worth a thousand words."

Even the best of designers may hit a "dry spell"—a period when no bright ideas are forthcoming. The reference collection acquired through the years can be the greatest aid at such times. It can act as a force of renewal, open up new design horizons, help one not to go stale or repeat oneself. Throughout your designing career, do not hesitate to turn to your reference material, including your own notes, sketches and photographs—especially when you're temporarily out of ideas and searching for a new direction.

HOW TO USE REFERENCE MATERIALS

Let us say you have before you a few pieces of reference material. You are inspired by them, you admired their colors, something about the look of them interested you enough to collect them. What do you do now? How do you design from them?

Begin with your own inner feelings—what you like. What pleasure and satisfaction do you derive from these reference materials? But consider also that you want to work close to your abilities: do what you feel you can handle successfully.

You can start with the *colors*. Depending on your material, and the result you want to achieve, you could increase or decrease the number of colors in the original document, retain the general color effect, or alter and enhance it as you see fit.

You can change the *size* of the original to larger or smaller, or change the *coverage* and general layout, still keeping some elements of the original motifs. Studios often have a *lucy* which is a projector used to enlarge and reduce images (scaling). You may use the layout from a piece of fabric from the thirties but substitute flowers from a botanical print, and paint the design in colors from a color forecast in a current magazine, thus ending up with a totally new look.

Technique is another way into the design work. A textural effect may get you started, a loaded brush with a bold, blobby gesture may inspire you; a cross-hatch effect or dry-brush technique could be just the look that is right for the painting of the design. (More about techniques in **Chapter 6.**)

Some ways of modifying reference materials are:

- Use silhouettes of the forms, painted flat.
- Try variations of motifs (different views of a single flower).
- Show the motifs in different sizes, or two-by-two, overlapping, with alternating colors.
- Change the medium (respond to what different media can and cannot do).
- Introduce a new technique.
- Use only one or two motifs from the many found in the reference material.
- Simplify complicated material.
- Adorn and embellish severe, plain forms.
- Re-color to suit current needs.
- Change color relationships (substitute dull for bright or vice versa).
- Alter value relationships (substitute darks for lights or vice versa).
- Introduce background motifs and interest.
- Combine motifs from different sources (new relationships of motifs can create an unusual juxtaposition).
- Use a mask or "window": Cut a mask from a piece of bristol paper with a mat knife and metal edge. Try an opening 1″ × 1¼″. Then

With the use of a "mask," a segment of a microscopic photograph was translated into a turning-square pattern. (© DOROTHY WOLFTHAL.)

place the mask over your reference material. This isolates sections of the reference and suggests new layouts and scale changes. Try a larger window and look at some seashells or bird feathers. It is exciting to discover new patterns and layouts with this simple tool.

Another type of "window" is a mask in the shape of a product. Cut the mask silhouette of a cup, for instance, and place it over the reference or your final croquis. This helps enormously to visualize the design on the object. The mask may be a silhouette of a tie, a shirt, the back of a high chair, a toddler's jumpsuit. Many examples of masks are used throughout this text.

Seed catalogues can be used to create designs like "Meadowsweet" by GREEFF.

Start by applying some of the above suggestions for using and modifying reference material. Soon your own imagination will take over. Combine what you have learned in your exploration of the marketplace with your intuition. Find inspiration from your research as well as your reference material. From the multitude of source material at hand, be selective. By combining, altering, selecting and modifying—in time you will create new ideas, new directions, and new textile designs in your own original idiom.

TOOLS & SUPPLIES FOR A TEXTILE DESIGNER

One of the greatest joys of designing textile patterns is the craftsmanship acquired and practiced. The horizons expand continually as new techniques and new skills are added. And the tools and supplies used by the designer are part of this picture. The materials used in our field are filled with promise. Just to buy the tubes of paint, brushes, and paper can be an exciting experience of anticipation. Often for the beginner the materials are a real challenge and until we've had hands-on experience with them it is hard to know which color to choose, which paper is the best to express the design, which brush will do the job best. Getting the feel and control of the brushes takes practice, but there is no tool more responsive and more rewarding to use than a beautifully made brush.

The materials speak to us. We must learn to listen and especially to "feel" their language, to respond to what is happening when we place one color next to another, or how the pencil feels on the tracing or coquille paper. With this sensitivity comes the joy and originality of working. It can fire the inspiration as well.

In this chapter we will mention specific product names for art supplies because in our experience, we have found them to be the most satisfactory for one reason or another. Of course there are many manufacturers of many different art supplies and each artist will explore and choose those products most preferred. There is no need to limit oneself to the products and brand names mentioned in this chapter.

Listen to the inner dialogue between you and the brush.

THE PAINTS

Gouache The most commonly used paint in the textile design field is *gouache* (pronounced gu-*wash*)—an opaque watercolor (water soluble) sold in tubes. *Acrylics* and *oil* paints can be used but their properties are less suited to most design work. Polymer acrylic medium, spray varnish, and molding paste are sometimes used by professional designers to create special effects. It is best for the beginner to put off using these special techniques until you have more experience handling the basic paints. Although any medium the designer chooses is acceptable by industry, gouache has been the most commonly preferred for many years by most artists.

Gouache is available in a large selection of colors, and is made by

A one-color wallcovering design rendered in sketchy pencil technique.

several manufacturers, American, English, European, Japanese. Experiment with new brands and new colors, and you will gradually build a collection that suits your own particular needs and tastes. All brands are compatible and can be mixed and used together, if you make sure that the label says "gouache."

The lists here are recommended for the beginner—**List 1** is basic and essential, and includes the most frequently used colors. **List 2** has excellent additions and should be added to the collection as the student becomes more experienced. Two colors appearing on **List 2** are white and black gouache in tubes. Some artists prefer these instead of Richart White and Black poster paints which are usually less refined than the gouache found in tubes. It is a matter of individual choice. Ivory black and lamp black have special characteristics that become more evident when mixed with white or other colors.

Winsor & Newton™ *Designers' Colors* (English) has been the preferred gouache for many years but new products appear all the time. Try to obtain color charts published by paint manufacturers. They are useful in understanding the specific properties of each tube of paint such as staining power, opacity, the light-fugitive or permanance properties, and so forth. It is helpful to know these properties when experimenting with various colors.

Casein is a kind of opaque color, more permanent than gouache, but not often used except for special effects. It is hard on brushes, and you should not use your good red sable brushes with this paint.

Suggested Gouache*/Opaque Watercolors for Use in Textile Design

	List 1	List 2
Yellows	Lemon Yellow Golden Yellow	Cadmium Yellow Deep Orange Naples Yellow
Reds	Flame Red Bengal Rose (Grumbacher™) Carthamus Pink	Alizarin Crimson Rose Tyrien Cadmium Red Deep Scarlet Lake
Blues	Ultramarine Blue Sky Blue Blue Light 49 (Talens™) (If unavailable use Turquoise)	Peacock Blue Indigo Turquoise Cerulean Blue
Greens	Permanent Green Light Permanent Green Deep Cyprus Green	Linden Green Permanent Green Middle Windsor Green
Earth Tones	Yellow Ochre Raw Umber	Havannah Lake Raw Sienna Chinese Orange
Neutrals	Richart™ White (8 oz. poster paint) Richart™ Black (8 oz. poster paint) Bleedproof White (1 oz.)	Zinc White Ivory Black Lamp Black

*Colors are Winsor & Newton™ in tubes, unless otherwise designated. There are other acceptable brands such as Talens, Grumbacher, Pelikan and Turner.

THE DYES

Dyes (highly concentrated transparent liquid watercolor) are another, frequently used medium. The dyes most commonly used are made by Luma™ and are brilliant and fast to work with . . . the transparency aspect makes them dazzling and rich to the eye. Also, dyes manufactured by Dr. Martin™ are available in many art supply stores and have some interesting and unusual colors. It is wise to purchase these dyes in preference to other brands since matching colors for repeats and other purposes is greatly facilitated. (See **List 3**.)

Dyes for textile designs to be executed on paper are most frequently sold in bottles with droppers built into the caps. Again, acquire the basic

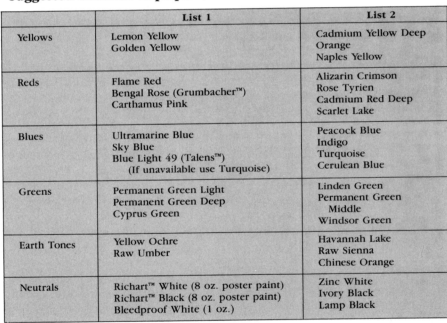

The brilliant concentrated watercolors are called dyes by textile designers, and should be distinguished from dyestuffs used in printing fabrics.

colors (see **List 3**) and add to your collection carefully and gradually. With dyes, a *special precaution:* there is a smaller group of "hot" colors, more luminous than the rest, that are used when unusual brilliance is required. Most of these "hot" colors are compatible with each other but *not* with regular dyes. Before trying to mix the "hot" with regular dyes, try just a few drops in combination. Mix them carefully, let the mixture sit a minute or two and test it. You may find that it has curdled and become unusable. With practice you will learn which dyes are "friendly."

Dyes are more subject to fading, especially when exposed extensively to strong light, some colors fading more than others. When working with dyes make it a habit to cover the unfinished work with a sheet of paper if you must leave it on your desk for any length of time. Store your finished designs in a portfolio or file drawer.

Fading may not be a problem if the design is sold and produced soon after it is created, as happens more frequently in the apparel field. Designs for the home fashions field often must survive longer; they may even sell years after they are painted. In addition, the "look" of the painted gouache surface is closer to the finished product (the printed inks on the fabric, vinyl film or paper) than is that of dyes. Therefore, gouache is the preferred medium when designing for draperies, upholstery and wallcoverings, and for the domestics field.

NON-CRAWL & WAX-GRIP™

Non-crawl is an additive which decreases the surface tension of dyes, inks and gouache, and allows them to flow smoothly and evenly onto non-absorbent surfaces such as waxed Masa. Without this additive the paints would bead up into separate droplets. Only a drop or two should be added; the less the better. The same product by Luma™ is called *Wax Grip*™. Soap or liquid dishwashing detergent can be substituted but may alter the colors somewhat. *Photo-Flo 200 solution*™ sold in photo shops can also be used and costs less.

Suggested Dyes* for Use in Textile Design

List 3					
Yellows	Reds	Blues	Greens	Earth Tones	Neutrals
Lemon Yellow	Scarlet	True Blue	April Green	Tobacco Brown	Black
Daffodil	Persimmon	Turquoise	Olive Green	Brown	Paynes Gray
Yellow	Tyrien	Ultra Blue	(Dr. Martin's™ dyes)	Sepia	(Dr. Martin's™ dyes)
Orange	Pansy	Slate Blue	Juniper Green	Saddle Brown	

*Colors are Luma™ Dyes, unless otherwise noted, and are available in ½ oz. bottles with droppers.

PAPERS

This is a special category of supplies. There are so many types that only with experience will you know which is best for the particular work at hand (refer to chart in **Appendix**).

When choosing a paper, the "tooth" or texture is an important consideration in relation to the medium to be used. For example, soft papers with a textured surface, or "tooth," such as Georgian or Seminole, accept gouache readily. Dyes need a less absorbent surface like Arches. The smooth surface of bristol is good for fine work and penline. The following is a brief description of some of the papers used in textile designing.

Papers for Gouache

- *Georgian*—excellent all purpose paper (35" x 46"), inexpensive.
- *Carousel*—similar to Georgian but more absorbent.
- *Seminole*—fair quality but usable, inexpensive.

The most commonly used paint is an opaque watercolor called gouache.

- *Fabriano*—fine quality, slightly textured surface.
- *Bristol*—several varieties and weights depending on purpose. *Kid* (or vellum) finish, two-ply by Strathmore™ or Fairfield™ is recommended for general use, especially good for gouache. Smooth (or plate) finish bristol is better for penlines; both finishes can take some erasing without damage to the surface.
- *D'Arches* (most often called "*Arches*")—very high quality paper with high rag content. Available in several weights and surfaces. Most commonly available size 22″ x 30″. Excellent for wash or "photo" techniques. Arches is less expensive if purchased in rolls, but curling is an annoying problem.
- *Beau Brilliant*—creamy white paper, textured surface good for gouache and watercolor techniques. Also made in several colors. Fairly inexpensive.
- *Pre-colored papers*—It is strongly recommended that you paint all grounds with gouache since you can achieve exactly the color desired. Also you then have the mixed color for touching up when necessary. However pre-colored papers are sometimes used for colored backgrounds. Some pre-colored papers are:

    Mi-teintes™—about thirty-five colors from pale tints to deep shades and black. Slightly "toothed" surface good for most media, especially gouache. Fairly inexpensive, 21″ x 29″.

    Color-aid™—These papers are available in almost any color you can think of. The colors are silk-screened onto the paper, hence have a flat, matte finish. Color-aid takes ink and gouache and the color does not "bleed" through. It does not take kindly to erasing and must be handled carefully to prevent marring the surface. Fairly inexpensive, 18″ x 24″.

    Pantone (PMS)™ *papers*—A lighter weight paper, available in hundreds of colors, including some metallics. The smooth surface takes gouache, crayon, ink, and can be erased with care, using a soft eraser. There is a range of color-coordinated Pantone products: coated papers, colored papers, markers, printers' inks, etc. Moderate cost, 20″ x 26″

Tracing Paper

Tracing paper is essential in textile print designing. Available in rolls and pads. Pads are preferable since they lie flat and do not curl as the rolled tracing paper does. Nevertheless, rolls are popular since the large sizes are often necessary for repeat layouts in the decorative field and are also less expensive. A medium weight is preferred. If the paper is too lightweight it tears easily, too heavy (like a vellum) is wasteful.

Saral™ Transfer Paper

Saral™ is similar to typewriter carbon paper and is used to transfer designs from tracing paper to the final rendering paper. It is available in *graphite* as well as white and several other colors. It produces a grease-free line that can be easily erased. Caution: *do not* use typewriter carbon paper since it will smudge. (See **Chapter 5** for complete discussion on use of Saral™ paper.)

Papers for Dyes

Some of the white papers for gouache mentioned above are also good for use with dyes: *Arches*™ (excellent for wash effects), *bristols, Strathmore*™ (two- and three-ply "kid" finish good for Liberty-type penline and dye designs), and *Beau Brilliant*™.

Various types of *rice paper* (unwaxed and waxed) are available from art supply stores, and are frequently used for dyes. Colors appear brilliant and intense. Rice papers have different textures and weights, some have "threads" or fibers embedded in them, and some have patterns woven into them. They are referred to by such interesting names as Troya, Mariki, and

Technique using tjanting pen and wax as resist with dyes. (© MICHAEL D'ELIA.)

Masa. Masa is the most frequently used in textile design, and is sold either in its original state (unwaxed) or waxed (impregnated with paraffin). *Pencil is not* used on waxed Masa. Instead the pencil work is done on paper or tracing paper. This must then be covered with a sheet of acetate or sprayed with workable fixative to isolate the graphite from the underside of the Masa. Since waxed Masa is translucent (almost like tracing paper) it is placed over the drawing and painted directly with dyes with no further preparation. Non-crawl, however, is necessary in dyes to make them adhere to the surface and prevent them from beading. The result is a brilliant, fresh color look. And the technique is fast.

Gouache can also be used on waxed Masa, always remembering that a few drops of non-crawl or a similar product must be added to break down the surface tension of the water.

Unwaxed rice papers can give special effects, colors running and bleeding together rapidly, for instance. Edges are harder to control unless one paints "dry."

The waxing process is done in Japan and in Western countries, on a mass-production basis. Originally, however, artists and studios did their own waxing, and it is a process that designers should know.

How to Wax Rice Paper

You will need, in addition to unwaxed rice paper:

- Cakes of paraffin (available in art supply stores, but cheaper in grocery-supermarkets where home-canning supplies are sold).
- A double boiler or an electric fry-pan *with temperature control.*
- Newsprint paper—low cost, off-white paper, most frequently sold in pads. Recommended size is 18″ x 24″. Do not confuse it with the *pages of a newspaper* which should *not* come in contact with rice paper at any stage of the waxing process, since the newspaper ink will transfer itself to your rice paper and make it unusable.
- Lots of old newspapers (large format size such as *New York Times* is better than tabloid) or brown wrapping paper to protect work area.
- A broad brush (about 2″ to 3″, hardware store variety, soft bristles).
- A large clean flat work surface.
- An iron.
- An electric hot-plate (if using double boiler). Your kitchen stove is likely to get wax dripped into places that are difficult to clean. If you use an electric fry-pan, a hot plate is not necessary.

Design inspired by woven blanket using tjanting pen wax lines as resist. (© DOROTHY WOLFTHAL.)

- A drop cloth would be useful.

1. Prepare the work area by covering the floor with a drop cloth, old newspapers or brown wrapping paper. Place a clean sheet or two of wrapping paper or newsprint paper on the work surface.

2. Melt one or two cakes of paraffin.

Double Boiler Method: Put hot water into the bottom half of the double boiler, making it as full as possible and still allowing top half of double boiler to fit. Put the paraffin in the top half, place it on a hot plate and then bring water to a boil. *Do not* use the pot cover. Monitor the level of water in the bottom half throughout the process, and replenish it as it boils down.

Electric Fry-pan Method: Put paraffin into fry-pan, turn heat to low-to-medium setting until paraffin melts. *Do not allow it to become so hot that it smokes.*

3. Place *two* sheets of unwaxed rice paper on prepared work surface. Dip brush into melted wax and stroke onto the top sheet of rice paper. You'll know the wax is hot enough when it penetrates through to the second sheet and makes both sheets look transparent. Keep the melted paraffin at this temperature. (If it starts to smoke it's *too hot* and should be turned down.)

Paint the entire surface of the paper. The wax will penetrate both sheets of paper at the same time. To prevent paper from sticking to work surface, lift both sheets together by one corner while they're still warm. Work fast, because paraffin cools quickly.

4. As soon as rice paper is waxed, *remove double boiler from heat* or *unplug electric pan.*

5. Lift the waxed rice paper off the work surface. The two sheets will be stuck together at this point.

6. Place a padding of newspaper on the work surface (five to ten pages thick). Cover with two or three sheets of clean newsprint paper, and put the waxed rice paper on top. Put two or three more sheets of clean newsprint paper on the waxed rice paper.

7. Plug in your iron, at low-to-moderate temperature setting. Start to iron over the entire area that covers the rice paper. You will soon see that the wax is being absorbed into the layers of newsprint paper. Change to fresh newsprint sheets, both under and over the rice paper as the newsprint becomes saturated with the excess wax.

It's a good idea to turn the sheets of rice paper over about halfway through the process. By the second or third change of newsprint paper, the two sheets of rice paper will separate from each other. At this point, very little wax will be seeping out into the newsprint as you iron. This is an indication that the waxing process is complete. Lift each sheet up to the light to find any thick spots of excess wax you may have missed, and iron them out.

8. Store your waxed rice paper flat, and handle it carefully. If you accidentally cause some slight cracks in the paper, these can usually be ironed out between two sheets of newsprint paper or paper towelling.

Notes

1. As you become more expert with this procedure, you will be able to process as many as four or five sheets at a time, by waxing the set of unwaxed paper from both sides. As they begin to separate from one another when you start to iron them, take them apart and complete the ironing operation separately.

2. Other types of rice paper can also be waxed by the same method. This provides you with different textures to work on which are not available commercially. Even tissue paper (white and colored) can be treated this way for special effects.

3. *Paraffin is very flammable. Do not* smoke while using it, and observe all sensible safety precautions. Turn off the heat units if you must leave them, even for a moment.

4. The plain uncolored utility candles sold in hardware stores can be substituted for paraffin block. Remove the wick once the wax is melted.

5. For a more flexible wax (less brittle) you can add beeswax to your paraffin, from a small amount to as much as 50 percent. Beeswax is available in craft stores or at dressmaker's supply outlets as well as some art supply stores. Some stores even carry a prepared wax which is a combination of paraffin and beeswax. This is more costly, and the proportions are pre-determined.

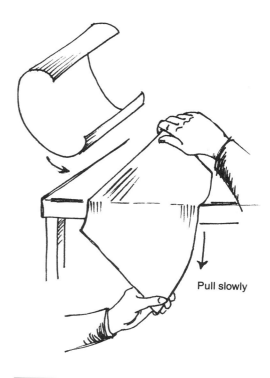

Pull slowly

Rolled or curled paper can be flattened out in this manner.

How to Solve the Problem of Paper Curling

Designs and unused paper may have been rolled for storage and transportation purposes. It is difficult to work with them since the *memory factor* of the paper keeps re-rolling them. Moisture will also affect the curling. It is possible to counteract this curling problem by pulling it across a sharp corner. The edge of a desk works fine. The design is placed on the top of the desk with the curl upward. One side of the design is pulled down over the edge of the desk at 90 degrees to the top. Pull down toward the floor. Sometimes one corner of the paper can be pulled downward in this manner, especially if the paper is fairly large. The sharp bend will counteract the curl and the paper will tend to lie flat again. The design can be rotated 180 degrees and pulled again against the edge of the desk to remove any remaining curl.

There is danger that the paper can be damaged. A bad crease can develop if the pull downward over the edge of the desk is *not* carefully or evenly executed. Start slowly and *re-start* if a crease begins to develop.

If the paper you wish to un-curl has artwork on it, never place it face down on the desk. This will damage the painted surface as you pull it across the edge of the desk. Always keep the artwork face up. Curled paper with artwork can also be carefully rolled in the opposite direction and rocked back and forth on a flat surface.

If a crease exists in the paper, it is possible to moisten the reverse side of the artwork and press it with a warm dry iron. This will remove almost all of the damage. With waxed Masa, ironing will remove small creases, but can destroy design-work (see **Chapter 7**).

OTHER SURFACES ON WHICH TO EXPERIMENT

Some studios and artists are presenting design ideas painted directly on silk. An advantage is that the fabric drapes and folds. It is close in appearance to

the final product. The silk is stretched on a frame. A resist called *gutta* is often used, and special dyes are applied directly to the silk. The finished design is steamed to remove the gutta and "set" the dyes. (Sources for materials and supplies are listed in the **Appendix**.)

Experiment with all types of novelty papers—gift wrappings, wallpapers with interesting texture, shelving paper, brown wrapping paper or other packing material, freezer paper, metallic papers. You may come up with some exciting new effects.

Other exotic *papers* with which to experiment, include shiny foils in an assortment of colors, and colored tissue papers. Tissue paper designs can be carried to a high degree of refinement. The overlap of these transparent colors creates a jewel-like effect. Spray adhesive is one way of mounting the tissue paper in this collage technique. Also experiment with clear, matte, and glossy polymer acrylic medium as a binder.

Flint Paper   High gloss coating on one side: white, black and colors. The paint may need some non-crawl to prevent beading, or Sobo™ glue for bonding.

Vellum   Translucent paper, similar to a very heavy tracing paper. Takes pen and ink, gouache, most media.

Prepared Acetate   Transparent, shiny not matte, useful entirely by itself or for overlays, especially good with gouache and ink. Can be washed and reused. Motifs, textures, and new colors can be painted on acetate and used as a visualizing technique to help evaluate a new color against existing artwork or to modify a design. Designs painted on acetate can also be placed on top of patterned papers, cloth, wood grains, cloud-textures, etc.

An interesting technique is to use gouache in a ruling pen and draw in a free-hand manner on prepared acetate (see **page 46**). Fabric weaves and woven designs can be meticulously interpreted on acetate using this method. Gouache used in a brush can also be used to create a bold, simulated woven effect. The Print-a-Weave™ collection is a good example of this technique (see **page 12**). A small amount of Sobo™ or Elmer's™ glue—two or three drops—in the paint will help the gouache to adhere more completely to the acetate surface.

Whenever using acetate be careful that the oil in the skin of your hands does not transfer to the acetate and cause an undesirable flaking of the gouache.

Plasti-vel™ (plastic vellum) and *Denril*™   A new breed of "paper" made entirely of plastics. Translucent, paper-like surface as transparent as waxed Masa and exceptionally durable. Excellent for gouache, ink, markers, and most media. Best used with smooth white paper (such as bristol) for backing. Plastic vellum clings to the backing paper because it is non-porous, and can easily be lifted off and repositioned. It is moderately expensive, and usually sold in 100 sheet packages and pads, in various sizes.

A technique using Plasti-vel™ that is very rewarding is to work with a watery gouache which is then partially lifted with a tissue. Some of the gouache remains and a subtle texture is created in the process. It is possible to texture a puddle of gouache with tissue *on regular paper,* but the non-absorbency of the Plasti-vel™ is a more successful surface on which to work. Inks, dyes and gouache can be moved and modified more readily when still wet on the *plastic* paper.

Try combining this technique with a penline, as in a Liberty print, mixing the India ink with some red Luma™ dye for outlining the motifs first. The watery gouache is then applied. The water will "soften" the line work since the Luma™ dye is water soluble and of course the India ink remains unaffected since it is waterproof.

The textile designer should constantly experiment, painting on all surfaces: photo back-drop papers, brown wrapping paper, shelving paper, window shades, graph paper, canvas (with or without a gesso coating), fabrics (silk, cotton, linen), etc. The designer has to remember that some papers and materials which are extremely fragile will deteriorate quickly and valuable artwork may be lost. So keep in mind the durability and lasting aspects of the materials you use.

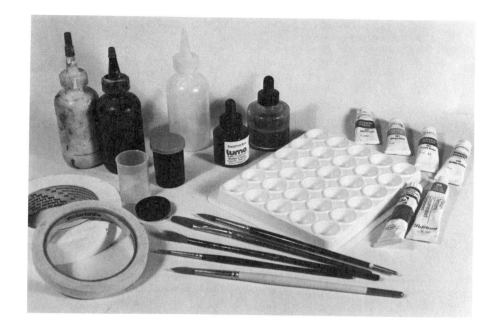

BRUSHES

The most frequently used brushes in textile design are *red sable*. There are several good brands; the most well known are Winsor & Newton™ and Grumbacher™, but there are some less familiar, very good quality brushes as well (Isabey™ for instance). As a standard for size and shape, when buying brushes, see **illustration.** The sizes #4 and #6 are recommended for the beginner. Brushes with a longer taper, #5 and #6 are also available. English and American brushes are numbered upward in size from #000 (small) to #14 (large).

Synthetic Brushes *"White sable"* brushes with synthetic fibers perform just like traditional red sable hair with regard to the spring, and sharp point (see **How to Buy a Brush**). Simmons™ are very acceptable brushes, and less expensive than the red sable type.

Quill Brushes Some designers prefer to work with *quill brushes.* If you would like to try these, make sure to ask for *designer's quill brushes.* Those made in France are the most satisfactory and a #4 or #5 would be a good size to start with. The French quill brushes have a size range from #00 (very large) to #8 or even #9 (very small). Quills work especially well with dyes because they hold a lot of the dye and yet come to a perfect point.

Ground Brushes A broad flat brush about 2″ to 3″ wide is helpful for painting colored grounds. Ideally, natural hairs would be best but these are very expensive. Some acceptable wash or ground brushes (as these broad brushes are known to textile designers) are made of nylon or a combination of synthetic fibers. You might find a good wash brush for a reasonable price in a hardware or paint store. Just be sure the bristles are not too stiff. Another tool for painting colored grounds is the "brush" made of flat rubber or plastic foam. This is fairly soft and flexible, and is available in several widths.

Other Brushes Available to Designers

There are many types of brushes available and designers must experiment with them in order to create special effects. Brushes are available in all sizes and shapes and each perform in a special way.

Fan Brushes These unusual brushes can be used to create interesting shapes and textures. Simply placed flat on the paper, they can represent flower petals, sun rays, seashells, etc. Using just the tips of the hairs, you can create stripes, textures, feathery effects, and more. They are available in several sizes, are usually made of synthetic hairs.

Some of the tools and supplies frequently used by textile designers. The 30-hole palette is most practical; dispenser bottles for black and white gouache and for clean water facilitate mixing colors.

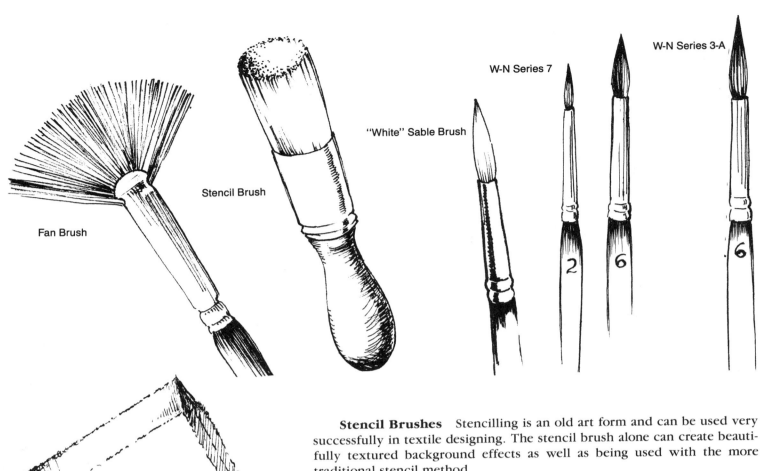

Fan Brush

Stencil Brush

"White" Sable Brush

W-N Series 7

W-N Series 3-A

Foam Ground Brush

A selection of good sable brushes is necessary. A white "sable" brush can be used for mixing as well as for painting.

Stencil Brushes Stencilling is an old art form and can be used very successfully in textile designing. The stencil brush alone can create beautifully textured background effects as well as being used with the more traditional stencil method.

Bristle Brushes Bristle brushes, used when painting with oils and acrylics, create good dry-brush effects but are not commonly used in textile designing.

How to Buy a Brush

Red sable, the recommended hair for designer's brushes, should be *springy* and bounce back with a snap if you press the hairs sideways with your finger (as illustrated).

Most art supply stores will leave a container of water and some plain paper somewhere near the brushes. A test of a good brush is to dip the brush into water and shake off the excess. The brush should form a single *point,* and not "split" into two or more points. If it "splits" upon repeated tries, it will probably cause you trouble. Forget it and try another.

On a piece of plain paper test the wet brush as if painting. Draw it across the paper using its full thickness, try using a light touch with just the tip. Take time to get the "feel" of it. A good brush is your most important tool and a most worthwhile investment. If you take proper care of it, it will last for years. Apply the *Do's and Don'ts* to all your brushes and they should serve you long and well.

PALETTES

A 30-hole palette is the type most frequently used in textile design. The holes or wells are about an inch in diameter and deep enough to hold a good amount of paint. You may see quite a variety of palettes at the art supply stores. It would be best to get a white ceramic type. However, the white plastic ones are inexpensive and generally satisfactory if you are careful not to pierce the rather thin plastic. It is a good idea to secure the light plastic palettes to your work table with tape, to prevent them from moving around as you are mixing paint in them. Avoid the ones made of aluminum. The gray surface is unsatisfactory and may be misleading when mixing colors; also they tend to corrode if they are used extensively with dyes. Plastic ice cube

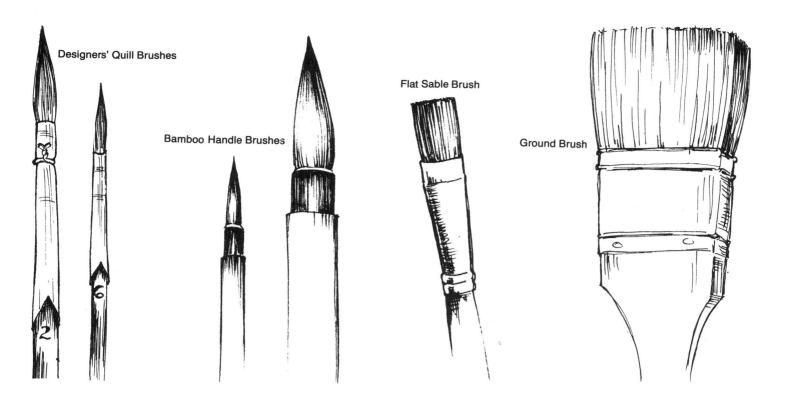

Designers' Quill Brushes

Bamboo Handle Brushes

Flat Sable Brush

Ground Brush

trays also make good palettes if larger quantities of paint are needed.

To save your mixed colors in a palette, cover it with a sheet of vinyl film (plastic wrap from the kitchen is fine).

Other Paint Containers For extended projects or for large areas where a greater amount of paint must be prepared, various types of jars are available. Many stores carry the "nesting" jars with tops and bottoms threaded so that they can be stacked for storage. Plastic 1 oz. cups are made with hinge-attached covers and with snap or screw-on covers. Avoid the flimsy inexpensive cups that crack easily and don't transport well. Also useful are 35mm film containers with covers and are usually free at photo shops. Save your empty small paint bottles with screw-on caps. Baby food jars are popular with some artists. Clear, transparent containers are preferred so that you can see the colors inside.

Dispenser Bottles These squeeze bottles are available in many forms and are essential when mixing dyes or gouache. We recommend that you keep *three* handy—one for clean water, one for Richart™ White, and one for Richart™ Black. The last two should have caps that close when not in use to prevent the paint from drying out.

PENCILS

An everyday #2 lead pencil, with a red eraser tip, is very useful. And try the #1 for sketching and extra softness. A #2H is good for tracing detailed artwork and will not smear easily. A #3H or #4H is helpful for transferring your artwork to final paper. The "Eagle™" Drafting pencil #314 is excellent for sketching.

A good mechanical pencil or lead holder with an assortment of leads ranging from #2B to #4H is useful and convenient.

Colored pencils and wax crayons are used for certain techniques, and a collection of colors can be acquired gradually. Almost any art material can be used to create textile designs. *Cray-pas™*, which is an oil-pastel stick can be combined with dye or gouache or used by itself. *Wax crayons* from our childhood days combine with dyes very well. *Colored wax pencils* can create a range of values for each color by the pressure used when drawing. Some designers like to use colored pencils on tracing paper to explore the placement of color in a design. Preliminary sketches on tracing paper are

Care of Your Brushes

DO
• *Rinse* thoroughly after each use and shake out extra water.
• *Form* brush into its natural taper and let it dry in a vertical position.
• *Protect* brushes if you have to carry them around (use a piece of a drinking straw for small sizes). See various carrying devices available in art stores.
• *Wash* sable brushes *gently* with mild soap and cool water if you want to remove all traces of previous color.
• *Purchase* a few nylon or other synthetic brushes for mixing paints, for use with bleach, acrylics, lacquer, etc., (and clean these promptly after use!).

DON'T
• Let brushes dry with any paint in them.
• Let brushes "sit on their heels" or soak in your water jar.
• Use India ink with a good sable brush. (Save the old ones for this medium.)
• Mix colors with good brushes.
• Carry brushes around loose in a handbag or pocket.
• Use hot water on brushes.
• Use your designer's sable brushes for bleach, acrylic, lacquer, or any other harsh medium.
• Clean your brushes with chemical solvents.

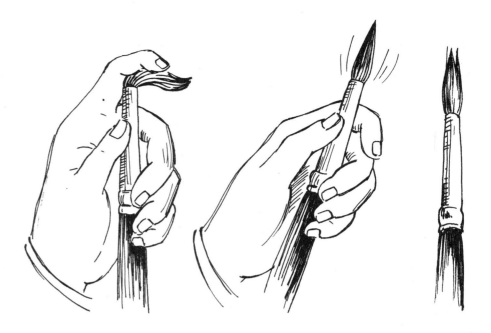

worked out in colored pencils to study the *color spotting* before the croquis is painted. These studies help the beginner to plan the croquis more thoroughly. Markers and pastels can also be used for color spotting.

Charcoal   Some artists like to use charcoal sticks or charcoal pencils, especially for preliminary rough layouts on tracing paper. Charcoal is fast, can be rubbed off or erased easily, and gives a good allover effect. (There is also a white "charcoal" pencil, a sort of highly compressed chalk in pencil form. This is helpful in backing tracings to be transferred to dark grounds as discussed in **Chapter 5**.)

PENS

The ordinary pen holder made of wood, aluminum or plastic is versatile and economical. An assortment of pen points (nibs) can be inserted and removed as needed. The pen holders are available in two sizes—the standard, which takes most pen nibs, and the smaller size especially made for the smaller crowquill point. The pen points are reasonably priced so that you can readily acquire a broad assortment.

Technical Pens   You will eventually want to acquire technical drawing pens. These have interchangeable tips of various sizes. For purposes of textile design, the range should probably be from #00 to #4. Popular brand names include Rapidograph™, Faber-Castell™, and Staedler Mars-matic™. They all function on the same principle, having a well or container built into the pen to hold the ink which feeds evenly down to the pen tip.

Generally, a steel pen point that's too fine or flexible, such as a crowquill, is difficult to use on waxed Masa or other rice paper, as it is likely to catch on the minute fibers and blot or splatter. However, these pens work fine on most papers. For a design that requires considerable pen work with rather small areas of color such as Liberty prints and paisleys, you might prefer a less textured surface such as two-ply bristol, or similar smooth-surfaced paper. They are very receptive to detailed line work. When used with Luma dyes, you *must* be sure the ink is waterproof.

These pens cannot be handled carelessly and when they are used according to the manufacturer's instructions they are very useful and a welcome addition to your supplies.

Ruling Pens   These consist basically of two steel prongs that can be brought closer or farther apart to make a thinner or thicker line. They can be used with ink or with gouache, and they are the recommended pen for use with a ruler or T-square. Some designers also use them as a drawing pen

Many types of containers are available for storing and transporting mixed paints. Test brushes before buying. Avoid brushes that "split."

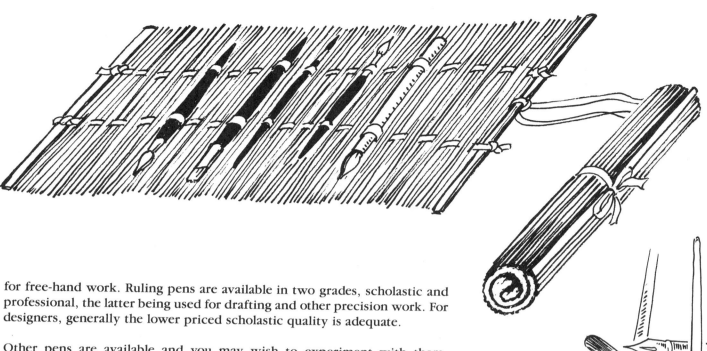

for free-hand work. Ruling pens are available in two grades, scholastic and professional, the latter being used for drafting and other precision work. For designers, generally the lower priced scholastic quality is adequate.

Other pens are available and you may wish to experiment with them. Fountain pens with special nibs, calligraphy pens, and ballpoint pens, all can be used in designing.

INKS

Black ink and colored inks (either permanent or water soluble) are used depending on the technique. The colored inks should not be confused with dyes. For ordinary "dip-in" pens and for ruling pens black waterproof ink is common. Some familiar brand names include Higgins™ India ink, Pelikan™ waterproof drawing ink and FW™ waterproof inks. Several companies make waterproof inks in black and assorted colors. These may be used with all the pens mentioned above. The colored lines drawn in the waterproof ink will remain undisturbed when the Luma dye is brushed up to it.

   With most types of pens it is advisable not to use the same ones for black India ink as for dyes and colored inks. It is almost impossible to remove all traces of the black ink from the pens and you would be wise to keep the "black" pens separate from those to be used with colors.

MORE MEDIA WITH WHICH TO EXPERIMENT

Felt-tipped Markers

Permanent or *water-soluble* markers, in black and assorted colors may be used. Fine-line permanent markers work well on waxed Masa. Pilot™, Sharpie™, Design Art Markers™ by Eberhard Faber™, and AD Markers™ are all used. There are other manufacturers to choose from and you will eventually decide on your preference.

   A very effective technique is possible using fine-line markers and dyes. When creating a design with outline (e.g., a Liberty-type or a paisley print), do the outline first. (They *must* be permanent and waterproof. Water-soluble markers will smear and run with disastrous results.) The fine-line markers can keep a very uniform thickness if you maintain even pressure. It is good practice to keep a sheet of paper towelling under your hand as you work. The lines made by waterproof markers need a few minutes to "set" and become really permanent. Don't rest your hand on newly drawn motifs. After the dyes have been applied, you can also come back with additional

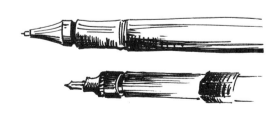

Experiment with many kinds of pens, using inks, dyes or gouache. A useful and efficient carrying device to protect your brushes can be made from a bamboo placemat. Thread two elastic bands through bamboo and knot all ends. Attach tape at one end for tying roll.

line work on top of your colors if necessary. On most papers they are likely to spread and bleed unless you work very quickly, although sometimes you may deliberately wish to create that type of line effect. Workable fixative sprayed on the paper beforehand will control this spreading effect.

When using markers, keep in mind that you can draw with a *broken* line or a *textured* line for more character and interest. This practice is quite common in the decorative field and is also found on Liberty prints. *Nervous, shaky* lines such as a Paul Klee line are also possible, and fun to use.

Liquid Frisket (lift-off)

This is a substance that is applied with brush, stick, toothpick, etc., in liquid form and dries somewhat in the manner of rubber cement. It acts as a mask or cover to the area. You can then use dye or paint over it, and when the paint dries you peel or lift the mask off, leaving the area it protected untouched. Liquid mask is also hard on brushes, and they should be washed out with soap and water immediately after use. Most designers limit certain brushes to be used exclusively with frisket.

Air Brush

Air brush is a skill that is growing in demand again. More and more design work is being executed with this technique. Compressed air is used to create a mist or spray of paint, ink or dye creating a soft graded look. Stencils can be used to control edges but the typical look is a sprayed, cloud effect. Professional equipment is costly but there are less expensive tools available. A can of pressurized propellant replaces the air compressor and can be purchased for a moderate price. It is wise to enroll in a course of instruction to learn this skill.

Transfer Sheets

Letraset™, Zipatone™, Formatt™ are some of the names of a very useful type of product. The principle for all is the same. These sheets are printed with different textures, designs, motifs, numbers, and letters as well as many symbols. Some are transferred to your paper by light burnishing, others have an adhesive backing and are cut out and pressed lightly onto the paper. They can add fascinating and novel effects to your designs. You can paint over most of these with dye or gouache; some may require the addition of non-crawl for the paint to "take."

Line Tape

Also called *chart tape,* these tapes are made in black as well as in colors—with a shiny surface as well as matte. Some are as thin as a pencil line, and are helpful when you want a very even continuous line. They can be placed in a straight line, but the thin line tape can also be fed around in graceful curves. They will adhere to almost any paper, on dye- or gouache-painted surfaces. Care must be taken to be sure of their placement. Some surfaces may be damaged if you try to re-position them. Similar tapes are made in metallic colors and also with decorative lines, dots, stars, etc.

Acrylic Spray & Workable Fixative

Acrylic spray is a polymer acrylic medium (glossy or matte) and is used as a protective coating on artwork. It is available in a pressurized spray can and is sometimes refered to as *picture varnish.* Krylon™ *workable fixatif™* is a clear protective coating which allows reworking after application. Gouache can be painted on top of workable fixative.

To prevent a felt-tipped marker from "bleeding" or spreading on most paper, try using acrylic spray on the paper beforehand. Two light applications should cut down on the paper's absorbency.

It is helpful to spray workable fixative onto newly painted gouache grounds. This isolates the ground from the painting which follows. The ground color will not be picked up or mixed with the new paint. It also

Ruling pens are used to draw straight lines with T-square or freehand lines.

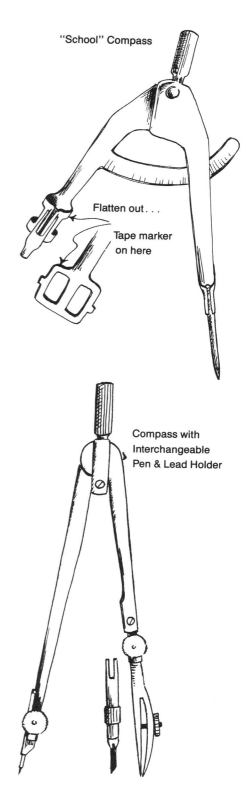

"School" Compass

Flatten out . . .

Tape marker
on here

Compass with
Interchangeable
Pen & Lead Holder

protects the ground from smudges and damage. *Caution:* the workable fixative spray will darken the color slightly and you may wish to compensate for this. Take precautions whenever using spray products. *Do not* inhale the spray fumes. Work in a well ventilated room. *Do not* smoke near flammable sprays.

Adhesives

Rubber cement is used on most papers, *except waxed papers,* for mounting purposes. Rubber cement *thinner* is used to control consistency of the rubber cement. Rubber cement in a spray-can is also useful but as with all spray-can materials be careful not to inhale it.

A rubber cement *pick-up* (a square chunk of hardened rubber cement) is used to remove unwanted rubber cement from artwork and mounts.

Elmer's™ glue, Sobo™ or their equivalent, or polymer acrylic medium (clear) can be mixed *sparingly* with gouache to enhance adhesive properties of the paint. This is especially useful when painting on acetate or other nonabsorbent surfaces. Crackling of gouache may occur if a thick layer of paint is added to an already painted surface. Glue in the second layer of paint will help control the crackling problem.

Erasers

Kneaded Eraser   A gray pliable *rubber* eraser which can be shaped into a point for reaching small areas is inexpensive and will not produce particles. It is excellent when working repeat layouts on tracing paper. The warmth of your hand helps to soften it for easier working. *Don't* buy the bluish plastic variety—this does not knead well.

Artgum™ Eraser (soap erasers)   This familiar tan eraser is safe on all types of paper and does not mar or scratch. If used gently on a painted gouache surface, it will remove pencil lines in the unpainted areas without marring the gouache. However, it does crumble and leaves particles that must be brushed away, and it wears away rather quickly.

Compasses

A bow compass is used to draw circles. Interchangeable pencil and pen parts are needed, the pencil when planning layouts and the pen attachment

Air-brush technique used to render a design for dinnerware. (© ROBERT CARBERRY.)

for use with gouache and dye. The trick is not to let the compass line dry before you paint in the circle if you wish to have a smooth effect.

An inexpensive school compass which holds regular pencils and colored pencils can be modified to be used with felt-tipped markers. If the marker is too large for the pencil clamp, it is possible to tape the marker to the compass. Also, the clamp can be bent and shaped so that the taping is made easier.

Rulers

Metal rulers are the most accurate. A good size to start with is 24″. You may want to add a 12″ ruler for smaller work, and a 36″ metal ruler is especially useful for larger repeats and for trimming paper with a razor blade.

Triangles

A large *triangle* (16″ to 18″ hypotenuse) and a small one (4″ to 6″ hypotenuse) are recommended. These can be 45° or 30°/60°. Clear plastic is commonly used. Some triangles are made with beveled edges which are helpful for inking and ruling pen work.

T-Square

A *T-square* is not essential, but it is a very helpful tool. For accuracy it should be used with a drawing board that has a metal edge. Wooden T-squares are not accurate and cannot be used for trimming paper with a razor blade. Metal is recommended, and a beveled edge is useful when using a ruling pen. 24″ is a good length.

Templates

A useful tool is a template, usually made of plastic. A circle template is easier to use than a compass. Templates come with many shapes from geometric and ellipses to objects and letters. It is also possible to cut your own shapes (two-ply smooth bristol paper works well). All templates work well with pencils, markers, and pens.

Tapes

Two types of tape commonly used are *masking tape* and *Scotch Brand Magic™ tape*. The masking tape is tan and is available in several sizes—½″, ¾″, or 1″ wide is an individual preference. A major use for the masking tape is to stabilize tracing paper on the final croquis paper or the drawing

Design rendered using a dispenser bottle as a designing tool. (© KAREN CONDON.)

board when making accurate copies of artwork. Scotch Brand Magic™ tape is clear with a matte surface. It is excellent for repairing tears in artwork and tracing paper. (See **Chapter 7** for techniques on repairing artwork.)

Tape Dispensers These are very handy and the double-roll type with two wheels can serve to hold masking tape and clear tape.

Knives & Cutting Tools

An *X-acto™ knife* with a #11 blade is a necessary tool. A *mat knife* will be useful for heavy cutting. In addition a package of industrial-type, *single-edged razor blades* will be helpful for general studio use. A *paper cutter* is a good tool in a large studio, but not essential. A good pair of paper scissors, 8″ to 12″ long is standard equipment.

Sponges & Tissues

Keep a flat synthetic or household sponge near the water jars, but it must be damp to be of any use. It will soak up the excess water from brushes after cleaning them when working with dyes or gouache. The tip of the brush is re-formed if you twirl it in your fingers as you draw it across the sponge. Several layers of paper towelling will work well also.

Facial tissues, bathroom tissues (roll), and paper towelling are extremely handy for general studio use.

Be on the lookout for interesting, unusual materials. Try materials that are not ordinarily considered as artist's supplies. Craft-supply materials sometimes suggest new techniques that can be modified and adapted to the design process. Art supply dealers are usually alert for new products, and are able to give you helpful information as to their use and applications. Try them out, experiment with the unorthodox combinations.

More exotic materials have been tried: coffee and tea work well to stain paper for a background color. Sand and salt when sprinkled on wet dye create their own special textures. The grains won't adhere, and can be brushed off when dry. Gesso and acrylic-based molding paste have been used successfully to simulate embossed and relief effects and can also be used to create a printing surface for unusual textures and patterns. The raised surface is allowed to dry and gouache is applied in a manner similar to inking a wood block relief and then pressing paper to its surface for printing. A number of impressions can then be assembled in a collage design. It is also possible to paint directly on the gesso surface to create special effects.

The list of art supplies available to the artist is endless and part of the joy of designing is to explore these materials.* Just why we choose and prefer certain media is a complex question. For the beginner it is best to become secure with the more traditional materials and techniques, and then gradually expand into the new. Trying new media can release unsuspected new skills. So take risks, be daring and have fun doing it!

---

*Send for catalogues listing art materials. A few suppliers are listed in **Appendix.**

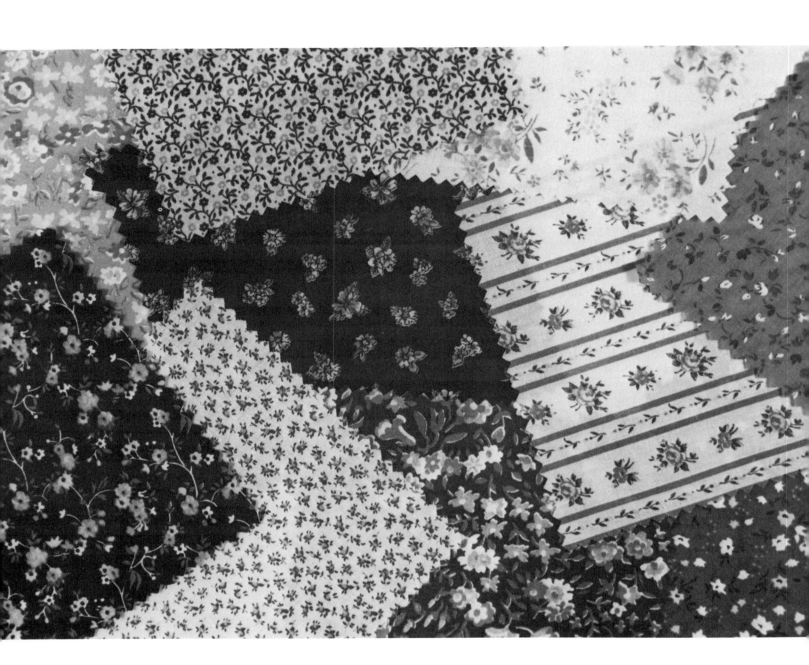

Some Elements of Textile Design

If one were to ask you to describe the designs on some printed fabrics, you might say "It has a lot of colors; it's made up mostly of imaginary looking big flowers going in all directions." Or perhaps "It's mostly blue and green; it's rather small and it looks very even and regular, somewhat geometric." Or again "It's bright with autumn colors. It seems like a big, bold, wavy abstract design, but when I look closely I see it's made up of ferns, grasses and leaves."

Examine these responses and you'll find some important elements of textile design. *Color* is mentioned, (blue, green, autumn); *scale* is included (big flowers . . . rather small, etc.); indications of *layout* (going in all directions, even and regular) as well as *motifs,* (flowers, ferns, grasses, leaves).

These elements and others which are used in creating designs are part of the artistic vocabulary of the textile designer. They are the traits that make designs distinctive and different from one another. They are the characteristics that will help you analyze and understand what you see. They are also the tools that you will constantly use in designing printed textiles.

This chapter will examine and discuss the elements of textile design.

COLOR

We talk extensively about color throughout the book since it is such a basic and very important aspect of textile design. It is color to which we initially respond when first seeing a design and before we intellectually become aware of *layout, motif,* etc.

Hue, Value & Chroma (Hv/c)

There are many aspects and considerations to color, and it is a fascinating and extensive study in itself. For example: the eye can see two million colors, more or less. *Hue* is the name for the color—red, yellow, blue. *Value* is the lightness or darkness of a color as measured against a gray scale. If we mix white with black we can make a gray scale of values. A workable scale would be 0-10 (0 = black and 10 = white).

We have mentioned *hue* (the color) and *value* (the range from light to dark). The third major aspect of color is its *chroma*. Chroma is the degree of brightness or brilliance of the color. Flame red or turquoise right from the

Design is creating order out of chaos.

Marjorie Bevlin

Calicos have become an American classic.

tube and unmixed with black, white, gray or their complementary colors will be extremely high in chroma. Color saturation is another way of putting it. We use words like *high* and *low, bright* and *dull* to refer to chroma.

Tints, Tones & Shades

When we mix a hue with black we have a *shade* of that color. When we mix it with white we have a *tint. Tones* are more subtle. If we mix a gray with a hue we get a *tone* of that color.

The formula Hv/c ties these three basic elements of color together and helps us to analyze a color, breaking it down into its three components. Every color, *hue,* has a *value* in relation to the gray scale (light to dark), and every color has *chroma,* its chromatic intensity (bright to dull).

It becomes apparent that value now refers not only to the gray scale but to the color itself. Any color may range in value from very light (a tint) to very dark (a shade). The value of a color then is how light or dark it is. The formula Hv/c is especially useful when mixing colors (see **Chapter 9.**)

Perhaps the most important aspect of color is its relation to other colors and its interaction with other colors. Each color influences or modifies the color it is placed next to, even when the color is on white paper. (The white interacts with the color as well.) The same is true of black. When a color, for instance a one-inch square of orange is placed on a dark blue ground it looks totally different than when placed on a pale green ground. And so it is when we paint a color falling on another color in a design. . . . they enrich each other and the whole design begins to "sing." (For additional information refer to *The Interaction of Color,* Joseph Albers.)

Carried to the extreme we can place bright red on bright green and the edges where the colors touch begin to vibrate dramatically. Any complementary set of colors of the same value and chroma will dance and jump. This is essentially an impression in the eye and is the basis of Impressionistic painting which originated in the French school of art in the 19th century when the principles of light and color were scientifically developed.

Another important aspect of color is the effect of the light source on color. Without light there would be no color. In a dark room we have difficulty distinguishing one color from another, especially if these colors are subtle tints, tones and shades of that color.

The light source has a *temperature* factor and may be warm or cool. Late afternoon sunshine is very warm—an orange glow that warms up the entire color spectrum. Winter light is cool, as is light through a north window. Incandescent bulbs are warm and yellowish, fluorescent tubes may be cool or warm. It is best to balance these light sources if possible. Daylight is considered the most balanced light if it is not direct sunlight. With artificial lighting it is important to come as close to daylight as possible. Colors will read most accurately and will tend not to vary too greatly when seen in different rooms with different light temperatures.

Color is the most joyous of all the elements of design for the artist. It has endless possibilities of combinations and variations and is the most sensitive element to the expression of the artist's personality. We all tend to prefer certain combinations of colors which reflect our preferences and our uniqueness. In the textile industry, designers learn to use all colors, in all kinds of combinations: analogous, monochromatic, pastel, darks and brights according to changes in season and fashion, to suit the demands of the marketplace. As professionals we respond to industry needs.

CROQUIS OR SKETCH

A commonly used term in the textile design field is the word *croquis** (pronounced *kro-kee*). It is the French word for *sketch,* not a sketch in the sense of a pencil drawing or study as used in fine arts, but *a finished, fully*

---

*The word "croquis" has been used traditionally to mean a fully painted design which is not in repeat. This is the word we use throughout the book. More recently "sketch" is being used as a working term, and is interchangeable with "croquis."

executed rendering of a design, painted in full color. It is as close to the final product as possible and is used for selling the design idea to the potential buyers.

A characteristic aspect of a croquis is that the design "falls off the edges" of the paper, so to speak, looking as though it had been cut out of a larger piece. It simulates a fabric swatch of a pattern which would have been cut from a bolt of printed cloth.

In general the word *design* will be used to refer to artwork that is painted on paper. *Pattern* will refer to a design that is printed on fabric. However these two terms are often interchanged and have come to mean almost the same thing to textile designers. The word *pattern* can also refer to the repetitive use of a *motif* or motifs within a croquis—which adds to the confusion.

MOTIFS

Motif is another commonly used word in the field. A motif can be several things—recognizable objects such as a cup, a pencil, a figure of a child, a rooster, an egg, a ball—these are called conversational motifs. Also a motif can be a flower, a leaf, a seed pod, a tree (things from nature). Others are squares, triangles, circles, wavy lines, and are called geometric or abstract motifs.

Motifs are the building blocks of a design. Their repetitive use creates the "pattern" look which is basic to designs on fabric. This ongoing, continuous aspect is necessary if we are going to print hundreds of yards of fabric.

For the beginner it is helpful to simplify the motif to a flat silhouette. It can then be placed next to itself or next to another motif. This process continues until a pattern is formed. Here an interesting phenomenon occurs: the individual motif recedes in importance and the pattern tends to dominate. In a sense the whole becomes greater than the sum of its parts! (For additional information see *Education of Vision,* Anton Erhensweig.)

LAYOUTS

When you were asked to describe a printed design on first sight, you noticed almost at once that the design was "going in all directions" or "it looks very even and regular" or "it's bold and wavy." What you were talking about is the *arrangement* of the motifs of the design, whether they are flowers, abstract shapes, animals, etc. You were talking about the *layout.*

Layout is another frequently used term in textile design. It is the same idea as *composition* which is a term used more commonly in fine arts.

Layout is the placement of one motif relative to another. It takes into account the distance as well as the direction the second motif is from the first. And, of course, this applies to all the motifs in the croquis.

A sketch or croquis can vary in its layout. A *repeat* also deals extensively with layout since we must extend the original croquis so that it "connects-to-itself" and can then be printed continuously on fabric and other flat surfaces. We will talk more about repeat layouts in **Chapter 8.** For the moment we'll discuss layouts as used in designing croquis (a painted design intended to be developed as a fabric pattern).

Direction of Motifs

One Way   Motifs are all up or "right-side-up," and are common to wallcovering and drapery designs.

Two Way   Motifs are both up and down in the same design which is desirable in apparel.

Four Way   Motifs are both up and down and left and right in the same design.

Tossed   Motifs are in all directions. When using this layout avoid

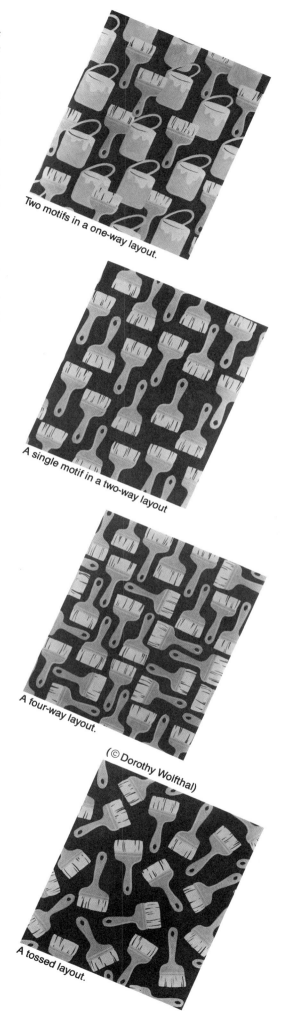

Two motifs in a one-way layout.

A single motif in a two-way layout

A four-way layout.

(© Dorothy Wolfthal)

A tossed layout.

motifs parallel to the edge of the paper—that is straight up or down, left or right. Tossed is a most usable layout for apparel. The manufacturer of a garment can nest the sleeves, yoke, front panels, back, etc., of the garment close together when cutting the cloth without worrying about the direction of the design, thereby using most of the fabric and avoiding costly waste.

Coverage: Another Aspect of Layout

When motifs of a design are placed closely together the layout is called *tight* or *packed*. If the motifs are separated and there is a lot of ground between motifs, the layout is called *open* or *spaced*. Even if the white fabric is printed, a solid color between motifs *(a blotch)*, the layout is still *open*. *Spacing*, then, is used to refer to the tightness or openness of the layout, actually the distance between motifs. Fifty percent coverage is an equal amount of printed areas relative to the background (non-printed areas). Sixty percent, seventy percent, etc., is more coverage. Forty percent, thirty percent, etc., is less coverage.

Coverage may also refer to an uneven or irregular placement of motifs, some clustered closely together in some areas, and more open (or spaced) in others. This is sometimes called an *open-and-closed* layout.

Types of Layouts

Set Layout   The set layout has an invisible grid, with the motifs of the design arranged in squares, or triangles, or rows or some other definite plan, perhaps interlocking in some clever way. Abstract and simple conversationals are especially suited to set layouts, but almost any type of design can be worked into a set layout.

Random Layout   (sometimes called tossed or allover) Since there is no underlying (invisible) grid, the motifs are scattered in *seemingly* random relationships to each other and go in all directions. This type of layout does not look "arranged," but has a more or less loose, irregular appearance. However, it takes thought and care to make a pleasing, balanced, harmonious allover layout.

Stripe Layout   Striped designs may be bands of solid color or they may be composed of motifs arranged in rows. Flowers and leaves, abstract shapes, documentary motifs—all may be arranged in vertical stripes (common in wallcoverings), in horizontal stripes (known as a bayadere) or diagonal stripes (from upper left to lower right, or from upper right to lower left). The stripes, or bands can be very straight and accurate or they can be wavy and freely executed. They can be the same width or they can vary in width.

Stripe layouts offer other opportunities for variations. A band of flowers can be interlaced or separated by a band of flat color. Horizontal rows of little boats may be shown on a background of wavy horizontal lines. A textured weave may be worked into a diagonal stripe, alternating with some documentary theme. The spaces between the stripes (the negative spaces) need not always be the same color; these areas can be colored differently for still another striped effect.

Plaid Layout We usually think of plaids in terms of tattersalls and tartans woven into the fabric itself. But printed design also utilizes the plaid arrangement, either in a tight, controlled manner or more freely. Flowers, ribbons, dots, wavy leaves, and grasses, all can be designed in an interweaving, cross-over manner to create a plaid effect.

Intersecting lines or bands of color, painted very evenly, can create fairly accurately the look of a woven plaid. This is quite effective in itself. But since it is meant to be printed and not woven, it is possible also to include additional design elements within the squares, or related to the lines of the plaid.

Because we are working with printed designs, we have still further flexibility. The plaid layout may be planned on the vertical and horizontal, and frequently is. But a plaid layout may also be worked at a forty-five degree angle and become a diagonal plaid. There are certain advantages, both practical and aesthetic, to a diagonal plaid when used for women's apparel. The diamond shapes are usually more flattering to the figure. And the problem of *bowing* in the printing process is avoided. *Bowing* occurs when the horizontal threads of a fabric are stretched during printing. The fabric is held under tension at both selvages while being fed through the machinery. If a straight horizontal line is printed during the time the fabric is thus pulled, the horizontally printed line will have a slight curve or "bow" when the fabric is relaxed. The threads return to normal when the fabric is removed from the print machine causing the horizontal lines across the width of the goods to distort. This is avoided if the plaid is "diamond-like" as it repeats from selvage to selvage.

Border Prints In this layout, as the name implies, a border is worked into the design. It usually appears along one selvage, or edge, of the fabric. The border design is printed a few inches in from the edge to allow for cutting and sewing, and also to avoid distortion of the design at the edge of the fabric that may occur during the printing process. Sometimes the pattern is so designed that there is a border running along both edges of the fabric.

There are many types of borders. They may be only a narrow strip, a sort of "ending" to the design. Or the border may be the most important element, broad and extensive, and taking up almost the entire width of the fabric. Most often, a border is somewhere between these two extremes.

The main body of the fabric may simply remain a solid color. More commonly, though, there are some additional design elements or motifs that extend from the border across the goods. This area of the design (the *field*) may be worked so that it appears to "grow" out of the border and be strongly related to it in style, color, and subject matter. It can also start from the border quite abruptly, giving the effect of a different design attached arbitrarily to the edge of the border.

Border designs are most useful for women's apparel as well as for drapery and other decorative fabrics.

Engineered Design

Closely related to the border print is the *engineered design*. Although most textile designs are meant to be ongoing and continuous, the engineered design is an exception. In this case the design is considered as a single unit clearly separated from itself as it repeats along the length of the fabric. It is designed, or engineered, to fit a specific area or shape, for a particular end

Fabric held firmly at both selvages

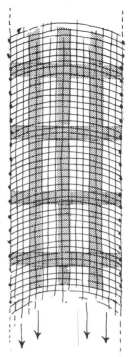

Direction of movement

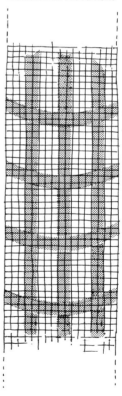

Bowing is a problem created when fabric is stretched during the printing process. The crosswise threads (filling) are pulled as fabric is moved along during printing. When the fabric is removed from the machinery, the filling straightens and crosswise bands, although printed straight, become "bowed." (Effects are exaggerated in these drawings for purposes of clarity.)

A stylized floral with stripe background (right, © FRESH PAINT STUDIO). Double border (below), shown from edge to edge. The field is a one-way set layout.

Scarves are a clear example of engineered design, which are laid out to fit a specific shape (facing page).

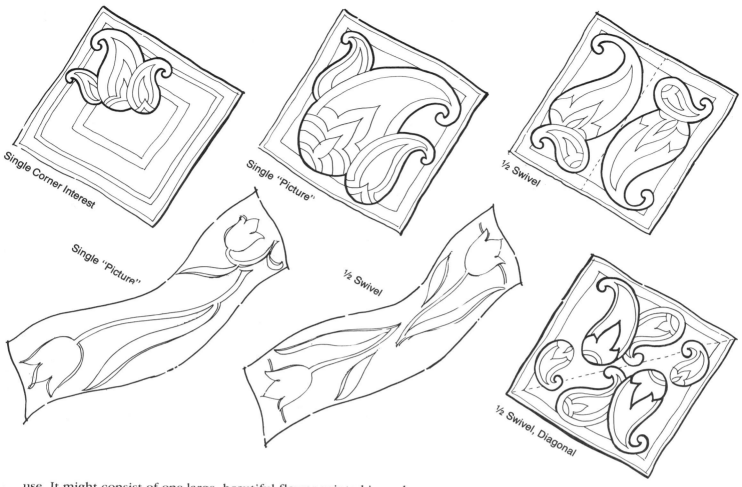

Single Corner Interest

Single "Picture"

½ Swivel

Single "Picture"

½ Swivel

½ Swivel, Diagonal

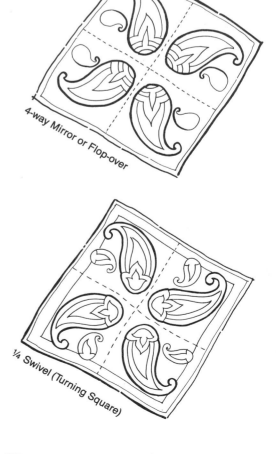

4-way Mirror or Flop-over

¼ Swivel (Turning Square)

use. It might consist of one large, beautiful flower printed in such a way on the fabric that when a dress manufacturer cuts it to make the garment, the flower always appears on one side of the skirt. It might be a conversational motif so placed that a men's loungewear manufacturer, for example, can cut the garment with the motif falling in the middle of the back of a robe. Often the textile designer works in cooperation with the fashion designer on an engineered print since special needs such as size, placement and direction must be met. An engineered design of this kind is often printed in a limited amount of yardage for one individual client. It is rarely possible to adapt this type of engineered design to any other purpose and it is therefore usually more costly to produce.

Another type of engineered design is a design created for a scarf, either square or long and narrow. Within the center of the scarf there may be one large design or "picture." Or the square may be divided in half or in quarters and the design repeated in each section, rotated around a center point or mirrored (flop-over). This arrangement may also be worked on a long scarf or ascot. It may be designed as one single "picture" or divided in half or quarters with a design motif that is repeated in each section.

When designing scarves it is important to bear in mind the end use. It will probably be draped or tied around the neck or waist or over the head so that the corners are in view. Therefore, on a square scarf the corners are important and on an ascot both ends should be given careful thought.

There is a large group of domestic and home furnishings products that fall under the heading of engineered design. A partial list includes kitchen and bath towels, tablecloths, napkins and placemats, bedspreads, sheets and pillowcases, and bath towels. These are all designed to fit certain dimensions. The purpose, of course, is that when they are cut and finished each piece will be a complete, separate unit. Kitchen and bath towels are planned so that when they are folded (usually in thirds lengthwise) the center portion is an important part of the design. This is a consideration for marketing purposes (gift boxes, presentations, and store displays) as well as for use by the consumer.

TYPES OF DESIGNS

Floral Designs

Probably the most frequently printed type of design, as far back in history as the first piece of patterned cloth, is the *floral.* This includes not only flower motifs but motifs based on the entire plant kingdom: leaves, grasses, vines, seeds, pods, water plants, etc. Flowers and plants have been used as decoration in interiors and on clothing for adults and children in all parts of the world and across all levels of society throughout the history of mankind. Trends may come and go, but florals will always be with us.

Floral designs may be painted quite *realistically* as they appear in nature, in more or less natural colors and sizes. *One type* of plant may be used in a design—all daisies, or roses or petunias, perhaps with their own kinds of leaves and stems. These may be *grouped in clusters,* or shown *separate* from one another. Or *several or many types* of plants may be used together as a mixed bouquet or as varied field flowers.

Floral designs can also be *stylized, unrealistic,* painted with fantasy or whimsy, flat and poster-like, unlike anything you'd find in a garden or a seed catalogue. A few examples: geometric-looking Art Deco flowers, William Morris and decorative Persian flowers.

Conversational Designs

Conversational refers to designs with recognizable subject matter. A *conversational* design may depict a single motif: wooden shoes, kites, kittens, lipsticks, spaceships. Or a *conversational* may tell a "story"—a number of motifs related to one *theme.* Some examples of themes are: *circus:* clowns, performing seals, acrobats, balloons; *sports:* tennis players in various poses, tennis balls, racquets, nets; *current events,* such as 1976, U.S. Bicentennial, using many "Americana" themes; or the summer or winter Olympics: figures of athletes and the apparatus of their particular sports.

Designs intended for use in the kitchen or bath may include motifs such as spice jars and cooking implements, or elegant or amusing bath and cosmetic paraphernalia. These are all examples of conversational designs with a theme. (Themes and collections have been discussed in **Chapter 1.**)

Often the design is not purely a conversational. Occasionally floral or other decorative motifs are included to "soften" the look. This is especially true of children's patterns. The following are examples of conversationals:

Juvenile Designs Candies, lollipops, animals, Mother Goose and other legend and fairy tale subjects, school (schoolhouse, pencils and pens, blackboard letters and numbers); toys (dolls, teddybears, toy wagons, trains and cars, blocks); special activities (at the beach, at the playground, bathtime, going to the zoo); winter subjects such as skating or snowmen.

Adult Patterns, Apparel Dancing, animals, articles of clothing (hats, gloves, jewelry); familiar objects such as lipsticks, buttons, sunglasses; calligraphy, vehicles, buildings (skyscrapers, houses, castles).

Other Patterns, Home Fashions Kitchen implements (pots and pans, eggbeaters, cutlery); spices and spice jars, fruits, vegetables, breads and other foods; sports and sport equipment, animals and animal skins, rural and urban scenics (skylines, farm subjects, etc.); "period pieces" (Victorian costumes and settings, roaring twenties, nostalgic movies).

Traditional Designs

There are certain textile designs that have been treated in more or less the same manner over the years. They have not changed very much while fashions have come and gone. These are the traditionals—the *classics*.

Foulards Used for such purposes as men's neckwear, men's lounge- and sleepwear, linings, in certain "correct" restrained women's fashions. They are usually rather small geometric forms, often in a "set" layout, having a classic, conservative effect. Colors are subdued often with a dark or neutral background, and all in all, they are very elegant.

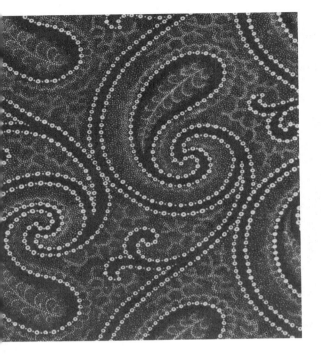

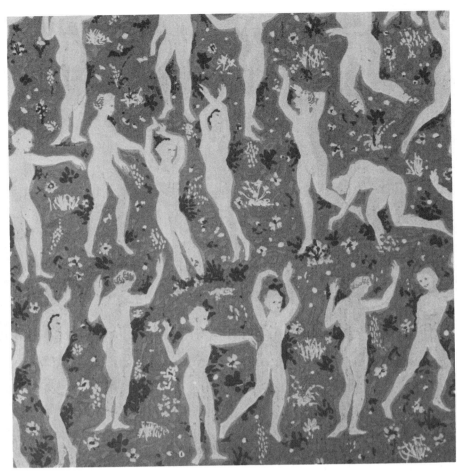

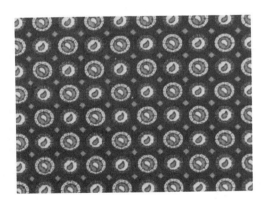

Paisleys   Using the standard paisley or Persian-palm shape. The classic paisley design has considerable detailed line work. It can range in size from quite small to medium-large. The traditional paisley colors are rich, deep, jewel-like.

Paisleys can also be interpreted more freely and in keeping with changing fashions in color and technique. But these are not the traditional paisleys, which are almost as classic as the foulard.

Calico Prints   These almost need no description. They have been in existence for centuries and frequently reappear as high fashion. The familiar calico print is a small floral, close coverage, usually three or four colors plus white, often with a bright or dark ground. Tiny geometric motifs as well as stripes and plaids are also typical. Their traditional use in the past was for dresses and aprons, children's wear and frequently for patchwork quilts.

Liberty Prints   Liberty of London, a venerable British department store, was for a long time known for a particular style of design. These patterns were usually florals, sometimes combined with fruits, birds or other charming motifs. They were in a small to medium scale, in soft colors, with rather even coverage. They often had a clean, thin outline to define the motifs. Liberty of London has since greatly broadened its range of designs and styles, but their earlier look was so distinctive and influential that it has become a classic type known as the *Liberty print*. Conservative in effect, they are used mostly for women's and children's wear.

The Lingerie Floral   This is a dainty, small, rather widely spaced type of design, sometimes in a scattered layout but also sometimes seen in a set arrangement. Rosebuds, little daisies, tiny nosegays, perhaps with a little ribbon or butterfly, in clean, delicate pastels; they are often printed on delicate cottons or dotted Swiss. These designs have been seen for generations and are used most frequently in lingerie, and clothing for infants and little girls.

Paisley design—a timeless motif executed in a delicate technique from the DESIGN LAB, FIT (top, left). Foulard design which includes a small, set paisley motif (bottom, left). Human figures used in a somewhat stylized manner with a flavor of the 1920s (top, right, © RICHARD FISHER).

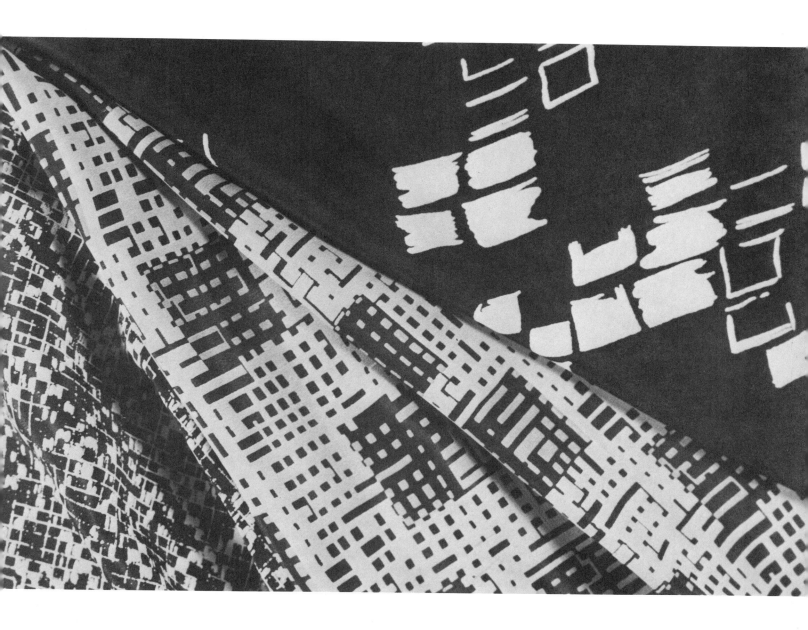

A group of geometric designs. The small scale creates textural effects. (© FISHER & GENTILE)

Typical William Morris patterns which are faithful translations from the original Victorian documents.

"Little Nothing" Designs   These might be called abstract, and they have become so familiar and constant in the textile design market that they are now traditional. They consist of *small,* rather simple shapes, usually having one to three colors. They may be simple geometric forms—triangles, circles, lines or irregular dabs or wiggles, crescents or commas. Occasionally there will be two or three of the same shape touching or overlapping. Usually these patterns are arranged in a tossed, openly spaced layout. Sometimes they are found as twin prints, that is, the same design in dark-on-light as well as light-on-dark. They have traditionally been used in women's and men's clothing, but have also begun appearing on fabrics and wallcoverings for the home—perhaps in a slightly larger scale.

Documentary Designs   These designs have their origin in certain periods of history, different countries, different cultures, and distinctive national or ethnic styles. A documentary design is a fairly close approximation of the original and is usually derived from research of documents and similar reference materials. Museum collections, books on fine arts and folk arts are typical reference material for this category of design. It is a great joy to be able to delve into documentary reference because we learn about the culture and history of other peoples, and our awareness of art grows with the research.

Some documentary sources are: Indonesian batik, African ikat, Japanese and Chinese (both ancient and modern), French, "toile de jouy" better known simply as *toile,* English, Italian and German baroque and rococo, Art Nouveau, Art Deco, Pennsylvania Dutch, Egyptian, North and South Native American, tribal decorations from New Guinea (primitive), Mexican, Peruvian, Byzantine, Celtic, Persian—the list is endless!

"Little nothing" designs with coordinate variations. (Top, © ANNE KRISTOF; bottom, © NATALIE MCLEAN.)

Textures & Weaves

Textures and weaves are often printed on wallcoverings and fabrics for home decorations, and are found on apparel fabrics as well.

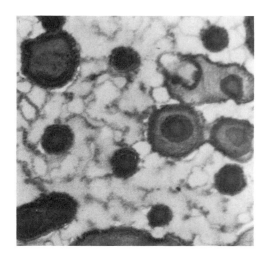

Organic Textures These are found in nature and include wood grains, reptile skins, sand and pebbles, grasses, clouds, seashells, bird feathers, fur, leather grains, and many more. The patterns found in nature are infinite, and a visit to a natural history museum or the seashore or any outdoor place will reveal exciting design possibilities.

Weaves Special effects can be printed on material to give the look of woven designs, such as straw, flax, bamboo, rattan, cord, wicker, basketry, as well as knits, crochets and woven cloth. When interpreted for printing purposes, fresh and exciting designs can be created. Often the scale is modified and the complexity of the threads and yarns are simplified. Printed "woven" effects can be used independently as well as for background interest in a larger design.

Artificial Effects Using a stipple brush, sponge, toothbrush for a splatter, tissues to blot a puddle of paint, or any combination of a number of techniques, can create a textured, irregular appearance. These techniques and others are described more fully in **Chapter 6**.

Graphic Textures Graphic textures are geometric in nature, having a simplified, clean and stylized look. They are not *motifs* in the usual sense of the word. They are the opposite of an organic texture but their appearance, especially from a slight distance, has a strong allover textural quality.

Abstract & Geometric Designs

Abstract designs are non-representational in content. Free-form and wavy shapes are typical. Although motifs may have been inspired by some specific form or object, they are so far removed from that object as to be no longer recognizable. The specific form or object has been completely "abstracted".

Abstract designs are so varied in appearance that their uses are universal. They are found in women's, men's and children's wear; home decoration for kitchen, bed, bath and in all living areas.

Geometric designs are comprised of squares, triangles, circles, cubes, cones, and spheres, and are made up of straight and curved lines and angles. The forms may or may not be connected, or may overlap or mesh with one another.

Other types of abstract and geometric design include *stripes, plaids,* and *checks.* Printed plaids, stripes and checks echo their woven origins. They include madras, tattersalls, tartans, roman stripes and gingham checks. (Plaids and stripes are discussed as layout considerations in a previous section of this chapter.)

Organic texture inspired by frog skin for rainwear. The design process allows for an element of controlled "accident"! (above, left, © RICHARD FISHER). A geometric abstraction with an architectural theme (above, right, © SANDRA COLON). Geometric motifs widely spaced on a diagonal stripe with linear textural interest (facing page, © FRESH PAINT STUDIO).

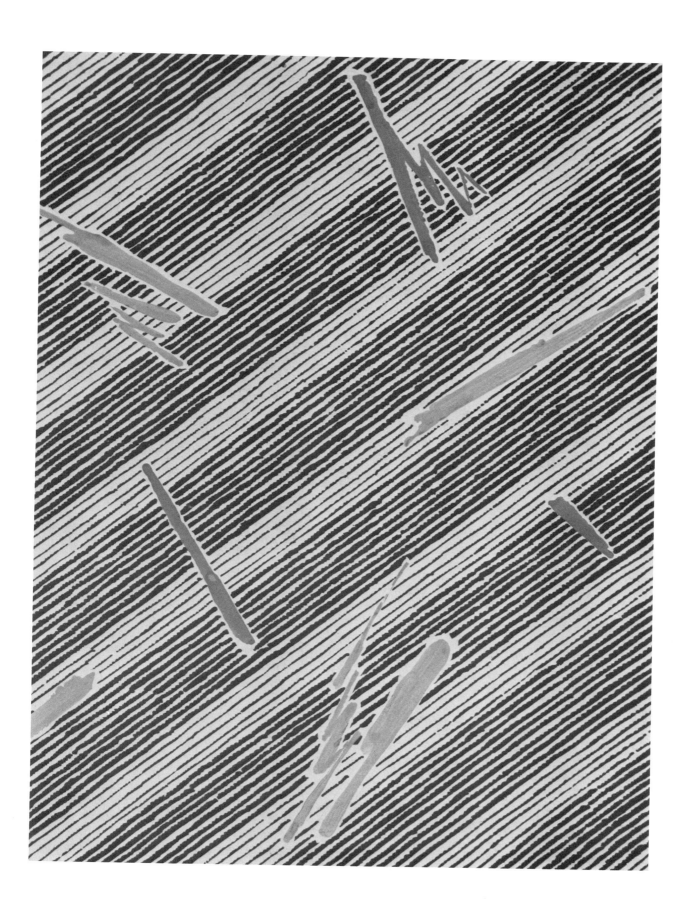

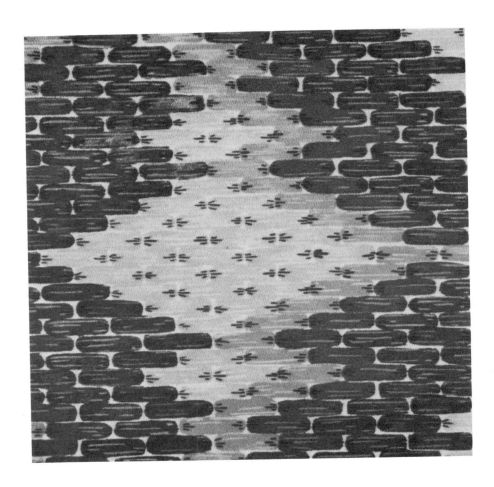

The Basic Types of Designs

- *The floral*—realistic or stylized.
- *The conversational*—recognizable objects.
- *The traditional*—foulards, paisleys, calicos, Liberty prints, lingerie florals, little nothing prints
- *The documentary*—Documents from other cultures and other periods of time
- *Textures and weaves*
- *Abstract and geometric*

These are clear, recognizable types, or categories of designs. Types are often combined: florals may be used with geometric or abstract elements; conversationals are superimposed on a textured or woven setting; florals and conversationals are often used together. There are *no hard and fast rules,* and the professional designer uses these categories freely and loosely.

A representation of a weave with a strong geometric effect.

CONCLUSION

We have discussed in this chapter some of the elements of design that are pertinent to the textile print design field. There are many aspects of design which have not been covered and can be learned in practice. It is the purpose of this book to focus on the special elements of design unique to the textile industry.

A special principle of design that needs highlighting is that of *unity.* Every successful work which is worthy to be called art has a wholeness and completeness about it. All elements of design must be in harmony. The subject matter, the color, the style as well as the entire pattern-look—all must fit the product for which the pattern is intended. The motif, the layout, the scale, the balance, the techniques must all work together, and be supportive of the whole. Without this integration—this unity—the work is not art; it is not satisfying to the artist and will not be truly successful in the marketplace.

Types of design have been examined to clarify the kinds of patterns so that newer designs have some reference to existing products. It helps to know what has been done in different product areas so that new design directions are more discernible.

There is an exceptionally high level of aesthetic content in textile print design, which is often closely related to the fine arts of museum collections. Indeed many artists in the field are also painters or printmakers or are involved with the visual arts in other ways. It is very satisfying to an artist to work with color possibilities and design ideas found in textile design patterns.

This chapter is intended as a foundation on which to orient ourselves to industry in order to work professionally as a textile designer. The purpose is to gain knowledge of the textile print design industry as well as other related product areas, so that we can apply our skills and talents to originating artwork. The following chapters will discuss steps on how to proceed with your actual textile designs.

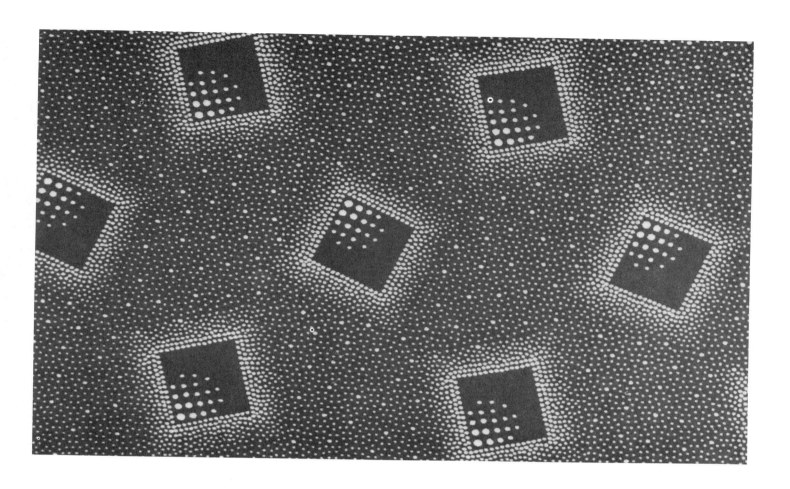

Geometric design for apparel from the DESIGN LAB, FIT. A stipple technique is used to create an ombre effect which defines the squares.

1. *Colors appear glowing on a black background. Tropical floral design from* FRESH PAINT STUDIO.

2. *Stylized floral on black squares for apparel. (© FRESH PAINT STUDIO.)*

3. *"Potpourri" by* GREEFF FABRICS—*the vine-like border imitates the central motif.*

4. *Floral border design with stripe layout within the "field."* (DESIGN LAB, FASHION INSTITUTE OF TECHNOLOGY.)

5. *A sophisticated conversational executed in a bold technique. (© FRESH PAINT STUDIO.)*

6. *A colorful, free plaid hand painted on silk.* (DESIGN LAB, FASHION INSTITUTE OF TECHNOLOGY.)

7. *Geometric apparel design from* FRESH PAINT STUDIO.

8. *Detail from "St. Etienne" by* GREEFF. *The entire design appears on page 144.*

9, 10. *For presentation purposes a border design has been shown in a fashion illustration. This is a dramatic selling device. (© KARNA SALEH.)*

11–13. *A reference photo of Chinese embroidery from a museum calendar (11), and exploration sketch (12). Below (13) is the final rendering. Unfinished edges can be completed when the design is put into repeat. (© RICHARD FISHER.)*

1

2

3

4,5

6

8

9

10

11

12

13

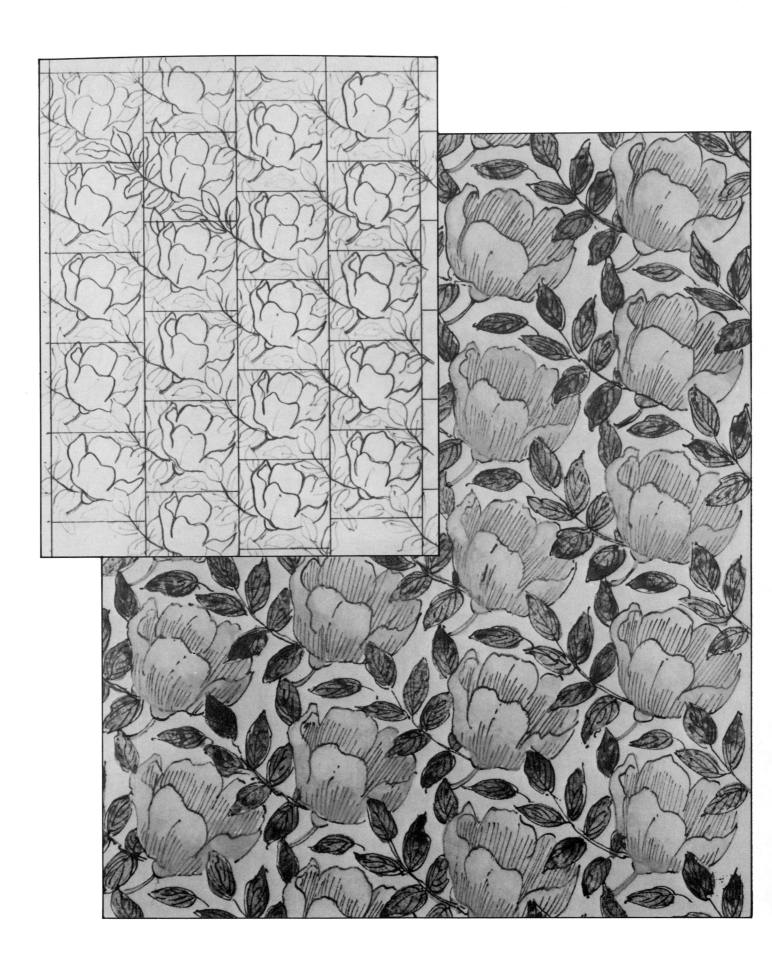

HOW TO MAKE IT INTO A TEXTILE DESIGN

An experienced designer may sometimes pick up a loaded brush and proceed to paint directly on paper, creating a new croquis boldly and spontaneously. But even the experienced designer often resorts to interim steps on the way to the finished croquis. For the beginner it is *imperative to follow a more controlled series of steps* to ensure a successful design. Using an orderly procedure will save time and avoid the frustration that can result from jumping in without looking.

Ideas won't keep. Something must be done with them.

Alfred North Whitehead

STEP 1. SEARCH & PONDER

The first step is to research the marketplace (see **Chapter 2**). This is in itself a fascinating process. You will look through current magazines and newspapers, examine what is being shown in department stores and boutiques, refer to your own growing collection of files and clippings, as well as the sketchbooks you have been filling with motifs, colors, and ideas for inspiration.

For example, let us assume you have zeroed in on a *stylized floral to be used for women's apparel.* Within this broad category there are many variables: many other decisions to make.

Is this going to be a design for junior apparel or misses' dresses or blouses? Spring or fall, or some other season? Mass market or high style? These questions must be answered before we can go further. For our purposes, let us say the design is meant for *women's moderate-priced blouses* for the *fall season,* to be sold in *department stores* and in several nationwide *catalogues*—in other words, *mass market.*

Next follows a number of further decisions:

1. *Scale of motifs*   Should they be large? Small? Since the design will be used for blouses and for a comparatively conservative market, the motifs should not be very large. The overall effect should not be too extreme or dramatic. We will choose *small-* to *medium-size motifs.*

2. *Layout*   For the purposes of economy we will choose a tossed *layout* for our example and make all the motifs go in different directions so that the garment can be cut with the least amount of wasted fabric (see **Chapter 4**). It is important to note that croquis for the apparel field usually are in a vertical, rectangular format. This relates to the verticality of the human figure.

A half-drop grid layout is used to create an apparel design with a single floral motif. The steps in the development can be seen on pages 84 and 85. (© RICHARD FISHER.)

3. *Coverage* (a further consideration of layout) Should the motifs be closely packed (close coverage) or more widely spaced (more ground showing)? Should there be even distribution, or rather irregular clusters (open-and-closed layout)? As a tentative decision let us say the coverage should be rather *close*. But to keep the design varied and interesting, let us make the layout somewhat irregular and uneven.

It is helpful for the beginner to look at the various print patterns on clothing in his/her wardrobe and in the department stores to see the types of layout being used. You will see the many possibilities. Examine these garments for color and motifs as well. This will help you design a croquis that is more suitable for printing on fabrics.

4. *Motifs* Of course we need reference material from our files and clippings. From our search of the market we come to the conclusion that for this design we will use several *different stylized floral motifs,* and *we will include stems and leaves for variation and interest.*

First, experimental drawings, sketches, and doodles should be started on tracing paper. Do not worry at this point about making a finished drawing or putting in a great amount of detail. Be prepared to sketch, scribble, select, eliminate in your search for potential designs. Try three, four or more sketches of various flower and leaf shapes until you have developed several possibilities.

STEP 2. FUN DOODLES/EXPERIMENTS/ROUGHS

Now we put the pencil aside and start to experiment with brush and paint. Using the motifs you have decided on, paint some preliminary experiments to help you make decisions on color, paper, medium, techniques, and other variables. *Don't* forget to use your reference material which will constantly give you fresh ideas and authenticity for the particular flowers you have chosen to use. Copying is not necessary unless you are doing a faithful reproduction of a document. We want to re-interpret the subject matter by using the reference material as a starting point.

You may get an idea for colors from one source of reference material, technique from another, background treatment from still another source. As you begin mixing colors and putting the brush to paper, these ideas will combine with your own creativeness, one idea leading to another, until they crystallize into your own unique and original concept. *Do not* stop until you have explored a number of interpretations.

An important rule: experiment on the *same* paper that you intend to use to paint the final croquis. Switching paper for the croquis introduces unexpected variables and can change the color as well as the technique.

STEP 3. WHAT COLORS SHOULD YOU USE?

Color is perhaps the most important element of a design and must be timely and market-oriented. The choice of what colors to use is often difficult since the eye can distinguish two million or more colors with their tints, tones, and shades.

In **Step 2** you have already started to experiment with color and have explored a few possible directions. All of us have our own color preferences which we tend to repeat unless we use reference materials in order to expand our color horizons. For the beginner it would be a good idea to take color from an existing blouse or swatch of fabric. Match them closely and try to use approximately the same proportions of each color in the swatch. Now you can see how the new color will look in the design you have begun. If you don't like the effect, try modifying the colors you have started with or try some new colors.

Matching Colors A 30-hole palette is useful when matching your reference color so that you can readily create new colors. Start with a tube of paint closest to the color you are matching. Add white and/or black to match the *value* of reference color. Then modify the *hue* with additional analogous colors.

Paint a small patch of the new color at the edge of a strip of paper. Cut a small "window" (a rectangle approximately ⅜″ x ⅝″) from another piece of paper. Place the newly painted color next to the color you are matching and then place the window over both of them. This isolates the two colors and it is easier to see if the match is exact. This procedure is especially useful if you are matching a color on a swatch of fabric or on an original design or a color in a book or magazine.

Other possible reference materials for color selection might be a page in a magazine, possibly a painting reproduced in a book or something in your immediate environment that appeals to you. An important part of color choice is to select reference material you like and respond to; sense that inner tug or feeling when you first see a promising direction and it will be a clue that it is worth a try.

Experiment with color looks, dark motifs on light background, or light on dark; a multicolor look, or more tonal or analogous colors. Try various techniques: flat, even colors, dry-brush, textured areas, bold blobs of paint with a loaded brush, outline or fine-line decoration. Should the background be pre-painted as a solid color? How about introducing some kind of secondary design feature in the background like a stipple or sponge treatment, some line-work, small geometric forms? Maybe a shadow effect? Take plenty of time at this stage to allow full range for your imagination and inventiveness. Try different types of paper to find the one most suitable to the development of your ideas.

The number of colors in any one croquis can vary from one (black is always dramatic) to five (a limit sometimes imposed by industry and based on the cost of engraving and printing). Occasionally you will find six colors. The fabric may be pre-dyed and if it is light in value (known as a *tinted ground*), it can be overprinted with the colors of your croquis. With drapery and upholstery more than six colors are often used. Eight is not uncommon and even twelve to fifteen can be found. For most apparel croquis, use no more than five colors.

STEP 4. PATTERNING—development of motifs into a pattern (layout considerations)

Patterning is a made up word to describe a very essential element of textile design. We use a single motif or several in combination with each other to create an allover effect. This is called the *pattern*. The individual motif(s) recede in importance and the allover look of the fabric dominates. In a sense the whole becomes greater than the sum of its parts.

On a fresh sheet of tracing paper, using the motifs you like, compose the final layout. You have the option of several ways to do this. Some designers work in charcoal at this stage, loosely indicating location, grouping, and direction of motifs. You can easily rub out charcoal markings with a tissue and continue to draw over the slightly smudged areas. An important advantage to this way of working is its flexibility. You can sketch, rub out, reconsider, and sketch again without wasting a lot of time and effort. The tracing paper can begin to look so messy that you may decide to place another sheet on top and continue your planning afresh. When the final layout is arrived at, a new sheet of tracing paper is placed on top of the charcoal layout, and a more careful tracing is made in pencil. Spraying the charcoal with workable fixative before the pencil tracing helps to keep your work clean and neat.

Another way of working a preliminary layout, especially when there are separate and distinct motifs and groups of motifs is as follows: the motifs are drawn several times on tracing paper, loosely or in silhouette, with a marker or dark pencil. These drawings are then cut or torn out so they can be handled separately. On a fresh sheet of tracing paper use the cut-out motifs almost like chess pieces on a board—move them around, turn them upside

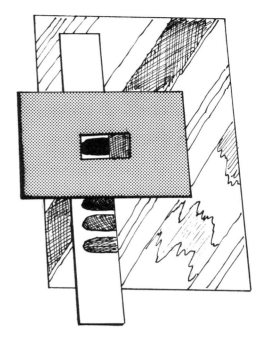

Use a "window" to facilitate matching colors. Be sure to paint test dabs at the edge of your strip of paper.

The original reference was a greeting card from the Metropolitan Museum of Art. Technique was explored on Denril® (a plastic paper). Penline was used and a watery gouache was modified by blotting with tissue. Using separate pieces of tracing paper, individual motifs were rearranged into the final layout. (© RICHARD FISHER.)

down, flop them over, group and re-group them until the arrangement seems balanced and "comfortable." Carefully tape these pieces in place (use invisible Magic™ tape). Place another fresh sheet of tracing paper on top, tape it down and make a more careful pencil tracing of this final layout.

Still another way of preparing a layout is to work directly on the tracing paper in pencil. At first, lightly and freely indicate the spotting—the areas and masses that will represent the locations of the motifs. Gradually begin to draw in the shapes you have decided upon in your preliminary sketches. *Do not* allow yourself to get involved with excessive detail at this point. Use simple silhouettes only. You are working for layout primarily. Keep in mind the direction and movement of the motifs, the general coverage and balance of the design. This method, like the others, must allow for flexibility. Be prepared to erase and change your mind about the arrangements. The work may become hard to "read" and from time to time you may have to place new sheets of tracing paper on top to continue.

It may take several layers of tracing paper before you arrive at a satisfactory layout, but this step—*working out the layout*—is crucial, and can make the difference between either a good and an unsuccessful design. Be prepared to use as much time (and tracing paper) as necessary to achieve the final layout.

You should become familiar with these various ways of creating a layout, and you may work out some method that is uniquely your own. You will probably find that different types of designs require different approaches to complete a layout.

It should be emphasized at this point that most textile designs are painted first as *croquis;* and a croquis is not a repeat! Unless you know beforehand that your design will go into production without any changes or corrections and unless you know exactly what size repeat will be required, you paint your design in croquis form only. Inexperienced designers impose unnecessary restrictions and limitations on themselves by trying to put their designs in repeat from the start. Of course there are exceptions. A design in a set layout, certain stripe or plaid layouts, planned geometric or grid arrangements—these are automatically in repeat just by the nature of the pattern.

Another exception is found in the decorative field where layouts are usually worked out in repeat from the start. Motifs are often large and repeat limitations require careful planning. When working closely with a stylist on *special-order work* quite often an exploration sketch, indicating the motifs, color and technique, is presented to the stylist along with the reference materials and a rough penciled layout of the repeat on tracing paper. After a "working" meeting with the stylist, the designer will either continue his design explorations or paint the final repeat.

However, it is common practice in the apparel field that all designs are in croquis form and the repeats are not executed until the design sells. Repeats take considerable time to do and a good designer can turn out several croquis in the time it takes to do one repeat.

When designing, the professional strives to make the final croquis look as much like the printed fabric as possible. Think of your croquis as if it were a section that has been cut out of a larger piece of fabric. Some motifs around the edges will be partly cut off and the assumption is that the design goes on continuously for yards and yards with no apparent break in the pattern.

Once you have a neat, clear layout in pencil on tracing paper, you're ready to complete the tracing by drawing the necessary details, the inner parts of the flowers, lines or veins on the leaves, etc. As a beginner you may feel more secure if you put in every last little line, but actually you'll find that some of these details would be covered and lost in the painting process and are just unnecessary work. Draw only the details that you will absolutely need to guide you in painting.

When beginning the layout on tracing paper, start with a 90 degree triangle and draw two lines in the upper left-hand corner, at least 1 inch from the edge of the tracing paper. *Do not* use the paper edges as guidelines for your layout.

Size of Croquis There are no concrete rules about how large or small a croquis should be. Size is determined basically by the various elements in your design. If the motifs are fairly small, and placed rather close, with even coverage and with no startling or dramatic changes in color spotting, your croquis could be approximately 8″ x 10″ to give the viewer an adequate picture of what the design will look like. If this same design has an occasional motif of a color different from all the others, or if a unique motif is introduced, say a bird or butterfly here and there in a floral design—then you must paint a larger croquis to give an idea of the distribution of this new element within the pattern. *Balance* of this unique motif must be maintained.

If the scale of your motifs is large, or if the motifs are widely spaced, or if there is some large, sweeping rhythmic effect, a larger croquis (22″ x 30″, or even larger) is required.

A general formula would be: *The size of the croquis is determined by the size of the motif and the distance between motifs.*

Balance Balance within a layout has several aspects. We can balance a particular *motif* within a design; we can balance *negative spaces* within a design; we can balance a particular *color* within a design.

•*For even balance*

Motif: If we are using oranges and grapefruit in equal amounts in a layout, they would be equally spaced from each other. If we wish to introduce an occasional banana, it would be placed among the other motifs approximately the same distance from itself each time it appears.

Space: If we introduce a space or opening into the layout, that space would appear again two or three times (approximately the same size and shape) within the sketch.

Color: Likewise, a spot of red color (an apple for instance) appearing in the design will usually appear again within the croquis and the amount of the red will be equally distributed throughout the layout.

•*For irregular balance*

Not all croquis are balanced in the manner discussed above. Quite often within a sketch only a single motif will appear (for instance a butterfly among the fruit). It may be a bright blue and it becomes a sharp accent. This is done to break the monotony and add excitement to the sketch. Irregular balance is also achieved by using uneven negative spaces.

Once the layout has been finalized, the next step is to transfer the design to the paper on which the design is to be painted.

STEP 5. TRANSFERRING THE LAYOUT FROM TRACING PAPER TO FINAL PAPER

There are several methods of transferring a pencil drawing from tracing paper to the final paper: • backing a tracing; • using transfer "carbons"; • using a light table (or light box).

Backing A Tracing

When a pencil drawing is clear and well drawn on tracing paper, label the front of the layout at the top, TOP. Then turn it over, with the drawing face down. Keeping your pencil (HB or #2) sharp, go over the lines of the drawing on the back of the tracing paper exactly as you see them. This is called *backing a tracing*. The result should be a clean and exact replica, *in reverse,* of your tracing-paper drawing.

Another way to back a tracing especially if your tracing paper has become somewhat damaged, is to use a fresh sheet of tracing paper of the same size or somewhat larger. Place it on the back of the tracing-paper drawing and tape the two layers together in several places to prevent shifting. With the tracing papers face down, and again keeping your pencil sharp, go over the lines of your drawing on the fresh tracing paper.

Position the backed tracing with the pencil-backed side in contact with your final paper in exactly the location where you want it to appear (check

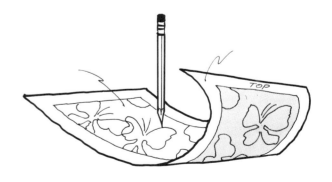

"Back the tracing" by going over the drawing on the back of the tracing paper.

Rub down the back tracing to transfer the image (left). *Pencil in the image instead of rubbing down (useful on painted grounds)* (right).

for the place where you labelled "top"). Tape it down in several places to prevent slipping.

The backed tracing is now ready to be used to transfer the graphite to the surface of your final paper.

Rubbing Down   You can use a dull knife or the edge of a teaspoon (not the round bottom of the spoon) to rub over the surface of the tracing-paper drawing in order to transfer the graphite to the surface of your paper. Lift a corner of the tracing from time to time to make sure the lines are completely rubbed down. If the pencil image on the top surface of the tracing paper smears because of the rub-down tool, it is possible to prevent this by spraying with workable fixative or by placing a piece of tracing paper over the area being rubbed down.

The *advantages* of this method are that with experience you can make several rub-downs, even as many as five or six which will be exactly alike, before the backing wears off (useful when making color combinations, see **Chapter 9**). In addition you have the tracing as a record. Some studios number and file these tracings for reference purposes. A new backing on fresh tracing paper can always be made from the back of the original tracing.

An important *disadvantage:* it is not advisable to rub down a tracing onto a background painted in opaque gouache or onto Color-aid or similar pre-colored paper, because the pressure of the rub-down tool will leave undesirable marks on the surface. Pressing too hard destroys the texture of the paper leaving an unsightly, smooth area on the final croquis. Rubbing down, however, works well with hard-surfaced papers such as bristol.

For work on white paper, on light wash or tinted grounds, and when a number of identical images is required, as for a set of color combinations, many designers and studios prefer the above method of transferring from tracing paper to final paper.

"Pencil-in" the Images   A variation of the above method that is useful on painted gouache grounds, is to *pencil in* the images instead of the rubbing down technique.

Back the tracing and place the tracing paper over the final paper as discussed above. Go over each motif with a 2H pencil with just enough pressure to transfer the graphite to the surface of your paper *avoiding too black an image*. This procedure encourages neatness and works well.

If a design is to be painted on a medium- or dark-value ground, you can back the tracing by drawing the images on the reverse side of the tracing with a white conte pencil, or a white pastel pencil. (*Do not* use a white crayon pencil or any other waxy material.) This may then be rubbed down on a

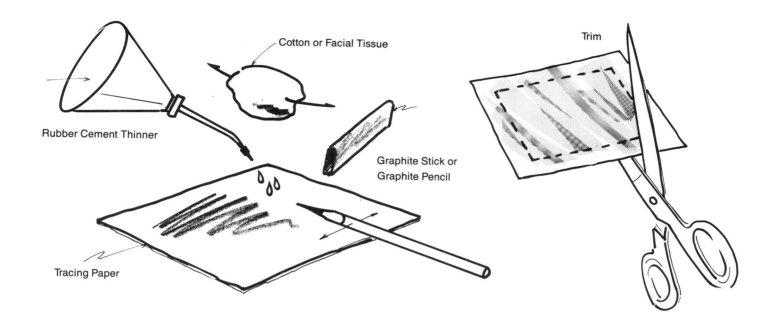

medium-value ground, or traced over with a sharp pencil on a dark ground, thus transferring your design in white lines.

Using Transfer "Carbons"

Saral™ paper is a commercially prepared tissue paper coated on one side with a chalk-like substance. It is available in several colors including dark gray (called graphite), red, yellow, and white. It is placed coated-side down between the tracing-paper drawing and the final paper on which the croquis will be painted. It functions very much like carbon paper used with typewriters. Using a sharp, fairly hard pencil (2H or #3), trace over the lines of your drawing. These lines are transferred to the paper. *A word of caution:* Do not try to use typewriter carbon which transfers a greasy line that is almost impossible to cover or erase.

Saral™ paper is heavily coated with material, and you must practice using a finely pointed pencil with just barely the right amount of pressure, or the image will be heavy and gross and hard to cover or remove.

An advantage of using Saral™ paper is that it is available in several colors, so that you can select the right one for dark or light backgrounds. The same sheet can be used many times before it is used up.

Making Your Own Graphite Transfer Paper Take a soft graphite pencil or graphite stick (2B or softer) and rub it over a fresh sheet of tracing paper, about 10″ x 12″ is a good size. You do not need to apply the graphite out to the edges. Next with a wad of cotton or facial tissue, smear rubber-cement thinner back and forth over the graphite surface to distribute the graphite evenly, at the same time getting rid of the excess graphite. (*Caution:* Rubber-cement thinner is flammable. Follow the precautions on the container.) Now trim the treated tracing paper with scissors and you'll have a "carbon" paper which can be used over and over again. This is used in the same manner as Saral™ paper, placing it treated-side down between your tracing-paper drawing and your final paper, and going over the lines of your drawing with a sharp pencil.

Advantages: You are transferring graphite onto your paper—the same material as in a pencil and not the coarse or waxy lines that present problems when you try to paint on them (as sometimes happens with the Saral™). Also the cost is minimal and the materials are readily available. One prepared graphite sheet of this kind can last a long time.

In addition, it is possible to make a white chalk version of the homemade variety substituting blackboard chalk or drawing pastels for the graphite stick. The chalk "carbon" is used with medium to dark grounds. It may be necessary to repeat the application of chalk two or three times to

It is possible to make your own transfer paper using graphite or white chalk.

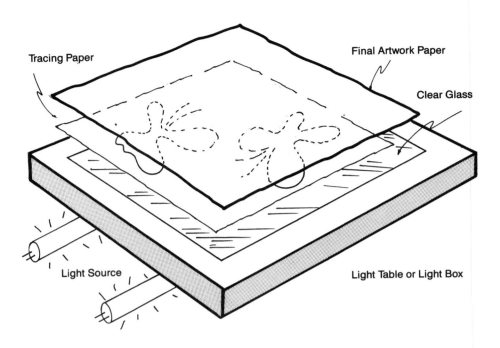

Tracing Paper

Final Artwork Paper

Clear Glass

Light Source

Light Table or Light Box

The light table is used extensively by professional designers. The image is pencilled onto the final paper, but sometimes the final rendering can be painted directly.

build up a sufficient amount. When distributing the chalk with rubber-cement thinner and cotton, use the same area of the cotton wad each time to avoid wiping away the newly applied chalk.

A *disadvantage* to both the homemade graphite sheet and the Saral™ paper as compared with pencil-backing and rubbing down a tracing is that you must completely trace over your pencil drawing for every copy you need. This is a slower more laborious process.

Using a Light Table (or Light Box)

If you have a light table or a light box, you can transfer your layout by still another method. Make sure the lines of your tracing-paper drawing are dark enough, then place it right side up on the light table. Put your paper directly over it, taping the two papers together in several places to prevent slipping. Turn the light on and you can trace the image directly onto your paper. Use a sharp, medium-hard pencil, *lightly!* This will work on most white or light-colored or tinted paper, but not on dark painted grounds, or dark Color-aid™ or similar pre-colored papers. The light table is used extensively in decorative design studios where plain paper is frequently used and dark backgrounds are blotched in.

Some textile designers have a strong preference for one of these processes to transfer their drawings onto the final paper, and use only that method. Others use all of them, depending on the particular circumstances. A beginner should become familiar with *all* the methods discussed above.

STEP 6. EXPLORATION SKETCHES

An important step, which is often neglected, is to make a series of *exploration sketches*. In **Step 2** you have explored preliminary ideas and have made some decisions as to color, techniques, paper, etc. Of course you have transferred your tracing layout to the same type of paper to be used for the final croquis. If a painted ground was decided upon in Step 2, you should have prepared enough paper for exploration sketches as well.

Now look back at your preliminary painted experiments again. Do you need further research for motifs and ideas, and further refinement of technique or color treatment? Are they exactly the way you would want them in the finished work? Of course if you make major additions or changes of motifs, you will have to revise your tracing-paper layout.

Next, transfer a representative section of your layout onto a separate piece of paper (identical to that which you are using for the croquis). The purpose of this exploration sketch is to finalize the color and technique. This step is a last chance to develop and refine your design ideas. All your mistakes and final experiments should be made in this phase of exploration in order to avoid problems on the croquis.

Several exploration sketches may be necessary. Have you included all the different motifs you want to use? If new and better solutions occur while painting the croquis you may have to begin again, and a lot of work and time is lost. If your exploratory sketches need further refinement, do it now. Be sure that the exploration sketches are developed sufficiently to the point where you are satisfied and excited about the design you are going to execute.

When all the explorations are completed, you should have before you a sketch showing a representative section of your design just as it will look in the croquis: all the different flowers, leaves and stems, and any secondary motifs, in exactly the colors you will be using, painted on the same type of paper, using the same tools (brushes, pens, sponges, etc.). Study it critically trying to envision it first as a larger painting (the croquis) and also as hundreds of yards of fabric. Make any changes you feel it needs. Now tack it up over your work area or in some other way keep it visible before you and keep referring to it as you work on the croquis.

This exploration step is commonly taken in the decorative field. In the apparel field it is less often used since the croquis are usually more spontaneous and executed with less planning than an upholstery design, for instance.

It is important to be flexible and open during all these steps and procedures. One designer may wish to start exploration sketches before the final tracing layout, since it might suggest other layout possibilities. New motifs and ideas often keep developing as we work. It is a good idea to get into paint as soon as possible and explore more directly the look of the motifs and techniques. But for beginners it would be well at first to follow the suggested steps in a methodical order

STEP 7. COLOR MIXING

So far you may have mixed small amounts of paint in a 30-hole palette, just enough for your initial experiments. Larger quantities of color will be necessary for larger designs, but usually the palette will be adequate for most apparel croquis. Using jars or other containers large enough and with air-tight covers, mix the selected colors again, this time making sure you have enough paint to complete your design. It is a time-wasting and frustrating experience to run out of a color in midstream; to spend precious time and effort trying to match it exactly (and it *must* match exactly; you can't get away with an "almost-match"). A good principle is to mix more paint than you think you'll need. When the croquis is finished you may need to do some final touch-ups, or perhaps you may have some minor spills, or make some errors that need to be fixed. And after your design is finished it is still good to have more of the mixed colors, possibly for painting the repeat or for minor last-minute changes after consultation with the stylist or client. Leftover mixed paints, are not wasted. They can be used as they are in combination with other colors, for new designs. Or you can use them for mixing new colors by adding additional paint to them.

If you are using gouache, be careful to mix the paints thoroughly—really homogenize them! Use a *mixing brush,* not your good red sable, for this process. Add just enough water, using your squeeze bottle dispenser to make the right consistency. The paint should not be watery, nor too thick and pasty; approximately the consistency of cream. Experiment with the thickness of the paint and decide for yourself what works best for you. But remember that in general, the paint is opaque and should cover evenly and flatly. Test the colors by making brush strokes on the same type of paper that you are using for your croquis. If the paint is too watery, the color of the paper will show through. If it is too thick the brush will drag and the brush

Exploration sketches are an important step in the design process. Variations in layout, technique and color were explored. The first sketch was too heavy and static (top). The style of a Liberty print did not seem appropriate (center). The third variation was the most interesting and a corner of the design was started on larger paper (bottom).

Early experiment sketch (left). *A further development of the technique, color and layout* (right). *Completed final layout in white chalk transferred to painted gouache ground* (facing page, inset). *Finished rendering* (facing page, © RICHARD FISHER).

stroke will dry with slightly raised ridges. If you have not mixed the colors thoroughly, you may pick up some particles of unmixed paint on your brush and the colors will be streaked. Mixing in a clear, transparent container is helpful in this respect because you can see any unevenness in the colors as you mix the paints.

As the painting proceeds, you may find that with exposure to air the colors in the containers will dry and thicken a little. Use your squeeze bottle to add a few drops of water to the paint when necessary.

Matching colors has been discussed earlier. When choosing a color to work with, start with the tube of paint closest to the color you want to mix. Don't be afraid of adding white and black to your colors to modify them. Also other colors can be added to the original. Tonal values can be mixed with the addition of the complementary color and gray. Try many combinations and variations in color in your thirty-hole palette. You can then mix additional quantities of any one color, or all of them, in larger containers *if* you think you will need a lot more of that color.

Another *word of caution:* If you plan to paint a ground in gouache, be sure to mix an extra quantity of the color and save it for touch-up work as well as painting the ground color into the motifs if that effect is desired. And *don't forget* to paint enough ground for the *exploration sketches.* Experience teaches you how much to mix. Beginners often don't mix enough.

Preparatory Steps

- Careful research
- Thorough preliminary explorations for color, technique, and interpretation
- Well thought-out layout
- Transferring the layout to the paper ready to be painted
- Mixing and preparing all the paints

STEP 8. PAINTING IT

You have taken the time to go through the preparatory steps—now all the planning comes together and you are about to make it happen!

In general the procedure when painting with gouache (or with dyes) is to start with colors of the lightest value and work in sequence through darker and darker values. Each darker color, if it is in contact with the lighter one, will cover and refine, or correct the previously painted form. It is not as easy to cover dark with light colors.

Of course this is not a hard and fast rule. There will be times when the nature of the design calls for light colors painted on top of dark areas, and if your paints are of the proper consistency this should not present a problem. However, the general recommendation is, proceed from light to dark. *And* if the design requires a *blotch,* which is the negative, or empty area, to be painted around and between the motifs, this blotch is almost always painted last, whether it is a light or dark color. This process—painting the blotch last—also helps to define and if necessary to correct the shapes of the painted motifs.

Use appropriate brushes. Usually bigger brushes are better than smaller ones. A good large brush can be formed into a fine point when necessary, can carry a generous amount of paint, and can cover areas with fewer strokes, which makes for a smoother, more professional looking result.

If you're using one brush with one color for an extended period of time, you may find that the paint is beginning to accumulate not only in the upper part of the hairs of the brush, but on the ferrule as well. It is a good practice to rinse the brush out in water from time to time, wipe off the ferrule and start "clean" again.

Incidentally—use large-sized jars for water, fill them at least three-quarters full, change the water frequently, long before it has a chance to become thick and muddy.

Take *risks!* Be bold! Beginners are often timid when first handling the brush and paint. A tiny bit of paint on the very tip of the brush is an inadequate technique. *Plunge* the brush deep into the paint well, *stir* and *twirl* the brush and *fill it* with paint. Then *wipe off* the excess on the edge of the paint-well. Be daring!

If you wish to make a delicate stroke, wipe the loaded brush on a scrap of paper, turning the brush in your fingers, in order to remove a bit more of the paint and at the same time forming the tip to a perfect point.

As you paint the croquis, keep your eye not only on the individual areas you are working on, but on the larger picture as well. Back away from it from time to time, and check for a balanced placement of the different colors (*color spotting*). Are you keeping the techniques consistent throughout? Refer frequently to your exploratory painting, which you have always in view before you. Watch the croquis as it "grows" with each step you add to the developing design.

Evaluating your croquis from a distance is a good idea. A helpful tool is a wall mirror. As you progress hold the design in front of you and stand before a mirror. You get a different perspective of your work, and it relates more immediately to the product (our example, a blouse) you are designing for. Turn it upside down as the final fabric will be seen from all angles. If a mirror is not available, put your design on the floor and walk around it.

If you do not finish painting the croquis in one sitting, but must leave it for any length of time, remember to cover all your jars of paint. Protect your croquis! Wait until you're sure the painting is thoroughly dry, then either turn it face down (of course onto a clean surface!) or put a clean paper or cloth cover over it. *Do not* leave it where it will be in full sunlight, exposed to heat, or in danger of wetting or other accidents.

When you return to continue painting, you may find that your paints have dried out a little. Add a few drops of clean water from your squeeze bottle, mix thoroughly, try it out, and proceed until your croquis is finished. How do you know when it is done? Refer to your exploration sketch. Are you satisfied? Now is the time to study and re-evaluate. Does this croquis please you? Can you see it as a pattern on fabric? As a blouse? Also, ask yourself if there are possibilities for additional designs, establishing and developing a theme.

A word about *perfection*. Cezanne said, "Be willing to paint a bad picture." The same can apply to a design. It allows us to make mistakes and takes the pressure off as we work. Mistakes can also be very useful if we can suspend harsh judgment and learn from them. So be willing to let the croquis "paint itself," and know that if it comes out "bad" we have the privilege of starting again.

STEP 9. PRESENTATION

No mention has been made so far of ruling or measuring off the final dimensions of the croquis. Generally, the designer will paint an area that is roughly *rectangular*. Since the pattern in our example is meant for apparel, it would probably be a vertical rectangle. For decorative design, this may not necessarily be so; often the artwork has a horizontal format.

There are now two possibilities for this croquis. If it is being done on assignment for a particular client, the croquis may be left untrimmed, with irregular edges to the painted area so that the painting can be continued directly on the same paper when put into repeat. This informal manner of presentation is usually the procedure when there is an on-going, working relationship with a stylist or studio.

If the croquis is to become part of a designer's portfolio, it should be handled in a more formal, finished way. In this case, you will proceed to "square it off" as follows: Take your triangle and place it with its right angle at the upper left-hand corner of your croquis. Don't worry if you cut through some of the motifs at the edges of the croquis. This will merely help to give the finished product a more realistic, fabric-like appearance. With a pencil draw a line along both sides of the right angle as far as the triangle extends. Now, using your metal ruler, carefully extend the pencil lines still further, somewhat beyond the painted area. Take your triangle again and place it at the upper right-hand edge of the croquis, and again do not hesitate to cut off some parts of the painted motifs. Draw the pencil line to the limit of the triangle and again carefully extend this line with your ruler.

Repeat this procedure until you have "framed" the croquis with pencil lines. Measure these lines to check that you have truly squared the corners and have not strayed from vertical and horizontal.

Look carefully at the newly framed edges of your croquis. If there are some unfinished-looking spaces, paint in appropriate motifs. Do not distort

Preliminary explorations to study both negative and positive shapes.

the design to make it fit inside the frame, but rather let it run over the edges, as would naturally happen on fabric. (In the vernacular of the studio, this is sometimes referred to as "faking it in around the edges.")

You're now ready to cut out the croquis. If you have a paper-cutter at your disposal, this is probably the best method. Otherwise, using your ruler and a sharp single-edged razor blade or X-acto™ knife, you can cut clean, straight edges. Hold the ruler firmly to prevent slipping, keep the blade vertical without tilting it at an angle, and bear down firmly with the blade to be sure that it is cutting all the way through the paper. (*Caution:* do not cut in this manner on a surface that you do not want marred. A heavy cardboard makes a good cutting surface.)

You can also cut the edges with a pair of sharp scissors, if you have a really steady hand. Most frequently croquis are mounted using rubber cement applied along the back of the top edge. Mounting will be discussed fully in **Chapter 7**.

ADDITIONAL POSSIBILITIES

We have outlined nine steps that will guide you through the intricacies of creating an original textile design. There are limitless variations in subject matter, color, technique, scale, etc., and the design possibilities are endless.

In Step 1 we determined that a floral croquis for women's apparel would be a good place to start. Now let us consider a few other possible design directions. Remember that the wisest choices will be based on market research and market orientation.

A good second choice might be a *hidden conversational*. This type of design emphasizes the allover pattern while reducing the importance of the individual motif. The hidden conversational is useful in apparel for all categories—women's and children's wear as well as men's wear (it is a type especially appropriate for men's wear). It is also used on home fashion products as well.

We will use one motif only, a familiar object found in the house. Look for four or five different objects. Kitchen utensils, tools and other hardware, try an enlargement of a bolt or screw, etc. Keep your choices open. Do not finalize your choice too quickly, or select the first one that seems possible. Almost any object has potential. Make several pencil sketches on tracing paper of each of the objects. Draw them about 1½ to 2 inches in size. Keep the shapes simple—silhouette only at first.

If you choose a coffee mug, for instance, make several pencil sketches of the mug on separate pieces of tracing paper. Now using the separate pieces of tracing paper nest the mugs next to each other. Turn them upside down. Flop them over. The images can touch each other or may be slightly spaced apart. Possibly the handles may overlap and break up the body area of the neighbor mug. The negative areas between the mugs are part of the pattern also and are as important as the mugs themselves. Be sure the shapes of the negative spaces are as interesting as the shapes of the mugs. Try other variations and you will discover many possible relationships.

What is happening is that a *pattern* is beginning to emerge. Keep adding coffee-mug images onto the growing pattern. You will find that a rhythm is beginning to appear, and it usually forms itself onto an invisible grid. At this point you should extend the grid by carefully measuring and ruling light pencil lines. Or you may want to try graph paper. Graph paper is available with grids of various measurements and on small- to large-sized sheets of paper. If you place the grid under your tracing paper, you can easily transfer the necessary guidelines. This is to ensure an accurate repetition of the spaces and motifs. Use some method to rule accurate lines, measured precisely with a ruler, and establish a grid so that the motifs do not stray or go off on a slant. The set layout must be precise and even, allover. The grid is called invisible because it will not be seen on the croquis and is used only for structural purposes.

When you have a tracing layout about 9″ x 12″, place a triangle on the edges and define the limits of the croquis. It's a good idea to start with two

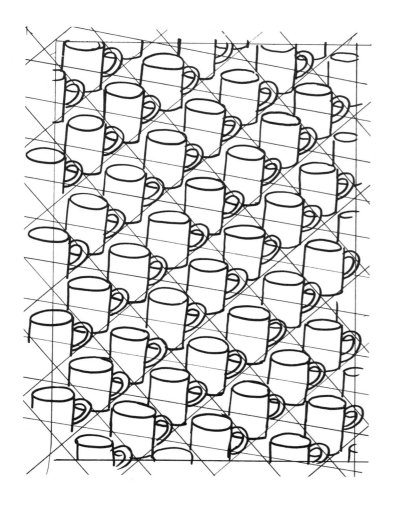

A grid acts as a "skeleton" on which to build the pattern. Another grid was used on page 81. In the final step the pattern is more important than the individual motif. (© DOROTHY WOLFTHAL.)

lines 90 degrees to each other in the upper left-hand corner of the tracing paper and then add on the succeeding images of the coffee mug downward and to the right.

Continue to follow the nine steps outlined above and you will have a second croquis for your portfolio.

You might want to try a variation of the hidden conversational using two objects instead of only one. Possibly add a decorative motif, such as a flower or a few bands which become additional areas for more colors. The colors of the negative spaces might vary, adding richness to the overall effect.

Other types of design that you may wish to experiment with might include a wallcovering stripe with flowers, an abstract with geometric shapes in a tossed layout; a group of small calico flowers or a paisley, or perhaps another floral, this time with only two colors. If you are feeling more daring or more secure, experiment by adding textures to the croquis.

Always a good place to begin is to research the market **(Chapter 2)** and develop a design reflecting a current trend. (Additional projects are included in the **Appendix.**)

TECHNIQUES FOR RENDERING WITH GOUACHE, DYES & OTHER MEDIA

Textile designers who are interested in professional growth and excellence will constantly practice with the familiar materials and media, using them in new and innovative ways. They also experiment with newly developed or less familiar products, trying them out in various combinations to discover their potential in order to make their work more efficient and their designs more interesting.

In this chapter we will discuss the two basic media—*gouache* and *dyes*—and the techniques that are most frequently used in textile design. We will suggest "tricks of the trade" that will help to save time and make your work easier. We will also suggest some techniques that can enable you to produce new and interesting effects. Try them out, practice combining techniques and media, use them in your designs. Soon variations of these techniques will suggest themselves to you and you will start on your own path of discovery and innovation.

PAINTING WITH GOUACHE

Gouache is the most frequently used medium for textile designs. It is used almost exclusively in the decorative field; in apparel, other media are also used but gouache is still preferred by most designers. Therefore it is an absolute necessity that you take the time to perfect your skill with this medium.

Normally gouache as it comes from the tube is too thick to be used *as is*. It should be squeezed out into a jar or palette-cup and mixed with a few drops of clean water to a creamy consistency. Designers have their preferences, some choosing to have the paint thicker, others somewhat thinner. Try making some brush strokes of the mixed gouache to test the consistency. You will learn by experience what suits your own "hand." However, gouache primarily is meant to be used as an opaque (not transparent) medium and should not be thinned down so much that it becomes watery.

Seldom is the paint used directly from the tube. If you want the color as it is in the tube, add a *very small* amount of white paint, which will not noticeably change the color of the original paint, but will help it to go on flatly and evenly.

When you open a new tube of gouache, you may find that a clear, gummy liquid (the medium—gum arabic) pours out. This should be discarded and not mixed in with the paint.

If we hear,
we usually forget.
If we see,
we might remember.
By doing,
we understand
and really learn.

Loosely rendered interpretation of the warp-print technique in gouache on painted ground. (© DOROTHY WOLFTHAL.)

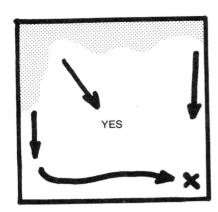

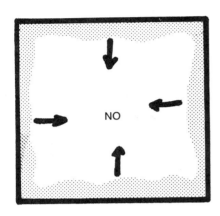

Start in upper left and work to lower right corner. Do not paint the outline and "fill-in."

Poster Colors These are opaque water-soluble paints sold in bottles, in many colors, and are compatible with gouache. They are not ground as finely as gouache and are occasionally mixed with gouache to achieve certain colors. White Richart™ tempera/poster paint (or other equivalent brands) is often used in place of white gouache from a tube or it can be mixed half and half with gouache. Black poster paint can be used as well.

As mentioned in **Chapter 3**, it is very helpful to put white and black poster paint into plastic dispenser bottles with closable tops. It will greatly speed up the mixing process. Add some water to the dispenser bottle as you introduce the poster white, to thin the paint to a creamy consistency for better pouring and mixing. A third plastic dispenser bottle is useful for clean water which is necessary when mixing paints.

Gouache and poster paint are *opaque* media. If you want to make a color lighter, you do this by adding white. You do not make it lighter by adding water.

Use a 30-hole plastic palette for exploring colors. Tape down the edge of the palette to your work surface so that it doesn't jump all over when mixing the paints. Experiment on several types of paper, from smooth bristol to slightly pebbled, to heavily textured paper. Start to practice using a red sable (#6) brush. Wiping a wet brush on paper towelling or a damp sponge removes the excess water from the brush and forms a desirable point. Dip the brush in your mixed gouache (draw it along the edge of the jar or palette-well to get rid of the excess paint), and start painting.

Paint a few rectangular shapes about 2" or 3". Do not paint an outline and "fill in" but rather work down, starting at the top, drawing the paint along as you go. Apply the paint evenly, so that as it dries there are no "puddles." Add paint to your brush as you work. Don't overload the brush or let it run out of paint.

Frequently, while an area of painted gouache is drying, it looks uneven and streaky. Don't panic! Wait until the area is thoroughly dry and you'll probably find that the gouache has evened out. When painted properly, gouache will dry flat and smooth, with a matte (not shiny) surface. It should be completely opaque with no lighter areas where the paper is showing through. If the area is streaky when dry, check your color and be sure that it is thoroughly mixed (see **Chapter 5**). Check the size of the brush. If the brush is too small, you have to use many small strokes to cover the area and this will cause streaking and unevenness.

Continue to practice painting, using more complicated shapes. Draw a silhouette of a flower, a curved paisley, a star, etc., and paint them following the same general procedure.

Notice how your brush has been responding to your hand. With a good brush, even a fairly large one, you can paint a thin line. Dip your brush into your mixed color, then stroke and turn it on a piece of scrap paper to form a point. Practice holding the brush so that just the tip touches the paper, and move it lightly across the surface to make a fine line. Next, press the brush down so that its whole fullness is in contact with the paper. Move it quickly across the page for a broad, sweeping stroke. Try working more slowly, raising and lowering the brush to create strokes of varying thicknesses. Cover a whole page with practice strokes of your brush—thick and thin lines, long graceful curves, short, jagged lines. Your brush is a remarkable tool. Make friends with it, respond to its characteristics.

Painting One Color over Another with Gouache

You may want to put some decorations *inside* shapes—lines of blue dashes inside a green paisley, an orange center inside a pink flower. One of the nice things about gouache is that, since it is opaque, you can paint over one color with another and it will "cover" completely.

There are a few things to be aware of however. Make sure the underlying color is *absolutely dry* before painting on top of it. The second color *must never be thinned down* so much that it becomes watery. If anything, mix it a *little* thicker than usual. *Do not make many strokes* with the second color or you may begin to pick up the color underneath. Instead, paint with a rather full brush, and as quickly and neatly as possible. Then leave it alone.

A darker color will cover a lighter one more readily than the other way around. Still, there are times when for the purposes of your design, you really want to paint light over dark, and even if you observe the precautions given earlier, you can't get the light color to "cover." There are some procedures you can try in order to overcome this problem.

1. If the lighter color is one that contains white as one of the components, use Bleedproof White. However, the Bleedproof White should not make up more than 50 percent of the total volume of the mixed color, otherwise the color may dry shiny, gummy and uneven.

2. If the lighter color is not mixed with white, the Bleedproof White may still come to the rescue. Mix white (either gouache or poster paint) with Bleedproof White, about half-and-half. Paint this over the area to be covered (too thick a mixture will cause ridges). When it is thoroughly dry, you can proceed to paint your desired color on top of it.

3. Paint quickly with a full brush. Avoid picking up the underneath color by using as few strokes as possible. Try *flowing* the paint on rather than *brushing* it onto the surface. The paint will look more opaque when it has dried.

4. Spray a workable fixative on the area to be over-painted (see **Chapter 3** for detailed directions).

Painting a Colored Ground in Gouache

If you wish to design on a colored ground, you can buy commercially colored paper, and hope to find exactly the color and texture you're looking for. Or you can mix the required color yourself, and paint your own grounds, on any paper you choose. This is a good procedure although it takes a little more time. Individual artists may have their own variations, but the following is the general procedure for painting a colored ground in gouache.

With your mixing brush, mix a very generous amount of the desired color, and this time use a jar or dish with an opening wide enough for your ground-brush (see **Chapter 3**) to dip in. Stir the color *thoroughly* to be sure the paints are completely blended and to avoid picking up a lump of unmixed gouache to streak the background.

Test your mixed color on a piece of the same type of paper that you plan to use, and wait for it to dry to be sure it's the color you want. Gouache colors may dry somewhat lighter (or darker) than they appear when wet.

Wet a ground-brush in clean water and wipe off the excess. Dip it into the ground color, and starting at the top and *working quickly,* draw the brush in broad, even strokes across the paper. The paper should be taped down at the corners and edges.

Now stroke in the vertical direction and then horizontally again, back and forth. This crisscross technique will help to even out the paint. Keep adding paint to your brush and more water, as well, as you work so that the paint does not begin to dry or get too thick. Dip just the tip of your brush into the water jar. The paper absorbs a great deal of water.

Grounds are sometimes called *washes* and as such should be as thin as possible and yet appear *even,* when dry. It is a personal choice of the artist whether or not to make a ground fully opaque or thinly painted. It depends on the effect you wish. Remember that a thinly painted ground is harder to touch up than a fully opaque one.

When the ground looks even and opaque, set it aside to dry. You may find it convenient to mount your painted ground on a wall by the four corners with thumb tacks or tape while it dries. Or you may prefer to tack or tape it onto a drawing board or a second table to dry.

It takes practice to master the knack of painting a smooth, flat, opaque gouache ground. Here are some hints:

1. Work as quickly as possible so that the paint does not begin to dry too soon.

Explore the many ways you can paint and draw with your brush.

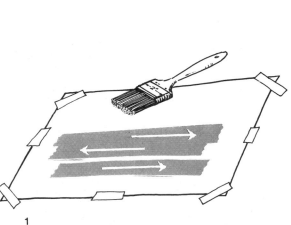

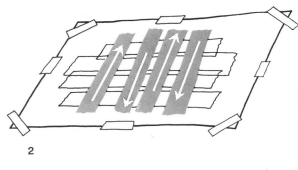

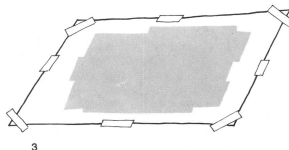

A procedure for painting a ground in gouache.
When painting a ground on paper in dyes, it is
advisable to moisten the paper slightly first (as
described in Step 6C). 1. Draw the brush in
broad even strokes back and forth across the
paper. 2. Now stroke in the vertical direction,
up and down. Then horizontally again, left and
right. Keep adding paint and more water to your
brush. 3. The criss-cross technique will help to
even out the paint. Leave a margin of unpainted
paper. Trim when dry.

2. Don't leave any "puddles" of paint. They will dry more slowly and leave a ring that will be impossible to repair. Smooth the paint out thoroughly as you work.

3. Stand up if you are painting a large sheet of paper. Use your whole body, arms, back and shoulders as you brush the paint left and right, up and down, back and forth.

4. Mix enough paint. The wash-brush drinks up a lot more paint than you may expect. Save the unused paint in a covered container for touch-ups.

5. Do not try to "stretch" the paint to make it cover a large area. Keep dipping into the mixed color to keep the brush uniformly full as you work your way down the paper.

6. If you're making a fairly large ground, the paint may begin to dry a little before you're done. There are several ways to avoid this.

A. Mix the paint to a slightly thinner consistency by adding a little more water than usual—but not so thin that it ceases to be opaque and the whiteness of the paper shows through the paint.

B. While you're painting the ground, dip the brush into clean water a few times, just enough to pick up a little moisture. The back and forth strokes will be easier with less resistance. Keep adding paint and water whenever necessary.

C. Wet your paper first. This can be done by "painting" the entire surface with your wash-brush dipped in clean water before you start to paint, so that the surface is damp—not soaking wet. Another way of wetting the paper beforehand is by using a *water mister* or *atomizer* (sold for plants).

7. Paint a larger area than you think you'll need. There are several good reasons for this: Often the wash dries a little unevenly around the edges and you have to trim this part off. Also a spare piece of the painted ground will be useful for practice and test purposes, for painting a reference piece, for splicing, if this should be necessary (see **Chapter 7**), or perhaps for making color tabs.

8. Do not try painting over the ground if it is not exactly what you wanted. Applying a second coat can result in a streaky, uneven look. If the color is wrong, save the painted ground for a future design. If the ground color is not uniform, try again, carefully following the list of suggestions.

Blotches *Blotch* is the term used to refer to a ground that is printed around and up to motifs in a design. (A separate roller is made to print the blotch, see **Chapter 8**.) When designing we paint the blotch directly into the background areas and it becomes the background color. Frequently a fine line of white paper may appear between the motif and the blotched ground which anticipates registration errors. If this gap is inserted as a designed element, the final effect is more successful.

Blotches are fairly commonly used when designing. They have been associated with less expensive fabrics as contrasted to discharge printing which is more costly and in some ways a more refined printing technique.

Mistakes When Working with Gouache & What to Do about Them

In the process of painting and designing, no matter how carefully you proceed step by step, you cannot avoid an occasional accident or mistake. We do the best we can to avoid accidents, taping things down, covering jars and tubes, keeping the work area organized, clean and clear of clutter. But accidents and mistakes are inevitable.

The following are some ways to repair or undo some common mishaps and errors.

Problem: Using gouache, you have painted a blue flower. Upon reconsideration, you realize it should have been painted red. You could conceivably just paint the red over the blue; however, you know this would build up the thickness of the gouache, eventually creating an unattractive, bumpy surface.

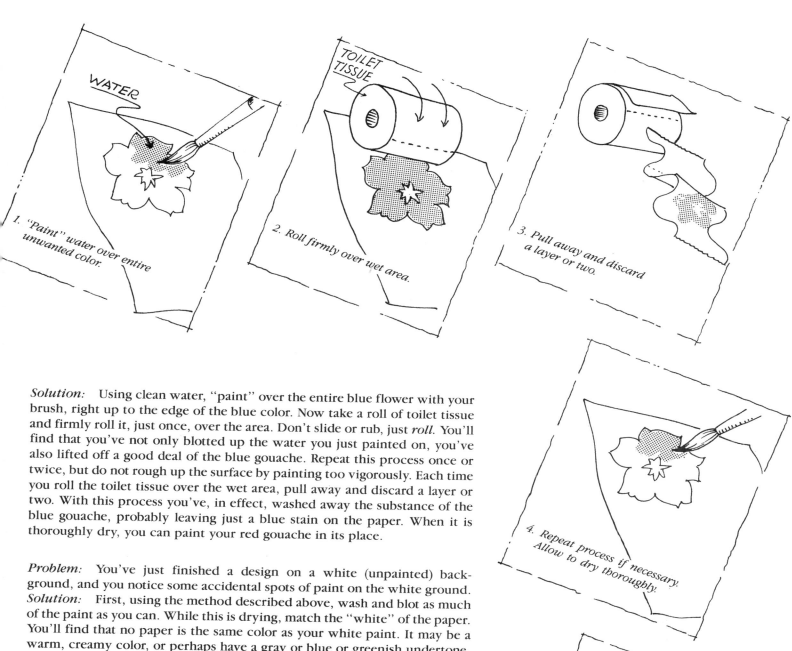

1. "Paint" water over entire unwanted color.

2. Roll firmly over wet area.

3. Pull away and discard a layer or two.

4. Repeat process if necessary. Allow to dry thoroughly.

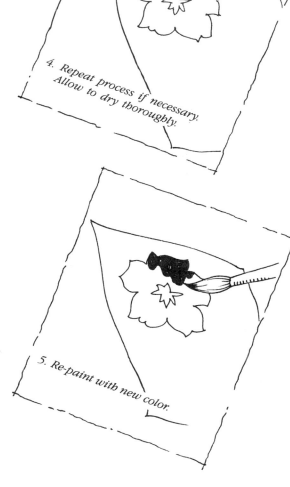

5. Re-paint with new color.

A technique for correcting mistakes.

Solution: Using clean water, "paint" over the entire blue flower with your brush, right up to the edge of the blue color. Now take a roll of toilet tissue and firmly roll it, just once, over the area. Don't slide or rub, just *roll*. You'll find that you've not only blotted up the water you just painted on, you've also lifted off a good deal of the blue gouache. Repeat this process once or twice, but do not rough up the surface by painting too vigorously. Each time you roll the toilet tissue over the wet area, pull away and discard a layer or two. With this process you've, in effect, washed away the substance of the blue gouache, probably leaving just a blue stain on the paper. When it is thoroughly dry, you can paint your red gouache in its place.

Problem: You've just finished a design on a white (unpainted) background, and you notice some accidental spots of paint on the white ground.
Solution: First, using the method described above, wash and blot as much of the paint as you can. While this is drying, match the "white" of the paper. You'll find that no paper is the same color as your white paint. It may be a warm, creamy color, or perhaps have a gray or blue or greenish undertone. With a little trial and error you can achieve such an exact match to the paper, that, when it's dry you can barely see where it was painted. Make your test "dabs" on a spare piece of the same paper, or if none is available, then use the back of the croquis. If you believe your "accident" contains a color that might bleed through (for example Carthamus Pink) use a little Bleedproof White in your mixture. When you are sure you have an exact match, paint over the spots and "feather" or blend out the edges so that no hard ridges will appear when your paint dries. Another option, if the "spoiled" area is small enough, is to paint your mixed "white" right up to the edges of the nearby motifs.

Mistakes and accidents may happen for a purpose although at the time we do not experience them in a positive way. Artists are, by nature, creative and even a mistake can be turned into a *happy accident* which might suggest a direction your work could take; possibly you can transform the mistake into a texture or new motif, something that was not pre-conceived. Be daring and experiment! Take a chance! In a sense, let the design "go where it wants to go" while you witness the process as it happens. This is harder for the beginner, who, during the early learning phase, has a real struggle for control of the media and the craft. In time, it is possible to relax and *allow* the creative process to have its own way and this can give rise to new and original work.

PAINTING WITH DYES *

Gouache has the consistency of paste, comes in tubes, and is opaque; *dyes* are clear, transparent liquid colors and come in small bottles with droppers attached to the covers. The bright dye colors are generally more radiant and vivid than gouache, and the overall effect of a design painted in dyes is fresh and clear. The colors are concentrated and a few drops will go a long way. *Unlike gouache, dyes are made lighter by adding water, not white paint.* Since they are transparent, dyes cannot be readily seen on dark colors. They should be painted on white or light-tinted paper, or on waxed rice paper.

Painting with Dyes on Waxed Rice Paper

There are various types of rice paper, with different textures and characteristics. They all can be waxed (this process is described in **Chapter 3**). However, the rice paper called Masa is sold already waxed, principally for textile designing. As you become familiar with this way of painting you will discover its many advantages; some designers prefer it to all others. Many textile designs are painted in a combination of dyes plus gouache and/or other media.

It is wise to experiment and familiarize yourself with dyes on waxed Masa before you start a finished croquis. Begin a practice session with a sheet or two of waxed Masa; several bottles of dyes in assorted colors (choose from the list in **Chapter 3**), one or two red sable brushes ranging in size from #4 to #8; a bottle of *non-crawl* (Wax Grip™); a #2 pencil or equivalent; tracing paper; white sketching paper; a white plastic 30-hole palette or equivalent (don't use an aluminum palette since the salts in the dyes will eventually eat pinholes in it); a generous-sized jar of water; a squeeze bottle with clean water (this will speed up the mixing process dramatically); facial tissues or a roll of toilet tissue; a damp, flat household sponge; and white blotting paper.

Waxed Masa should be handled gently to avoid causing cracks and wrinkles. With a sharp blade or scissors, cut off a piece, about 12" x 16", and set the rest aside carefully. Waxed Masa is almost as transparent as tracing paper; you can see anything placed under it. Therefore it is best to work on a white surface. Never trace or transfer preliminary pencil work on waxed Masa since it will severely damage the surface. Also, if you try to erase pencil or charcoal marks from waxed Masa, you will only create a gray smear that cannot be removed.

Incidentally you will notice that there is a slight difference in the two sides of this paper, one being a little smoother than the other. Both sides are usable. Generally the rougher side seems to produce a smoother effect for large flat areas, while the smooth side is more responsive to fine, delicate work.

Draw a simple shape, about 2½" in size in pencil on tracing paper. Place another piece of tracing paper over this, in order to protect the underneath side of your Masa from being smeared by your pencil marks. Clear acetate is more transparent and works better but is more costly. It is also possible to spray the tracing with workable fixative to isolate the graphite. Now take the piece of waxed Masa and place it on top of your penciled sketch.

Squeeze several drops of a bright color into one of the wells of the palette. Add some clean water from the dispenser, then wet your brush, dip into the dye, and paint a brush stroke onto an area of the waxed Masa. You'll find that it doesn't "take"—the color *beads up* and separates. The waxy surface is rejecting the water. Now drop a *very small* amount of *non-crawl* into the well next to the one with dye. Dip the tip of your brush into the non-crawl and mix some of it into the dye, and try again to make a stroke on the waxed Masa. If it still doesn't "take," repeat the process, adding a little

---

*The dyes used by textile designers are an artist's medium. They should not be confused with the commercial dyes that are used in factories to print fabric. See **Chapter 3** on **Tools and Supplies** for a description and color listing of the types of dyes used by textile designers.

more non-crawl until the Masa accepts the color. The object is to add only the amount needed to make it paint smoothly, *and not any more,* or the dye will dry gummy and the result will be unattractive.

Now move to the area of waxed Masa covering the shape you have drawn. Dip the brush into the prepared dye/non-crawl mixture, and start painting. Do not outline the whole shape and then fill it in. Rather, start at one corner of the motif, and gradually work down and across the motif to the opposite corner, drawing the dye over the area as you go. With the brush evenly loaded, working as fast as you can, keep the leading edge of the dye from drying before the entire shape is filled in by continually refilling your brush as you work. Avoid overloading the brush or "stretching" the dye as far as possible. This technique is more difficult with large, complex shapes. Repeat the process several times with various shapes and different colors.

Backgrounds which are to be painted as a *blotch* present other difficulties when they go off in *two* directions at once around a motif. End one of the directions at a narrow space between two motifs, if possible; it will be completed later. Continue painting in the other direction. When first learning any technique, it takes practice to gain control of the craft and the medium before you feel comfortable with it.

Now try mixing colors together. You'll find that it takes only a drop or two to make a real change in the color. When you add new dyes or water to alter an already prepared color, you are also diluting the non-crawl, so make a test stroke or two on the side of the waxed Masa to check that it still "takes."

One of the main characteristics of dye is its transparency, and this has both drawbacks and advantages. You have probably discovered already that you can't make corrections by going over your mistakes. Once an area is dry or almost dry, if you paint over it, it will appear darker. If you have allowed an edge to dry and you must continue with the same color, try to pick up where you left off by carefully bringing your brush *just up to* the dried edge without any overlap. It's like butting the edges of two pieces of paper together. If your brush does slip over a dried edge, you can sometimes pick the color up with a corner of a piece of tissue or with your fingertip. A gentle stroke will remove the unwanted wet dye where it overlaps the dry edge.

One of the very useful advantages of the transparency of dyes is that you can duplicate the printing process called *trapping.* This occurs when one color overprints another and gives the impression of a *third* color. For example, if pink is superimposed on yellow, the color created where the two overlap will be orange. Since both the dyes used for mass-production printing and the Luma™ dyes are transparent, designers can simulate this trapping technique; it is possible to produce richer, more varied color effects with fewer colors.

Return to your practice sheet of waxed Masa. Find a shape you have painted in a medium-value color—for example, a circle in *Cyclamen* that you may have watered down to pink. Now mix a couple of drops of *True Blue* with a few drops of water, and add the necessary non-crawl. Be sure that the first circle is completely dry; then shift your Masa so that the painted circle partially overlaps the penciled shape underneath. With the blue color, paint the new shape partly over the pink and partly on the white, unpainted Masa. Try to paint "dry" with the blue—that is don't flood the color on too wet. This will help keep the overlapping edges clean, sharp, and unsmeared. You will see that where the blue lies on top of the pink, you have achieved the *third* color, purple. (This third color is sometimes referred to as the "created color.") If this were expanded into a design, it would be a two-color pattern, pink and blue, even though it gives the effect of a third color, purple, where the blue "trapped" on the pink.

The fact that the waxed Masa is transparent also offers the option of working on both sides of the paper! For example, suppose you want to use a tinted ground, but are concerned about "picking up" the ground color as you paint your design over it. Paint the ground on one side of the waxed Masa, let it dry, turn the paper over and paint your design on the other side. Of course you must be aware that the color of the tinted ground, when seen

Without non-crawl on waxed rice paper the color "beads up."

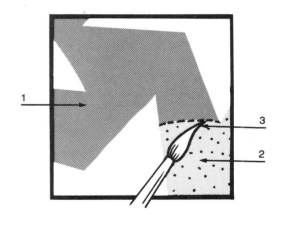

A technique for avoiding unsightly overlapping and creating a continuous appearance when painting a blotch with dye.
1. Dried blotch area.
2. Blotch to be painted.
3. Paint just up to dried edge.

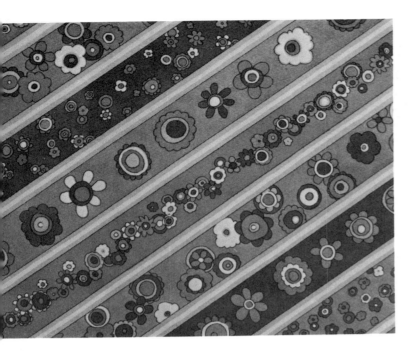

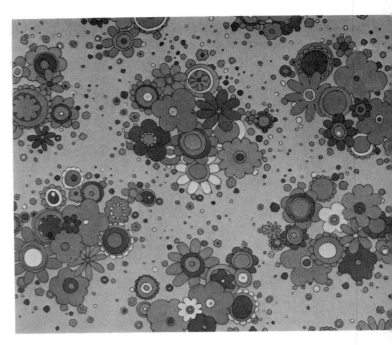

Two coordinating designs rendered in dyes on a tinted ground, with accents of opaque white gouache.

from the other side of the paper, will appear slightly muted, or "frosted," and you will have to adjust your color accordingly.

If you would like a darker background color for your design, you can apply a variation of the same principle. Paint a wash of the desired color on one side of the waxed Masa. Since you're working with dye, the wash will still be transparent. When it's dry, turn it over, place it on top of your drawing and paint your design on the other side. (*Remember* to protect the underside of your Masa from smearing by placing a sheet of acetate or tracing paper between your drawing and the Masa.)

The colors of the motifs in your design will be altered by the ground color underneath; if this is not the effect desired, you can easily correct it. Turn the design over again so that the painted ground faces you. Now get some liquid household bleach (Clorox or equivalent). Pour a little into a small dish or cup, and using a toothpick, a brush with synthetic bristles— *never* a natural-hair brush—a cotton swab or any appropriate implement, apply the bleach carefully to the areas behind the motifs (which are now on the underneath side). Do not saturate the paper excessively with bleach. As soon as the color is bleached out, blot up the remaining bleach with your roll of toilet tissue, a piece of white blotting paper, etc. If allowed to stay too long on the rice paper, it will begin to act on the colors on the other side.

When you turn your design right side up again, you'll see the original colors you have applied, unaffected by the background color, which now appears as an evenly painted blotch.

Mistakes when Working with Dyes & What to Do about Them

Once again, there is always the possibility of accidents or mistakes—or errors of judgment. With a little ingenuity, sometimes these can be incorporated into your design. Others have to be repaired or removed. Some examples and hints are presented.

Problem: You have painted a design on Masa with dyes, in which one (or more) of the colors turns out to be not exactly as you wanted. Perhaps the yellow is too bright, *or* the blue needs more purple in it.

Solution: You could paint over these areas, but there is the danger that the result will be blotchy, since you are likely to pick up the first color as you paint over it with a second. A neater way is to work on the reverse side of the paper. To dull down the bright yellow, mix a grayish-beige, or whatever color you feel is needed. Water it down to the necessary value, remembering the non-crawl. Turn the design over and paint the color only on the reverse areas where the yellow appears. When it dries, turn the design face-up again. The color painted "behind" the yellow shows through and softens its appearance. In the same way, the blue can be back-painted with a light wash of pink or purple. The original color can be altered with this technique. The value will become slightly darker since another layer of color is being added, even though it's on the back side of the paper.

Problem: One of the colors in the design is too dark. You'd like to make it lighter without re-painting the whole piece.
Solution: Somewhat in the manner of the solution described on **page 103,** with a thoroughly clean brush, apply clear water over the area you wish to lighten. Go over only one area at a time, bringing the water right up to the edge of that color. Immediately, before the water dries, take a roll of toilet tissue and roll it *once* over that area. Don't go back and forth, or slide or rub, just one firm *roll.* As you blot up the water, you'll blot up some of the dye too. Wait for it to dry since the hue may seem to have changed while it is still wet. This process works best on small- to medium-sized areas, perhaps about 3″ across at most. On larger areas control is more difficult. (*Note:* If color tabs are being used, remember to alter these in the same manner as in the design. The color tabs must be consistent in color with the artwork.)

Problem: By accident you've dropped some spots of dye on a white area of the design.
Solution #1: Study it carefully, and see if the spots can't be turned to your advantage. Perhaps they can be made into another bud or flower in a floral pattern; incorporated into the texture of an already textured area; turned into a bee or butterfly if it suits the look of the design. Of course these new touches must be added elsewhere too, so that they look like an integral part of the layout.
Solution #2: If Solution #1 just won't work, carefully touch the spot with bleach. As soon as the spot has been bleached out, blot up the excess. *Do not* allow bleach to sit on the surface of the paper any longer than necessary. When this is completely dry, if the bleach has left a whitish spot, try touching it lightly with a little clean water and blot again. Work one spot at a time.

Problem: You've used bleach on a part of your design and now would like to paint something in dye on that spot.
Solution: If you paint on that area immediately after the bleach has dried, the bleaching agent (chlorine) will still be active for a while, and will discolor the dye. You can wait several hours until all the chlorine has evaporated. This is not usually too practical. Or you can "paint" water over the bleached spot and blot it up with the toilet-tissue-roll method described above. When this is thoroughly dry, you can safely paint over it with dye.

Dyes on Paper

Painting with dyes on white or tinted paper can also be very satisfying. Papers vary a great deal in texture and absorbency. If the paper is very soft and acts like a blotter, it produces a different effect than one which is harder and absorbs the dye less rapidly. Arches™ is one of the best papers to use with dyes. Different effects are achieved by wetting the paper first, but usually dyes are applied when the paper is dry.

Non-crawl or other wetting agents are *not* used in the dye when painting on paper. Experiment with various papers and dye to learn how they interact. (Refer to the paper list, **Appendix.**) If you use the lightweight Arches™, you will be able to transfer the design from tracing paper using a light box or light table. Be sure the pencil outlines are faint. Transferring the design from the tracing paper is also possible using Saral™ or homemade graphite carbon, but again be sure the graphite lines are not dark and messy.

The choice of paper to use depends on the technique and special effects one is striving for. There are no absolute rules and whatever works is acceptable.

Method I

Method II

Two methods for rendering photographic effects using gouache (facing page). Similar technique is possible using dyes. In Method I, cover area with clean water, and paint and flow gouache while area is still wet. In Method II, paint a small dry area with gouache. Using clean water, "lead" gouache down while still wet.

SPECIAL EFFECTS WITH VARIOUS MEDIA

We have described the customary, traditional uses of gouache and of dyes with which you can develop countless beautiful designs from simple geometrics to paisleys and foulards, from florals to conversationals. During the process, you will become more and more proficient in the use of these two basic media and begin to feel the need to expand, to experiment, to stretch your artistic and creative muscles.

The following section will deal with:

- More varied techniques to be used with gouache and with dyes, including combinations of these two.

- Other media and techniques.

SPECIAL EFFECTS WITH GOUACHE

Photographic Effect with Gouache

We have stated that gouache is an opaque medium, meant to be painted flat and smooth and traditionally has been used in this manner. However, since it is water-soluble, it can also be thinned down, for the purpose of creating *shaded* areas that blend smoothly from dark to light, not unlike the look of a photograph.

To produce this shaded, *photographic look,* use the gouache *as if* it were transparent watercolor. On white paper (such as Arches or Strathmore), lightly draw a simple shape in pencil—an oval, a leaf, about 2″ to 3″ in size—and paint a small area inside one edge of your drawn shape. Quickly clean the brush in water or use another brush dipped in water, and continue at the unfinished edge, pull the paint across the shape with your wet brush. Allow the gouache to thin down and spread into the area that you are painting with water. Gently and quickly guide the gouache onto the wet area. You can add a little more gouache to the other side of the motif for additional shading. With practice you will achieve considerable control, so that your shading can bring out beautiful dimensional effects, especially useful in realistic floral designs.

When using this photographic technique to paint a flower, concentrate on one petal or area at a time, and let the brush strokes follow the contours of the petal. Study botanical renderings and paintings of flowers and other natural forms, or better still look at real flowers. Notice that frequently the color is deepest at the innermost parts of the flower, and gradually seems lighter toward the outer edges.

Another way of producing this watercolor effect is by *first* brushing clean water onto the shape, then painting gouache where desired, leading the color with your brush to flow and blend into the wet area. Experience will teach you how much water to use in proportion to gouache so that it's wet enough to allow the color to flow and blend, yet not so wet that it's hard to control. Tissues help you quickly dry the brush and pick up any excess wetness. Don't overwork the gouache with too much brushing or stroking. You want to retain the spontaneous, fresh look typical of watercolor painting. With practice you will be able to produce richly shaded dimensional effects using gouache in this manner.

The Blob

When you closely study wallcovering and home fashion fabrics, you will see that many of them use a technique that could be called *the blob.* It is a bold, silhouetted look, more related in spirit to painting than drawing. A brush (#6 to #8) is loaded with paint and brought directly to the paper without wiping it on the edge of the paint-well. Leaves and petals and all motifs are painted freely and spontaneously, feeling the wholeness of the motif rather than its contours. The consistency of the paint is like milk or light cream, and flows freely from the brush onto the paper. The paint is moved about to

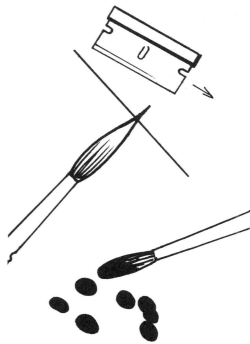

cover the motif-area, and the edges are formed with the long side of the bristles. The rounded tip of the brush is also used to shape the motif. Working in a *stipple* manner creates a bold dot or blob. An open, textural look can be created as well as solid coverage if the blobs flow together (as illustrated above). This is an important way of handling the brush and the paint, and should be practiced until you feel comfortable with it.

To achieve this technique, it is helpful to blunt the tip of the brush. This sounds a bit drastic, especially with an expensive sable brush. But you will not regret it once you have tried it. Use a #6 or #8 brush, wet the hairs and form a perfect point. With a single-edged razor blade, cut away *the point only* (as illustrated). It may be only 1/64″ with the first cut. It is better to cut too little than too much. So test the newly cut brush with gouache and see if there is a different feel to it. If not, cut away a tiny bit more— perhaps another 1/64″. Remove only the extreme tip of the hairs. Trimming the tip of your brush in this manner will allow you to paint *the blob* technique more effectively.

Spatter

Spatter is a technique done with a toothbrush and closely imitates the effect of air-brush. It is a way of achieving a shaded, *tonal* effect similar to a photograph while using opaque gouache. The gouache should be mixed to normal consistency, neither thick nor watery. A hard toothbrush which is flat on top and with at least four rows of bristles is used, with a "scraper"— such as an old metal table knife or spoon or try a plastic picnic knife. For practice use any white or light colored paper.

The method is as follows: With the mixing brush, paint some gouache onto the toothbrush. Now, holding the toothbrush in your left hand, bristles downward, about 3″ to 4″ above the paper, scrape across the toothbrush with the scraper. Tilt the toothbrush at a slight angle, and scrape towards you (as illustrated). You will see a fine spray developing on the paper.

If you're getting large-ish spots, your paint may be too thin or you may have too much paint on the toothbrush. If the spots are so fine that they are almost invisible, you may not have put enough paint on the toothbrush, or perhaps your gouache is too thick.

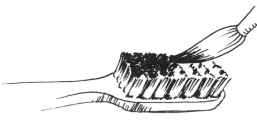

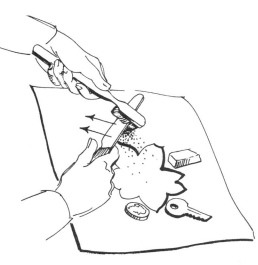

Some examples of effects achieved with toothbrush-spatter. Apply paint to surface of the toothbrush. Pull scraper toward you. Weigh stencil down around edges.

Instead of a toothbrush, a brush with coarse bristles will make a coarser spatter-dot, if that is desired. It will take a little practice to develop a satisfactory spatter technique.

This technique offers many potentials for variations. Try cutting out a simple silhouette on a scrap of bond or bristol paper. Special stencil paper which is treated to be water resistant can be used. Place this *cut-out* shape on your test paper and weigh it down with keys or coins or small objects. Spatter a color around it, and wait a few moments for the paint to dry. When you lift off the cut-out (carefully!) you'll find the shape outlined with a spatter "halo." You can use the negative shape (the "hole" left when you made the cut-out) in a similar manner. Place this stencil on your paper, weigh it down around the cut-out, and spatter around the edges. Shift the mask so that the opening overlaps the spattered form somewhat. Spatter again with another color.

You can imagine some other possibilities of this technique. For example you can cut out a long silhouette of a skyline or mountainous horizon. By moving this silhouette down the length of the page, shifting it sideways occasionally, or turning it over face down as you go, with the toothbrush spatter technique you can create a scenic-stripe effect, varying the colors as desired. You can create a misty ring around painted motifs in your design; with the appropriate shapes for your masks, you can enhance the look of Art Deco designs, conversationals, and florals as well as achieve novelty and special effects. As you practice and perfect the spatter technique, let your imagination go and you'll find countless ways to apply it in designing. *Caution:* To avoid smears, always give your spatter a minute or so to dry before touching it. Tweezers are also useful for removing the cut-out.

Stipple

Stipple is another way of achieving a shaded effect with dots. However, it provides much more control than the toothbrush spatter, since the dots are applied one at a time by hand, and precisely where you want them. Stippling can be done with brush and gouache, pencil, marker, and more often, with pen and ink. Select a brush that does not come to a very fine point, but has a rather rounded tip. Keep the brush fully loaded for this process, in order to produce rounded, "blobby" little dots. By painting the dots closer together you create the appearance of darker *shading;* gradually placing them farther apart will give the illusion of lighter and lighter shading with a more open texture. You can augment the illusion even more by gradually making the dots smaller in the less concentrated areas and larger in the areas you wish to appear darker or more covered.

Dry Brush

For this technique, the gouache should be mixed rather on the thick side. Dip your brush into the paint, then stroke it on a piece of scrap paper until the hairs are somewhat spread and the brush is painting "dry"—that is, not really covering completely, but allowing the paper to show through in small streaks and specks. Now, on your practice paper, make some short strokes. The result should be feathery-edged, fuzzy strokes, giving the impression of shading even though you've used only one color. Practice this effect with larger or smaller brushes: straight or curved lines, shorter and longer strokes. Try it on different types of paper, and notice how the dry-brush technique gives different effects on smooth and rough surfaces. For textile printing purposes, dry-brush helps to give a shaded, dimensional or textural look without having to use additional printing processes.

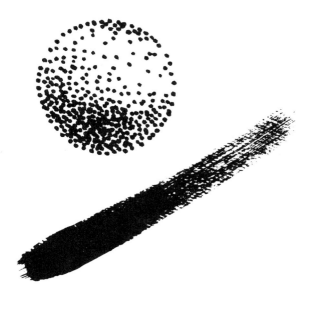

A variety of techniques produce other interesting effects such as stipple and dry-brush.

Sponges

Several types of sponges are available that can be used to create interesting effects with gouache. The synthetic household sponges sold in supermarkets, the fine-grained red rubber sponges found where cosmetics are sold, as well as the various grades of natural sponges—all are useful in designing. For creating irregular, textured areas, *tear off* a portion of the sponge (do not cut in order to avoid a straight, hard edge). Dip the sponge lightly into the color, and dab it onto the practice paper. Try varying the pressure as you touch down on the paper for different effects. Keep turning the piece of sponge, or use two or three different pieces, to avoid duplicating the same markings. With the more fine-grained sponges, you can rip off a piece about ½" or ¾" round, and holding it with a pair of tweezers, achieve enough control to create some fine effects with gouache. With the household or the red rubber sponges, it is possible to cut out a clear but simple form, cover the flat surface with your gouache, and use it as a stamp, either by itself or in combination with painted forms. A rich color effect is achieved by sponging two colors, one over the other. Experimentation is always necessary to explore the possibilities of any technique.

Stamps

It is possible to use many different objects to stamp shapes in gouache. Simply by painting the surface of any object, say a piece of cork or a household key with gouache, you can print the image onto paper or painted ground.

An exciting variation of this is to make your own stamps using *Artgum™ erasers.* They are tan in color and usually measure 1" x 1"x 2" although it is possible to buy them larger. First slice the Artgum eraser with a sharp kitchen knife into smaller sections if a small motif is chosen. Try to keep the cut surface flat and even. The pressure should be applied both at the handle and at the tip of the knife to ensure a steady, even cut.

On a piece of tracing paper, draw the image you want with a #2 pencil. This image is now transferred onto the Artgum eraser surface by "rubbing it down" in a manner similar to that described in **Chapter 5.** If there is a lot of detail, define the image on the Artgum eraser with a pen and ink line. This will not readily smear as does the graphite.

Cut away the surface of the Artgum eraser that you do not want to print. This is done with a #11 Xacto™ knife blade. Hold the knife at a slight angle so that the printing surface is not *undercut* which would cause it to break away. Lift out the small unwanted pieces of Artgum eraser from the areas that will not print. Around the edges, trim all the excess eraser away

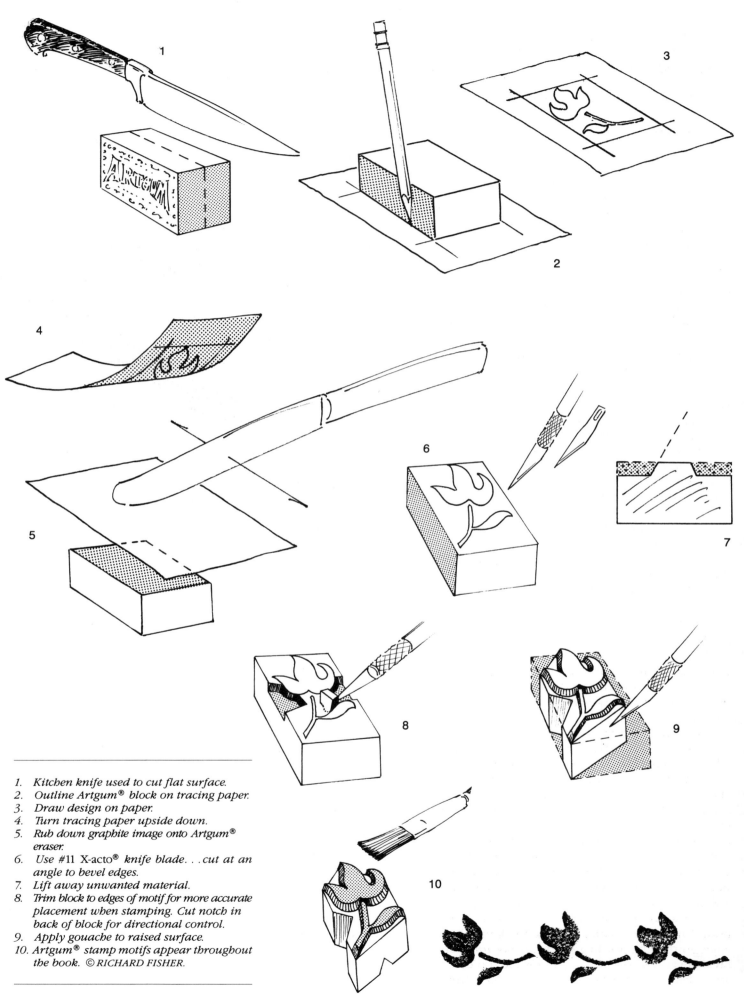

1. Kitchen knife used to cut flat surface.
2. Outline Artgum® block on tracing paper.
3. Draw design on paper.
4. Turn tracing paper upside down.
5. Rub down graphite image onto Artgum® eraser.
6. Use #11 X-acto® knife blade. . .cut at an angle to bevel edges.
7. Lift away unwanted material.
8. Trim block to edges of motif for more accurate placement when stamping. Cut notch in back of block for directional control.
9. Apply gouache to raised surface.
10. Artgum® stamp motifs appear throughout the book. © RICHARD FISHER.

from the printing surface. This will make it easier to place the printing image exactly where you want it to be.

Using a flat brush held at an extreme angle, brush on the gouache so that the paint does not fill into the cut-out holes but remains on the printing surface of the Artgum eraser. The consistency of the paint must be exactly right; too thick and it won't print, too thin and it will run down into the cut-out areas and destroy the image. The first two or three images will not print well since it takes a while to get the paint and the artgum "worked in."

A small notch on the back of the Artgum will help orient the image in a consistent, one-way direction. This is especially important when working with a grid layout.

The ideal surface for receiving the paint is unwaxed rice paper. The more porous the surface, the better the printing will be. However, it is possible to print on regular design paper (such as Georgian) as well as on painted gouache or dye grounds. The printed image may not be as flat and even as the rice paper image.

With practice very fine detail can be achieved. Once the stamp is made, the execution of the final croquis is quite simple. A rhythm of working is established: painting the Artgum eraser, stamping, painting, stamping, etc. Unusual effects which could normally be achieved only after endless hours of tedious brush work are quickly possible.

Textures

Textures for backgrounds as well as motifs can be either *organic* or *geometric*. *Organic textures* are similar to those found in nature. There is an accidental quality to them and they do not look hand painted or contrived. *Geometric textures* are created by small geometric motifs placed close together, usually in a set layout. The allover effect appears *textural*.

Spatter, stipple, sponges and dry brush can all be used to create *organic* textures. *Geometric* textures can be created with stamps as well as painting directly with a brush.

To create this effect, tape tracing paper, paper towelling or facial tissue together to retain shape and apply paint to top surface only.

A technique to create a texture on Plasti-vel™ is described in **Chapter 3** in which a watery gouache is partially absorbed with a piece of tissue. Tissues or paper towelling can be used to blot wet paint. For interesting textural effects, take a piece of paper, crush and wrinkle it into a crumpled mass, then brush paint onto the wrinkled surface. Use this either evenly, to create an allover effect, or here and there for a more irregular look. A variation would be achieved by repeating this with another color over the first. The crumpled paper can also be pulled across the paper for straight or curved lines—also with variations of color. Try crumpling different types of paper—tracing paper, a page from a notebook, tissue paper, paper towelling. Another variation of this technique is to dab clean wrinkled paper to a painted surface while it is still wet—turning or pulling it across for different effects.

Ruling pens can be used in a free-hand manner to create varied and unusual textures (see **Chapter 3**). Simulated *woven fabric design* effects can be rendered with ruling pens as well as brushes, on both prepared acetate or regular paper.

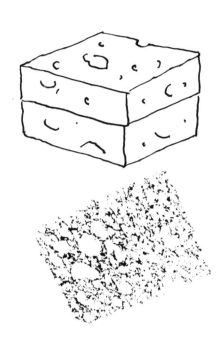

Rubber cement two pieces of synthetic sponges together to create another interesting effect.

Warp-print or Ikat Effect

Ikat is an ancient technique that has been used in Malaya, India, northeastern Asia, and Africa. It is a method of fabric decoration whereby the warp (the vertical threads) is tie-dyed or otherwise printed *before* the fabric is woven. This results in blurred edges in the design with a pronounced up-and-down direction. Occasionally the weft or filling (the horizontal threads) is also dyed in selected locations prior to weaving. In this case the result is called a *double Ikat*.

Warp printing is a similar process, used in modern printing plants. With the warp threads in place, the design is printed *before* the fabric is woven. As a result, on the finished fabric, the printed images have vertical thread-like edges.

Both these methods are time-consuming and painstaking, and the fabrics thus produced are usually of comparatively small yardages, and costly.

However, there is a way of painting that can *imitate* this effect with brush and/or pen for mass-produced printing on fabric. As a rule, the design, whether abstract or floral, should not be too fine or detailed. If you are working on waxed Masa, place it over a sheet of vertically lined paper and tape it down. If you're using any other type of paper, *very lightly* rule vertical lines in pencil, about 1″ apart. These will act as guidelines, to keep your painted thread-like edges vertically true. Without these guidelines the tendency may be to go off on a slant, with a tilted, crooked-looking result.

With all textures and techniques of this kind, *consistency* is of great importance. The textures *must* look the same throughout the design. *Variation* in direction, scale and gesture will look sloppy and unattractive.

The motifs are sketched and traced in pencil with clearly defined edges. When painting with gouache, you use only vertical strokes, imitating the dyed warp threads of the true Ikat or warp print. If you are painting with dye, you can intensify the vertical, thread-like look with broken, irregular penlines accentuating the design on top of the colors.

A similar effect can be achieved using only markers, either as a multi-colored design or with a single color. Keep referring to your guidelines as you work, using only vertical strokes with your marking pens.

Gouache on Waxed Rice Paper

Although gouache is usually painted on paper, occasionally waxed Masa is used. This is especially convenient when the artwork is complicated and would require an elaborate tracing if it were to be done on paper. Since the waxed Masa is transparent, it can be placed on top of the drawing and painted directly from the image underneath. When using gouache this way, you must add non-crawl to it, but, as with dyes, start by adding a minute amount and test it on your waxed Masa, adding more non-crawl in very

small amounts until it "takes" without beading up. You can then proceed to paint as you would normally on regular white paper. If your croquis requires white, unpainted areas, leave the Masa unpainted in these sections, but remember that the finished work must be presented on a white backing or mount.

Ombré or Shaded Effect with Flat Gouache

Ombré (pronounced *om*-bray) is the French word for *shadow* or *shaded,* and is a term frequently used in textile design. In textile design it is used to describe a special principle of design when there is a *transition* of color, motif or texture which is either smooth and gradual or through a series of steps. In a sense, an ombré is a *shading* illusion.

When a *shaded* effect is desired and you do not want to use the *photographic* or *wash* technique, you can achieve it with flat opaque gouache applied in a series of steps placed one next to the other. There are several ways to create an ombré effect.

Value Transition Using a single color straight out of the tube, with just a minute amount of white added to help it lie flat, paint a band about 3″ x ½″, and let it dry. Add some more white to some of this color in another well in your palette. Add enough so that you can see a value change from your first color, and paint this in a band right up against the first one, leaving no white space between them. While this dries, in another well of the palette take some of this second color and add more white, trying to make it about an equally lighter step to the previous one. Paint this alongside the second band in the same manner. Repeat these steps until your last color is a very pale tint of the original full color, always waiting until the paint is dry before painting the next color. In about four to six steps, you can create a group of stripes using separate, distinct *values of one color*. The engraver can interpret these values as several separate colors, as several percentones of one color (see **Chapter 9**), or as two or three colors, each with a half-tone.

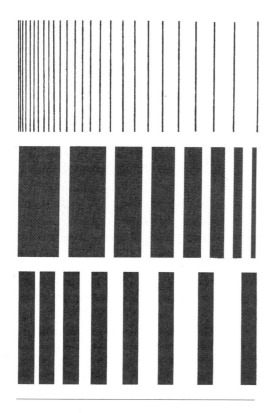

Analogous Color Transition   This time, let us assume you want to create an ombré stripe shading from red to yellow, in five steps. Let your first band of color be the pure red (again adding a tiny touch of white to help the red dry flat). While this is drying, mix some of this pure red in another well of your palette with some yellow to create a red-orange. (Since yellow happens to be such a pale color, it won't take much of the red to effect a noticeable change.) Paint this in a band up against the red. Now add more yellow to the red-orange until you have mixed orange; then mix a yellow-orange, then use plain yellow, each time allowing the previous color to dry before painting the following one next to it. You have created a five-color ombré design, again using flat colors to create a transition from one color to another through a series of carefully planned steps this time with *analogous colors.*

Layout Transition   A third type of ombré is created with the *layout* of the stripes or bands of a color. The spaces between stripes can go from narrow to wide while the stripe itself remains the same dimension. Or start with a narrow stripe and gradually increase its width as the layout widens. A combination of these two is also possible, with a transition of spaces from narrow to wide as the width of the stripes changes from wide to narrow.

A variation of this to achieve the illusion of shading is by using a single color and painting *lines,* starting very close together and gradually making them farther and farther apart.

Using dots or abstract shapes, start out crowding them close together and little by little *spacing* them farther apart. The same can be done with non-abstract motifs, such as flower and leaves, objects or geometric figures. In addition, an ombré can be created by changing the *sizes* of the motifs, starting out with large shapes and by degrees, making them smaller and smaller.

With this concept of transition, you can begin to see the many other possibilities of this *ombré* technique. By *stepping* values and colors it is possible to create the effect of *shading* in flowers and other natural forms;

to give a feeling of depth or dimension in geometric shapes; and to enrich the look of an Art Deco or abstract design. Frequently this manner of *shading* is used in stylized period florals for decorative fabrics.

SPECIAL EFFECTS WITH DYE

Photographic Effect with Dyes

In learning to use dyes, we stressed the need to *practice* in order to perfect your skill in painting smooth, flat, even areas. However, the brilliance and luminosity of dyes can also be used to great advantage in other ways. The colors can be blended from pale to deep, using a watercolor painting technique. Colors can be allowed to flow into one another, blended carefully or in a freer, more accidental manner. As described with gouache, the dye can be *shaded* from full color to a pale tint as it is blended into the watery areas. Introduce two or more colors. Allow some *accidents* to happen. Try to keep the fresh, spontaneous look that is the essence of the watercolor painting technique.

Take the time to explore this technique. Work on waxed Masa as well as on a good watercolor paper. Some of the most beautiful, lush floral designs, especially those meant to be printed on silk or polished cotton, are created in this technique. Dramatic effects can be achieved with this exciting medium.

Drawing & Painting with Bleach on Dyes

Several uses of bleach have been suggested earlier, but mainly these have been for the purpose of correcting mistakes or solving particular problems. Bleach can also be used to enhance or augment designs painted with dye.

Using a toothpick or a brush with synthetic bristles, try "drawing" some fine lines on the test sheets that you used for your explorations with dye. White lines will appear in a second or two. As soon as the bleach has

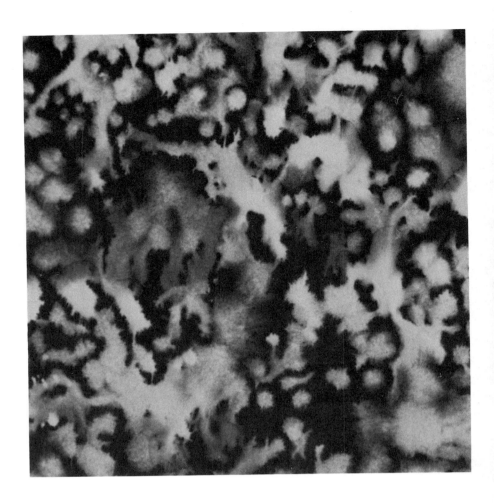

Bleach dropped onto a ground while the dye was wet, causing accidental and random shapes.

done its work, use the roll of toilet tissue as previously described to blot up any excess. If you prefer to have the bleach work more slowly, or if you want the lines to be off-white, dilute your bleach with a few drops of water.

An entire design can be created by painting or drawing with bleach on a dye background—and this ground can be a flat and even color, or swirled or textured with different values and colors. Little highlights—veins in a leaf or flower petal, stripes or dots or stipple effects, even some dry-brush effects—all are possible using bleach on dye-painted areas.

Spatter with Bleach A smock or apron will protect your clothing from accidentally being bleached. Paint a ground with dye and while it is drying, cut out a simple shape in two-ply bristol board or equivalent weight paper, creating a stencil. Place the stencil on the painted ground and weigh it down with a few coins around the edges of the cut-out. Spatter bleach in the manner described on **page 109.** *Do not* saturate the toothbrush with bleach or the spatter will be hard to control. You will soon see the white spatter-dots begin to appear.

Instead of using a stencil or a cut-out paper shape, try placing objects such as small scissors, a key, or some paper clips, creating interesting-shaped silhouettes. *Always* wait for the spatter to dry before lifting off the stencil or the objects.

Things to Remember When Working with Bleach

1. Keep all brushes with *natural* bristles away from the bleach. The active ingredient in bleach, chlorine, will destroy the bristles.

2. Protect *yourself* as well as *surrounding areas* when using bleach. Move any artwork or other papers out of reach or cover them. If you plan to be using the bleach for an extended period of time, ventilate the area to prevent fumes from accumulating.

3. If the bleach doesn't have much effect on the dyes, it probably is not fresh. On the other hand, if the bleach is acting so fast on your artwork that you feel you can't control it, dilute it with clean water to slow it down.

A steel pen was used with bleach wherever white appears. (© RICHARD FISHER.)

4. You can't paint with dye on a freshly bleached area. The chlorine remains on the surface of the paper, even after it is "dry." Either wait a few hours or better still, overnight, to give the chlorine a chance to evaporate. It is possible to "wash" the chlorine off with clean water and a brush as described earlier.

5. Bleach works equally well on dye whether painted on waxed Masa or on paper. You do not need to add non-crawl to bleach when working on waxed Masa.

6. Bleach does *not* work on gouache, ink or markers.

RESIST TECHNIQUES

Resist is a general term for a process whereby the painting surface is treated with a material (a resist) that will shield or protect that area from the paint that is to be used. The following are some examples of resist materials: liquid frisket, rubber cement, frisket paper, gouache/ink, wax (in batik method).

Liquid Frisket

Liquid frisket is a rubber-based liquid, not to be confused with rubber cement. It can be gray or pink in color, and is painted on with a brush. Most designers keep one or two brushes to use specifically with liquid frisket, as it is rough on good sable brushes. As a precaution, it's a good idea to moisten your brush and work a little soap into the hairs before dipping into the frisket. This will make it easier to clean out when you're finished. Paint with the frisket on your white paper, covering the shapes that are to be protected. (Liquid frisket works better on a hard, smooth surfaced paper, such as bristol, than on rough or textured paper.)

Wait until it is thoroughly dry (frisket dries rather quickly) then paint the gouache over the entire area, including the dry frisket areas. Allow the gouache to dry completely. Now lightly rub your finger along the edge of the "frisket-ed" area. You can also use a rubber cement pick-up (a small block of hardened rubber, sold in art supply stores). You will find that you can pick up an edge and peel away the frisket leaving a clean white image on the area the frisket had covered. This technique is especially useful when you want a colored background around rather fine or complicated forms, and would like to avoid blotching laboriously around these forms or painting your design on top of a ground. By using the frisket method, you can now paint a background as described earlier in this chapter, lift off the frisket, and have clean white areas within which you may now use light colors, dyes, pastels, crayons, etc.

Spraying the ground with a workable fixative before you lift off the frisket will prevent the gouache from smearing onto the newly uncovered paper. Spray two separate layers of Krylon™ workable fixative over the painted ground allowing it to dry between each application. The gouache will absorb quite a bit of the fixative and a moderately heavy amount can be used. However, do not saturate the surface to the extent that it looks like a wet puddle.

While spraying move the spray can back and forth, left and right, up and down to ensure an even distribution of the fixative. It is best to mount the paper vertically on the wall so the spray is directed perpendicularly at the surface of the paper. Hold the spray can *vertically* at all times. *Remember to protect your lungs by wearing a mask!*

Liquid frisket can be used with a ruling pen, either for straight, ruled lines or in a free-hand drawing manner. After these lines have been painted over and the frisket peeled away, thin, clean lines will be revealed.

Frisket can also be painted over areas that have been tinted with dye— but observe this precaution: peel away the frisket from such areas as soon as possible. If the frisket is left on for a few hours, it will tend to discolor or lighten the color of the dye.

Frisket cannot be used on waxed Masa since any material containing rubber is incompatible with the wax. However, when using *dyes on paper,* you'll find that frisket is very effective. You can use it on blank white paper to block out areas that are to remain white. You can also use it on areas you have painted, to retain that color in those places while painting a trapped color on another area. For example, say you've painted a pink butterfly's wing, but first masked off a few spots with frisket where you want to retain the white of the paper. When the pink is dry, you now paint frisket in a few spots that are to remain pink. When this is dry, you paint some blue over part of the pink including the second frisket spots. Allow the whole area to dry thoroughly. Then carefully, using your finger or rubber cement pick-up, lift off all the frisket. You'll have a pink butterfly's wing with some white spots, and some pink spots enclosed in a violet area where the blue trapped on the pink.

Things to Remember When Using Frisket

1. Be sure you have completely and thoroughly covered the areas you want to protect with frisket. *Too thin* an application of frisket will *not* block out the gouache.

2. When painting with gouache over frisket, do not paint too thick, and avoid going over the gouache with a second coat. In this way you will prevent the gouache from "cracking" around the clean shapes you want to create.

3. In removing the frisket, be gentle. Lift and peel away as much as you can; dab lightly with your finger or the rubber cement pick-up, do not rub. When you think you've removed all the frisket, lightly run your fingers over the areas to search out any parts you may have missed.

4. Keep the bottle of frisket covered between uses. It dries out very quickly. (There is a polymer thinner made just for frisket, but it is rather costly, and it too tends to dry out quickly.)

5. Wash out your frisket brush promptly. If it has been allowed to dry you can try rinsing it in rubber-cement thinner, but frisket is hard on brushes—clean them as soon as possible.

Rubber Cement

The resist principle of rubber cement is similar to liquid frisket. The rubber cement is applied to the areas you want to resist the paint. Allow to dry, then paint with gouache. When the paint is dry the rubber cement is carefully peeled and rubbed off, leaving unpainted the areas that were covered. There is more control with liquid frisket than with rubber cement,

which is not really meant to be used for detailed brushwork. However, bold, strong brush strokes with the regular rubber-cement applicator or with a brush can create interesting textural and directional effects. Similarly, other improvised *tools* have been used, such as cotton-tipped swabs, drinking straws, or chopsticks. With the latter, you can dribble the rubber cement in drops or winding trails across the paper, allow it to dry, then paint over the page, and peel away the rubber cement. Experiment to develop your own ideas.

When using frisket or rubber cement with dyes, remember to *work fast.* Plan your time so that you do not leave frisket on a dye-painted area for more than an hour or two. The frisket tends to bleach or discolor the dye the longer you leave it on. Frisket also tends to *set* and adhere more firmly with time, so that when you start to remove it, you may tear the paper underneath, creating an unattractive appearance, and preventing any further work on those areas.

Frisket Paper

This is a thin film that can be cut easily into any sort of shape. It has a layer of adhesive on the back, covered by a protective backing sheet. When the backing is removed, the cut shape will adhere firmly to your paper, yet can be re-positioned if necessary. You can paint over it or spatter around it. When your paint is dry the frisket paper can be lifted away, leaving the area under it untouched.

Gouache/Ink Resist

A very attractive effect having somewhat the appearance of a wood-cut or linoleum print can be produced with *waterproof* India ink and either Richart white or gouache white. Colored gouache may also be used. You will need, in addition to these materials, a strong good-quality paper, approximately 8″ x 10″ with which to experiment (two-ply bristol works well), running water, and one or two brushes. (*Note:* Many designers keep a brush exclusively for use with India ink, as it is a rather harsh medium and difficult to wash completely out of the hairs and shank of the brush.)

Step 1   Paint a few motifs with gouache mixed slightly thicker than usual. Paint with a "full" brush. Make some parallel lines, a circle within a circle, a bold daisy, a few leaves. Try two or three different colors (but only one layer of paint. Don't paint one color on top of another.) Allow them to dry thoroughly.

Step 2   When you're sure the gouache is dry, paint the entire surface with India ink, covering the gouache as well as the unpainted parts of the paper. We suggest that you use a fairly large brush for the India ink—the larger the croquis, the larger the brush—and apply it as quickly as you can, with smooth, even strokes. Allow this, too, to dry thoroughly.

Step 3   Run a gentle stream of water over the painted surface. A shower nozzle would be useful. Use *cool* or cold water, never hot. Gently stroke across the paper under the running water, using a soft brush or your fingers. The areas you painted with gouache will rinse away, taking the India ink with it. Where the ink lies directly on the paper it will remain, since it is waterproof. Where you had painted gouache, the paper will be exposed and remain white. The gouache has acted as a resist to the ink. Handle the paper gently—do not scrub it, or hold it under the water any longer than necessary.

If you used only white paint, the result will be a black and white pattern. If you used color, most of the color will be washed away along with the substance of the gouache, but some color will remain on the paper as a tint of the original color. To some extent, you will be able to predict how much stain of color the various gouache paints will leave.

Gently *blot* off the excess water, using a roll of toilet tissue or paper towelling. Put it aside to dry flat. Tack it at the corners and edges on a drawing board.

With experience you can develop considerable control with this technique. You will learn to leave little "accidental" unpainted places in the gouache, which fill in with India ink and simulate a block-printed look. Or you may choose a more controlled, finished appearance. And with experience you will be able to work with larger areas.

This technique is possible with various types of papers with different textures, as long as the paper is strong enough to withstand washing with water without damage to the painted surface. Designs executed with this technique can be used for apparel as well as for home furnishing products.

THE USE OF WAX IN DESIGNING

Batik is an ancient process of fabric decoration that probably originated in Indonesia. Variations of this process have spread to Africa, Japan, China and India, and in recent years batik has enjoyed considerable popularity throughout the world. To put it very simply, batik is a resist technique in which melted wax is applied in designs on fabric. Then the fabric is dipped into a dye bath, and the areas that have been waxed are shielded from the dye. The waxing and dipping are sometimes repeated several times, each time covering additional parts of the design with wax and using additional colors, thereby enriching and enhancing the final result. In the traditional batik method, the melted wax is applied to the fabric in several ways—with blocks or stamps (called *tjaps*), with brushes and most frequently with a *tjanting-pen*. When the design is finished the fabric is steamed to set the dye. Finally the last remnants of wax are removed, and the fabric is ready for use.

Modern textile designers have adapted some of the techniques of traditional batik. The melted wax resist is applied to unwaxed rice paper, most frequently Masa. Instead of the laborious process of repeated dippings in dye baths, designer's dyes (Luma™, Dr. Martin's™, etc.) are simply painted into the unwaxed areas. The dyes are rejected by the wax. When the design is finished, it is sandwiched between several layers of newsprint and the wax is ironed out.

You will need, in addition to the wax "set-up" listed in **Chapter 3:**

1. One or two tjanting pens (sold in craft and art supply stores). Tjanting pens are available in several sizes.

2. Brushes—two or three, various sizes. The oriental bamboo brushes are preferred by many designers. These brushes will not be usable for other

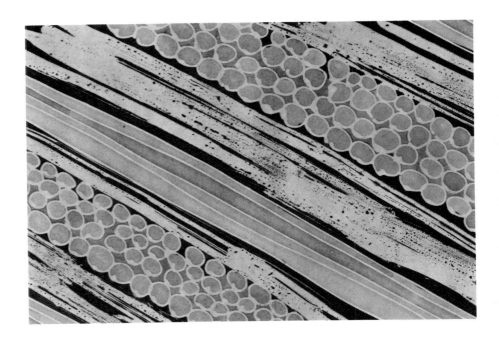

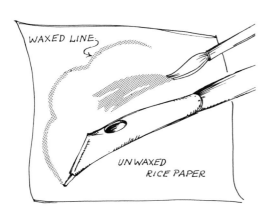

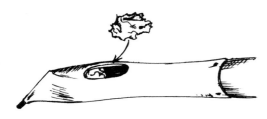

A design using "batik" method. Folded paper towelling helps to catch drips on the way from hot wax to work area. If wax flows too fast. . .put a bit of crumpled paper towelling inside "cup."

purposes, and you do not need very fine expensive brushes for use with wax. (Synthetic bristles are not recommended, as they will get frizzy or melt together under heat.)

3. Tracing paper, pencil or pen for drawing your design.

4. A sheet of acetate as large as your drawing.

5. Luma™, Dr. Martin's™, or equivalent dyes.

6. Paper towelling.

7. A large pad of newsprint paper (not newspaper).

Designing with the "Batik" Method

1. Draw your design clearly on the tracing paper. Never draw on the rice paper (refer to **Chapter 5**).

2. Place a sheet of acetate over the tracing paper drawing to protect the underneath side of the rice paper, then place the unwaxed rice paper on top of the acetate. Tape all sheets together at the top. (You do not need to use *prepared* acetate, which is more costly.)

3. Clear the work area of unnecessary clutter, and protect the work surface with brown wrapping paper or newspaper.

4. Melt the wax, using a double boiler or electric fry-pan *with heat control,* as described in **Chapter 3**. The wax should be about *2″ deep,* so that you can dip it up with the tjanting pen.

5. Fold a sheet of paper towelling into a square of about 3″ to 4″. When the wax is melted, dip some up into the tjanting pen. Do not overfill it or the wax will spill out over the top. As you lift it out of the melted wax, with your other hand hold the folded paper towelling under the spout of the tjanting pen. This will prevent melted wax from dripping onto your work as you move the tjanting pen.

Make a test line or two with the spout. If the rice paper becomes transparent where the line was made, this means the wax is penetrating the paper, and is hot enough. If the line remains white, the wax is not ready yet. If the wax pours too fast, it is too hot. Take the time to practice getting the melted wax to flow out of the spout at a comfortable rate.

With a little practice you will develop a rhythm of filling the tjanting pen, moving it across your paper with the paper towelling held underneath with the other hand, making the lines and strokes of melted wax, and returning to dip up more wax. Always keep your hands close together so that you can quickly put the paper towelling under the spout to avoid blots of melted wax on your work as you move back and forth to refill the tjanting pen. *Note:* Try to make your design with forms that are completely en-

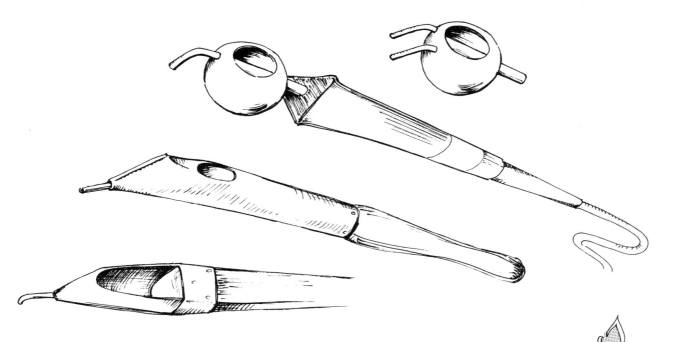

closed. These can be long narrow shapes, such as stems and branches, stripes or meandering pathways; rounder shapes, such as flowers, petals, leaves; geometric shapes, circles, triangles and squares; irregular shapes such as paisleys, stylized animals or figures. The lines of wax will act as the enclosure within which you will later paint the dye.

While using the wax, occasionally lift the rice paper gently away from the acetate underneath. As the hot wax penetrates the paper and begins to cool, it will adhere to the acetate, but can easily be lifted off.

6. When you think you're through with the wax, empty the tjanting pen of any melted wax back into the pot and put it aside to cool. Immediately unplug the pan or hot-plate and let the wax cool and harden in the container, ready for use the next time.

7. Remove the tracing paper and acetate from underneath, and put clean white or newsprint paper under the waxed design.

8. Prepare the dye colors, mixing more than you think you'll need. The unwaxed rice paper is very absorbent, and will take a lot of dye. The colors will look somewhat lighter when they dry, but in the later steps when you wax the final paper they will again become darker and more luminous.

9. With the mixed colors, start to fill in the white, unwaxed portions of your design. You'll find that the colors spread quickly, and it is easy to paint them flat. When you reach a waxed line, the dye will bead up and "roll" off the wax. If a few drops stay on the wax, lift them off lightly with a bit of tissue or blotting paper. Do not paint too "wet," or the dye will soak through to the paper underneath.

10. When you have finished painting, give the design plenty of time to dry. You now have two options open to you:

A. You can immediately iron out the wax, using a method similar to the one described in **Steps 6** and **7, Chapter 3.** Place your design on two or three sheets of newsprint, put two sheets on top of the design, and using a low-medium setting, iron on top of this "sandwich." Usually, once is enough and you don't have to replace the newsprint and iron again. This method results in a darker colored "halo" around the lines, where the wax melted and seeped into the adjacent unwaxed paper. Sometimes this is a very attractive effect. If it is not desired, you have another option.

B. Reheat the container of wax to the proper temperature. Place the design on a clean sheet of newsprint. Using your large brush, paint the melted wax over the entire design. Remember to lift it up by a corner before the wax cools completely, so that it

Various types of tjanting pens are available. The most frequently used is the one illustrated at the bottom of the group (top, left). Electric tjanting pens are also available. When wax is hot enough line becomes transparent. Halo effect can be retained or eliminated as desired (above). (Refer to Step 10, A and B.)

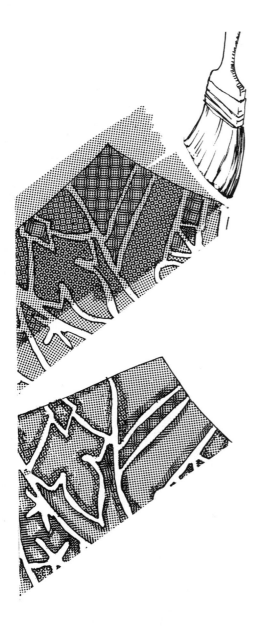

doesn't stick to the newprint underneath. Now iron it out in the same manner as described in **Steps 6** and **7, Chapter 3,** making sure to change to clean newsprint as you work. The result will be a design on translucent paper, and the colors will be rich and glowing.

Precautions & Reminders When Using "Batik" Method

1. Do not use pencil or charcoal on rice paper that is going to be waxed. You *cannot* erase it.

2. *Do not* use markers or gouache in this technique. Gouache will discolor and char, and markers will smear and streak when subjected to the heat of the melted wax or the iron.

3. Keep the wax constantly at the proper temperature. If it is not hot enough to make the paper transparent, that means it hasn't penetrated the paper sufficiently. In this case the wax will not act as a resist, and the dye will seep under and spread.

4. If the wax flows faster than you want from the tjanting pen, making too heavy a line, you may be able to slow it down. Take a small piece of paper towelling (about 1″ or so square) crumple it into a loose ball, and insert it into the cup of the tjanting pen, down near the opening to the spout. (Remember to remove it when you're finished.)

5. When working on a lengthy project, you may have to use more paraffin. Break it up into pieces and put it into the container of melted wax. This will cool the wax somewhat, and you'll have to wait for it to heat up again to the proper temperature before you can proceed.

6. If you have followed **B** in **Step 10,** when the design is all ironed out you can treat it like waxed rice paper (which it is). You can now use pen or marker or gouache. You can paint with dye on the design, perhaps filling some of the white lines with color. (*Remember* to add non-crawl.)

In addition to using the tjanting pen, you can also create designs by painting melted wax with brushes. Bring the wax to the proper temperature, dip the brush into it, and start to paint. Remember to use a square of folded paper towelling to catch any drips as you move back and forth. You'll find that the dry-brush technique is easy to produce and especially attractive when handled in a free, painterly manner. You can also experiment with objects used for stamping: cork, wood, nailheads, as well as stamps cut from Artgum™ erasers.

Crackle Effect If you would like to create the veins or crackle characteristic of traditional batik, this is done when your rice paper is coated with wax, after the design is painted (**B** in **Step 10**). It takes courage to crackle a newly painted design, so experiment with some plain rice paper until you feel confident (about 9″ x 12″). The procedure seems drastic, but is really fairly simple.

1. Wax the rice paper. Let it cool.

2. *Do not* iron it out. Instead, carefully but firmly *crumple* it in your hand. Open it out flat, and if only a few white cracks appear, crumple it again, and again flatten it out, being careful not to tear it.

3. Put some dye into a small dish. Use a dark color, like sepia or ultramarine. Make a dauber by crushing paper towelling or some tissue into a ball. Holding it at the top, dip this dauber into the dye and firmly press it into the creases on the waxed rice paper. The dye will seep into the creases and closely imitate the veins that appear in traditional batik.

4. Place this crackled rice paper between layers of newsprint, and iron out as in **B** in **Step 10.** The colored veins have now become an intrinsic part of the paper.

Notes

1. When you master the *crackle* technique, you can even design with it. You can wrinkle or fold the rice paper into striped or plaid arrangements;

Wax can be applied with brushes as well as with the tjanting pen.

make more concentrated areas of crackle in certain sections of your design; fold it into sunbursts, fan shapes, etc.

2. In some cases, depending on the effect you want, it is possible to crackle the rice paper, apply dye to the cracks, iron the paper, and then paint your design on top of the crackle. To do this, remember to use the necessary amount of non-crawl. Also, keep the design simple, and paint quickly and "dry," to prevent picking up the crackle color as you paint.

3. It is possible to create a "negative" crackle. Paint a dye ground on a piece of unwaxed rice paper, and let it dry thoroughly. Coat this with melted wax, allow to cool, then crackle it. Next, instead of daubing the cracks with dye, use household bleach. If the bleach acts too fast, dilute it somewhat with water. The result will be white veins on a dark ground, or negative crackle.

USING DYE & GOUACHE TOGETHER

It is easy to get "locked" into thinking of media one at a time. If you're thinking of dyes, you use *only* dyes; gouache is put aside for another design. In fact, dyes and gouache are *frequently used together* in the same design. Usually the dye areas or motifs are painted first. When this is dry, gouache is used on top of or next to the dye.

When the design requires a large area to be blotched around the motifs, you can achieve a more even blotch with opaque gouache, even though the motifs are painted in dyes. If the gouache blotch is to be a very pale color, and if the dyes are especially high in chroma (bright and intense) you may want to use some Bleedproof white when mixing your blotch color; but generally gouache, if painted sufficiently opaque, will cover dye.

Gouache can be used to add detail or embellish forms painted in dye. However, since dyes are clear and transparent, you *cannot* paint them on top of opaque gouache.

Dyes and gouache can be used together on waxed Masa as well as other papers. Remember to add just barely enough non-crawl to both media when painting on waxed Masa.

Copying

At first a helpful exercise would be to copy already printed designs carefully to get the "feel" of the gesture. Copying can be helpful for many reasons: we get deeper into mixing and matching colors as well as understanding the subtleties of the layout. But the purpose of copying is to improve *crafts-manship*. The hand, or gesture of the painting technique is what we are reaching for here. For the same reason, painting *repeats* of other designers is a good learning experience (see **Chapter 8**). The only danger to be aware of when copying existing designs is that you don't become limited to this practice alone but continue your growth toward *original* work.

Experiment with the techniques and media discussed in this chapter. Let your imagination go. Combine photographic, spatter, bleach, resist. There's almost no limit to the variety of possibilities. When examining the infinite variety of techniques and materials available to the textile designer we realize it is not possible to cover the entire range of variations. Many techniques have not been discussed here, and it is the role of the artist to explore, experiment and search out those most useful to his/her purpose.

A detail of a design using dye motifs with gouache. (© DOROTHY WOLFTHAL.)

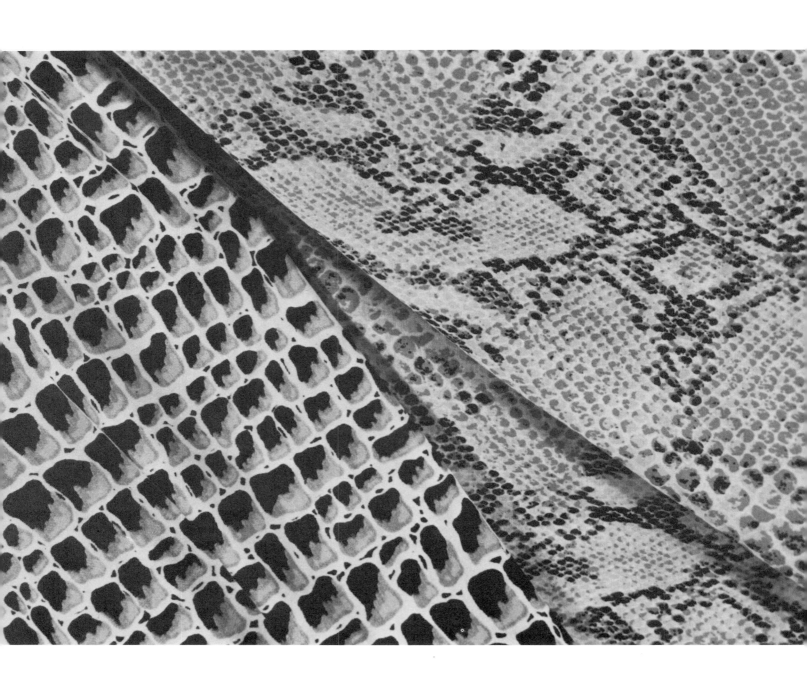

PRESENTATION & SELLING YOUR WORK

NEATNESS & MOUNTS

From time to time we have stressed the necessity for gaining control of the media and techniques of our profession. With poor control there is an air of carelessness; an attitude of non-caring is communicated. When we take pride in our efforts and hard work it follows that we want to present it in its best possible light. As professionals, we are a service to an industry and are trying to communicate design ideas to a stylist and/or manufacturer, and these ideas should be presented in the most ideal way.

This is why *neatness* is essential when we assemble our work for presentation. And this neatness must be an ongoing effort. If a design has an unsightly grease spot in the middle of a motif, the eye spots it immediately and the feeling it projects is quite negative. If the mounts are frayed and smudged, the design is less appealing. Dog-eared and battered mounts must be replaced whenever necessary. Dust and paper particles that collect inside the portfolio must be removed.

When trimming a croquis, use a metal straight-edge ruler or T-square and a sharp single-edged razor blade to cut a straight line. A triangle helps to establish 90 degree (square) corners. Some designers will use scissors, cutting along a lightly drawn pencil line. Be careful to cut the edges straight.

A cutting board or cutting table with a hinged blade mounted on the right-hand edge can also be used to trim a croquis; square corners can be accurately cut.

Designs on waxed Masa are quite fragile and a good practice is to back the edges of the croquis with clear Magic™ tape or its equivalent (1″ wide). This will reinforce the edges and help to extend the life of the design. Use wider tape for larger designs.

Neatness also applies to the way the designs are mounted. If you scatter a group of designs in a haphazard pile, one design tends to confuse and cancel another and the whole is less inviting to explore. When you mount each design separately on mount paper, the design is immediately enhanced and becomes more *readable*.

Do not mount two or more designs on a single mount paper since it will hinder selection and also tend to reduce the importance of each design. One exception to this rule is when assembling *storyboards* which might include a fabric, two or three thumbnail sketches, a croquis, and similar visuals that

80 percent of Life is showing up!

Woody Allen

Fabrics printed with reptile-skin patterns. (© FISHER & GENTILE.)

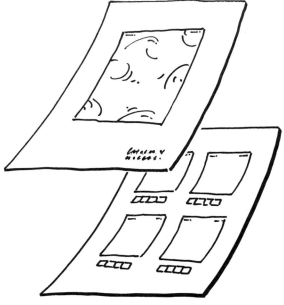

coordinate to tell a story. Another exception is when mounting color combinations; two or three could be mounted on a single mount.

Mounting Papers

Fairfield bristol or Becket mounting paper has a surface which is smooth and hard to the touch (plate finish) and will repel dust, dirt and fingerprints more readily than a soft paper such as Georgian or Seminole. Also it is easier to erase smudges and smears from a smooth surface. Clean your mounts immediately whenever they are dirty. If you have a spot of dye try bleach to clean the mount.

The size of the mount paper is an individual choice. Artists can purchase mount paper which is 22″ x 28″, and mount all large scale croquis on this size. (These will fit into the portfolio described on **page 134**.) Cutting the paper in half will give a size of 14″ x 22″ which works well for small scale croquis. Using only *two* sizes will help keep the presentation of your designs neat and consistent and more organized. *Do not* have many different size mounts or single designs floating in the portfolio. Even the smallest designs can be mounted on the 14″ x 22″ size mount.

An alternate size paper might be 20″ x 30″ for large croquis and cut in half will be 15″ x 20″ for smaller ones. The only important consideration is to standardize the mount sizes. Consistency is the key.

Mounting Designs

There are several methods of mounting designs onto the mount paper. Rubber cement works well. On the back of the design brush the rubber cement *across the top only*. Allow the major part of the design to hang freely. This will allow the mount and design to be rolled without damage. Rolling occasionally happens during the sales period. Also removal is easier if only the top has been rubber-cemented.

Another common practice is to staple the designs onto the mount. Again, staple the work only in the upper two corners of the design. For larger work three or four staples are needed; across the top is sufficient. A large size stapler is available, and will reach across the mount paper to the smaller designs. Be aware that the sharp ends of the staples on the reverse side of the mount can scratch other designs in the portfolio. Small pieces of masking tape placed over the points of the staples on the back will prevent any damage from occurring. Waxed Masa rejects rubber cement and stapling is necessary.

A third method for mounting designs is the use of double-coated tape. It is fast and efficient, but designs are more difficult to remount.

The design is usually placed in the center of the mount (left and right) and slightly above center vertically. The designs for apparel are mounted vertically. In part this relates to the verticalness of the human figure for which the design is intended.

A rubber stamp with the artist's name, address and phone number can be ordered from a stationery store and stamped in the lower right-hand corner of the mount. If a studio or agent is involved, then that information is placed on the mount instead. In this case, the designer can have a stamp with his/her name only which is placed above the studio information. Also the name, etc., should be stamped on the back of each design to avoid loss. If the croquis is on a transparent paper (Masa or Plasti-vel), the stamp-pad ink may show through and spoil the design. Stamp your name on a separate piece of lightweight paper and tape it to the back of your design with Magic™ tape.

Presenting Designs Un-mounted

Parameters for decorative designs for the home fashions field are somewhat different. Designs can be worked up on paper, which is *always* the same size. If all sketches are done on the same size paper, *mounts can be eliminated altogether* and the overall weight of the portfolio is much lighter. Also the costs of mounting are eliminated. These designs will then fit into the standard size portfolio, 23″ x 31″. A good paper size to use for the standard size portfolio when designing is 22″ x 28″.

When designs are created for the wallcovering industry, a horizontal format is recommended. This relates to interior walls (which generally are more horizontal than vertical) and reflects the standard repeat size of this *mass-market* type of design which is frequently 18″ vertically and 27″ horizontally. These dimensions are fairly typical, but are by no means the final word. Repeat sizes vary considerably and could be 25¼″ for rotary screens, 32″ or 36″ vertically for flat-bed presses; side repeats could be 22″ or 28″. (See **Chapter 8** for further information.)

If the design is not fully executed in repeat, part of the design may be presented on this standard size paper, somewhat like "creating a corner" discussed earlier for initiating apparel designs. An adequate amount must be painted for the purposes of communicating the design ideas.

When the design is sold, the original artwork can be extended to finish off the repeat often on the original paper (as illustrated). But the main purpose of the standard-size paper is to eliminate mounts, to maintain consistency and neatness, and to present artwork in an organized manner.

Color Tabs

Color tabs are small patches of color, one tab for each of the colors used in a design. They help the stylist and engraver to count colors and estimate production costs.

In *home fashion design:* color tabs are used on croquis as well as on color combinations. If a croquis completely fills the paper, interrupt the design at the lower edge to make room for the tabs. They should not extend beyond the edge of the paper, as they may get torn off and damage the design as well. And do not put them on the back of the paper, only on the front.

For *apparel design:* color tabs are always used with color combinations and can be used with repeats, and original croquis. Some studios ask their designers to indicate the colors as well as the "recipe"—the combinations of

In home fashion design, color tabs are always painted on the front with the artwork.

paints they used to mix these colors. This is meant as an aid to the repeat artist in matching the original colors, and in this case it is put on the back of the croquis. (*Exception:* not on the back of rice paper, which is translucent.)

Color combinations and color tabs will be discussed more fully in **Chapter 9**.

ERASING, CLEAN-UPS, FIX-UPS

Erasers are graded from very soft to very abrasive. Artgum erasers (the softest) crumble readily, and with gentle strokes can be useful when erasing smudges on mounts as well as gouache croquis. It is the only eraser that will not scratch the surface of gouache, but be gentle since it can cause an unsightly shine to the surface of the paint if used with a heavy hand.

The next grade of abrasiveness is the kneaded eraser, which is particularly useful when working with pencil and tracing paper. (Be sure to use the *rubber* kneaded eraser which is gray and not the plastic variety which is bluish.) Pearl pink and ruby red erasers are next up in abrasiveness and are commonly found on the ends of pencils. Most abrasive is the gritty typewriter or ink eraser. This will remove gouache and ink spots and usually destroys the paper as well.

If your kneaded eraser doesn't get the spot off, try a Fiberglas™ eraser. It's really a Fiberglas brush tightly enclosed in a holder. It must be used with care, in order to protect the surface of the paper. To erase a small area, protect the rest of the work by using a template, which is a small metal shield with various-shaped holes.

Another method of removing unwanted paint is a single-edged razor blade. The paper on which the paint is to be removed should be hard-surfaced and strong (rag content preferred), and the technique with the razor blade should be gentle. Large areas of course are impossible to erase, but small spots and specks can be removed with the sharp corner of the razor blade. Even an area up to ½ " in size can be scraped away with the flat part of the blade, but again it may damage the surface of the paper.

Pounce and other erasing powders can be used to clean up mounts and background paper areas, and a drafting brush is useful for dusting away the powder.

To remove grease or scuff stains, do not use an eraser. This would probably just smear the stain even more. Instead, try some rubber cement thinner on a tissue or cotton swab and dab it gently over the stain. The rubber cement thinner dries very quickly, and leaves no mark.

To get rid of accidental creases and wrinkles on waxed rice paper, place the creased part of the paper on one or two thicknesses of paper towelling, put another paper towel on top, and iron it *quickly* with the iron at low-to-medium setting. The creases will usually simply disappear. This can even be done with designs painted in dye. *Do not* try this on areas that have gouache or felt-tipped marker, or that have been spliced with tape.

To remove a croquis that has been mounted with rubber cement, use rubber cement thinner. Place the mounted work face down on a clean work surface. Use a cotton swab or a brush, depending on the size of the work; saturate it with the thinner and gradually work it in between the mount and the artwork, lifting the mounting paper gently. Keep the brush or swab saturated as you work. The rubber cement thinner will dry without leaving a mark. A rubber cement thinner dispensing can with a long spout is useful for flooding thinner between the artwork and the mount. This method is faster and works well with larger designs. *Caution:* Rubber cement thinner is a white gasoline product and is highly flammable.

Do not use this method on designs that have crayon, wax or felt-tipped marker.

To remove work that has been mounted with rubber cement, double-stick tape or any other adhesive, it is always better to place the work face down and gently *pull the mount away from the artwork,* rather than the other way round. If any damage occurs it will be to the mount, and if necessary, some shreds of the mount can remain on the back of the design.

SPLICING & MENDING PAPERS

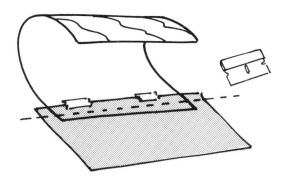

There will be times when you will need to add paper to a croquis in order to extend it to add on more design work, or perhaps to finish it off in repeat. The cleanest way to do this is to *splice* it. The procedure is almost the same whether you're working with waxed or unwaxed rice paper, or with heavier papers.

To splice paper, you will need: Scotch Brand Magic™ tape (or equivalent *frosted* transparent tape—*do not* use the *glossy* clear tape); standard tan masking tape; a sharp single-edged razor blade or X-acto™ knife with a #11 blade.

Experiment with rice paper first since it is easier to cut through *two* pieces of rice paper simultaneously, than through two pieces of Georgian for example. With the artwork face down on a clean working area, place a second piece of rice paper over the edge to which you will be adding, with a generous overlap (1″ is sufficient). On the wrong side, tape these two pieces together with small pieces of masking tape in several places to prevent slipping. If you use this procedure with a heavier paper such as Georgian, it is important that the *grain* of the added paper *matches* the *grain* of the original and that the same sides of both papers also match exactly.

Now, with the artwork face up, cut a straight line with a razor blade and a metal ruler. Cut through both pieces of rice paper *simultaneously*. This assures a clean and *identical* cut in both pieces.

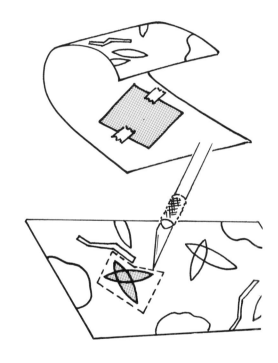

Lift away the excess strips of rice paper along with the small pieces of masking tape. Turn the papers face down and *match* the cut edges exactly. Apply the transparent tape to the back side of the artwork. Tape the entire length of the splice. The cut edges will be almost invisible.

A slightly more complicated variation of this procedure is used if you wish to replace, for instance, an area in the middle of the design. Essentially we will remove the unwanted section and replace it with clean unpainted rice paper. Again, working on the back side of the artwork, tape a fresh piece of rice paper to the original design. Be sure to plan the rice paper patch larger than the area you wish to replace. (Also be sure the surfaces match and any grain, as well, if there is one.) Turn the design over, right side up, and with an X-acto™ knife blade, carefully cut through both pieces of rice paper *simultaneously*. Wherever possible make the cut at the exact edge of an *adjacent* motif. This will help to hide the cut edges.

You may wish to replace one motif only, say a single flower. In this case place the clean piece of rice paper behind the flower. Tape it to the back in a few spots and cut away the motif through the fresh paper underneath at the same time. You can lift out the unwanted flower, fit the new piece into the cut-out space and again, on the back side of the paper, apply the transparent tape to the *entire* length of the cut line. *Do not* leave any cut edges untaped. The final result should be a clean patch within the design area whose edges are almost invisible.

If you are working with a design that has a colored background, then pre-paint the patch before you cut and splice it into the artwork. Be sure to match the ground color exactly.

Caution: Try to avoid applying dye where there is a cut edge. It is apt to appear darker and unsightly. It is possible to paint the motif before splicing it into place.

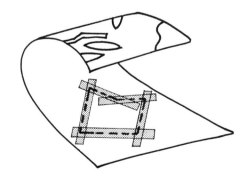

When splicing heavier weight papers, the blade *must* be sharp and enough pressure exerted to cut both pieces at the same time. Make the cut slowly and carefully, and be sure the grain of both papers is running in the same direction. Masking tape may be used on the back in place of the transparent tape but either is satisfactory.

To prevent artwork from bending and cracking at the splice, a common practice is to reinforce it. A "patch" of the same paper is rubber cemented onto the back, overlapping the splice a few inches. To make this extra firm, let the rubber cement become nearly dry on both surfaces before sticking the "patch" on.

If the surface of the design is painted entirely in gouache, it is possible

Additional paper may be spliced onto existing artwork (top). Also a section of the artwork can be removed and new paper spliced in. Cut along edge of adjacent motif to hide cut edge. Tape entire length of cut line with masking tape (½″ wide).

to tape the front as well. This assures a very strong splice and a completely invisible patch is possible. Once the standard splice is taped on the back of the paper, apply Scotch Magic™ transparent tape to the front side of the design, directly on top of the gouache along the cut edge. Next, burnish the tape *firmly* onto the surface so that the edges are completely tight and there are no blisters in the tape. It is now possible to paint gouache on top of the transparent tape and complete the design.

PORTFOLIOS

The actual size of the portfolio depends on the work to be carried and is relative to the size of the mounting paper. A currently available, standard size portfolio is 23″ x 31″. This size will accommodate almost all of the designs created for the apparel industry and is also usable for decorative designs. Larger sizes are also available, but are bulkier to carry. A zipper edge protects the design in rainy weather. The material of the portfolio can be leather, canvas, synthetic fabric, or vinyl. Less expensive portfolios made of paper and cardboard are also available but do not last very long.

Very often decorative designs are larger in scale and will not fit into the standard 23″ x 31″ black-zippered portfolio. Rolling is the usual way of carrying these larger designs and various solutions to protecting them are possible. Standard kraft wrapping paper is commonly used. Masking tape or a rubber band is used to keep it together. A plastic bag such as a common garden leaf bag will protect the work against the weather. However, all this is less professional and a roll-type portfolio can made.

To make a roll-type carrying portfolio, leather or laminated vinyl film (the kind used to upholster furniture or automobile interiors) can be used. Two straps hold it together and a handle is added to help carry it. The ends are exposed and a piece of soft vinyl material or Scotch-guarded™ fabric can be attached to the edges of the leather. When rolled this material can be tucked into the ends to protect the artwork (as illustrated). A great many designs can be carried with such a device. (Commercial variations of this type of portfolio are not available.)

Tubes are also used to carry large designs but if the diameter of the tube is small (4″ to 6″) the artwork is too tightly rolled and is hard to manage when it is removed. A large diameter (8″ to 12″) is awkward to carry, unless a handle is added. In any case be sure to close the ends of the tube with waterproof material.

How Many Designs Should Be Put into Your Portfolio?

The number of designs in your portfolio can vary and may depend on what is appropriate for the company or the customer you are about to see. In general, for an interview for a salaried position, twelve to fifteen designs are adequate. They should include florals in a variety of styles, color combinations, and a few repeats if you have them. Even a nature study or similar type of drawing is acceptable if it shows skills and artistic sensitivity.

The number of designs in a portfolio for free-lance is different. Here you are selling designs and a greater number is called for—twenty to forty designs are appropriate.

Sequence of Designs in Your Portfolio

When assembling your designs, be aware of the sequence of the work. Start with an exciting design and place your strongest pieces on top. The more specialized types of work should follow (color combinations, examples of repeats, etc.).

One of the privileges of the designer is that we can eliminate the work we are not pleased with. If you have any doubts about the quality of a design, re-do it or put it aside. Present your best work only.

It is a good practice to group the designs by type. For instance, put all the calicos together, all the paisley types together, all the florals, and designs with a similar technique—together. This tends to suggest collections. In fact

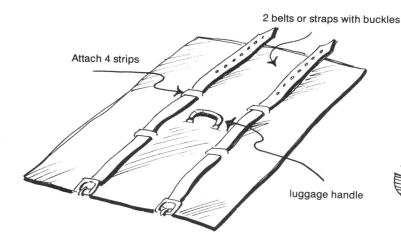

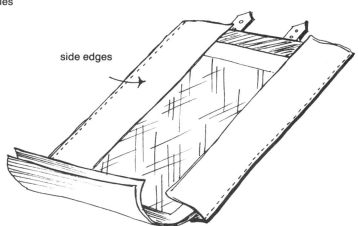

it is wise to work up groups of designs with a similar theme. Each design is separate and independent, but the group together is considered a collection. The advantage is that each design reinforces the others and the whole is greater than the individual works when alone. Also there is a better chance of selling more than one design.

Between interviews, clean up the portfolio and put it in order again. Remount, revise and continually update the work and keep it current.

In order to enhance your design ideas, a small *fashion sketch* of a figure with the design incorporated (as a dress or blouse, etc.) will add excitement and help the buyer visualize the design in context. It should look current in style and technique. Of course the look may soon be dated, but if it is timely it will help sell your design. The sketch need only be 10″ to 15″ high but it must be well-rendered or else it will hurt the sale of the design. If poorly drawn it is better not included at all.

This idea of a selling sketch works well with home fashions and domestic products as well. A photostat could be used (since it takes gouache well) or even an ad from a magazine or newspaper. The bedsheet pattern or a wallcovering is painted directly on the picture. It means translating your design into a three-dimensional view with radical scale changes. What is necessary is to suggest the pattern in context. This idea can be applied to other products as well.

Any ideas or methods you can think of to add excitement to your portfolio are valid. Anything goes if the portfolio is more interesting—and of course it must look professional.

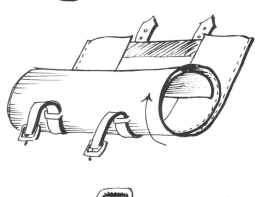

KEEPING RECORDS OF YOUR WORK

A good habit to get into is that of taking photos of each design as it comes off your drawing board. Each designer will have his/her own preferences on methods for keeping these records. A 35mm transparency or slide of each design is a good beginning. A film that best reproduces the color should be used. Kodak™ Professional film 50 ASA has a good color accuracy if you use the proper lighting.

35mm Kodachrome™ slides can be used for reproduction of the design in magazines and trade publications, for publicity purposes as well as communication of ideas in lectures at schools or company meetings. (Trade publications are magazines and other printed matter geared to specific product areas, e.g. wallcoverings.)

A *print* (4″ x 5″) on paper of the slide could be made of each design, and placed in a *photo album* which becomes a valuable record of work accomplished. A Kodacolor™ picture or a Polaroid™ shot could be taken of each design.

A roll-type portfolio can be made for carrying large size artwork as well as large quantities. (© DOROTHY WOLFTHAL.)

This photo album can be used as a selling tool to prospective customers as well as a working tool when developing new designs on special order with a stylist. There is an immediate visual reference to techniques, layouts, colors, and subject matter for discussion.

A record book or a 3″ x 5″ or other file card system should be established and maintained. Each design is assigned a *name* and *number,* and all the information about the design such as reference source, date of execution, who purchased it, the selling price, and so forth is recorded. If the file-card system is adopted, a second print of the design could be attached to the back of each card.

There is also a personal reward for the artist, in keeping records: to be able to see the artistic growth through the years of his/her career. Designs will sell and artwork can be misplaced. A visual record of your work is invaluable.

INTERVIEWS

Interviews are often filled with apprehension for most beginners. Is my work good enough? Will they like my designs? Will they hire me? How do I measure up? And perhaps, unconsciously, am I getting into something I'll regret? Fortunately this kind of negative questioning soon disappears with experience in being interviewed. More constructive questions will arise: What are the needs of this company? Where am I strong and how can I make a contribution? What can I do to grow? What can I learn? How can this or that design be adapted to fit an immediate need?

Interviews are a two-way affair. You are interviewing the customer or potential employer as much as they are interviewing you. You must decide if you will like the type of work and products of this company; if you want to be in that office or environment; if you can contribute significantly to this business. Ask yourself, "What do I want?" Ask about the company; about sales and manufacturing facilities. Does the job involve teamwork or will you function more or less independently? Find out as much as you can and give yourself time to know whether or not this position is for *you.*

Personalities are very important. Compatibility is important. If you like the people there, chances are they will like you. Perhaps fifty percent of the interview will focus on your work; the other fifty percent will have to do with you and the way you talk, and look, and how you present yourself. But when it comes to the sales of your work, the designs will speak for themselves. It is not necessary to sell your work in the more traditional sense of salesmanship. Once a design has been completed and mounted it will stand on its own merit.

Of course we are always involved with the price and the worth of our work. (Pricing is discussed thoroughly in **Chapter 10.**)

Be aware of the persons or company to whom you are presenting your work. Show mostly apparel design to apparel buyers (maybe one or two decorative pieces could be included if they seem appropriate, for "hand," or possible adaptation purposes). The same for designs for home fashions. If your "audience" will be a drapery or wallcovering house, adjust your collection of designs to suit the probable interest of the person you are about to see. Always be aware of your next presentation and gear the sequence and selection of work accordingly.

It is best to telephone the converter or manufacturer for an appointment. Most places are willing to see you and your work and talk with you. And one contact can lead to another.

Being late for an interview is annoying to the customer who usually has a tight schedule. It can cause bad vibrations and spoil the meeting. Be on time—or even a little early.

A business card is always useful. And letterhead stationery is necessary for correspondence as well as invoices. A resumé is not always required but for salaried job interviews it is good to leave one with the company. *The Graphic Artists Guild Handbook** is a good guide in these matters.

Interviews can be relaxed and in the spirit of cooperation and information-seeking. When freelancing and selling your own work and services, be willing to negotiate, to make changes in your designs, be flexible. (See **Chapter 10** for limitations and financial aspects of changes.)

The Graphic Artists Guild Handbook, Robert Siver Associates, 95 Madison Avenue, New York, N.Y. 10016.

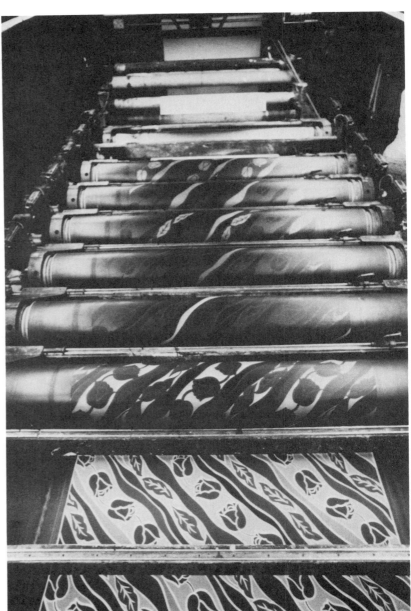

Production Considerations & Repeats

PRODUCTION CONSIDERATIONS

Graphics is a word that has many applications which can lead to some confusion. Semantically, *graphic* originally meant drawing, writing. The dictionary definition includes the words "lifelike and vivid" to describe graphics. If someone says a design looks *graphic* it usually means bold and strong. In the printmakers' world the word *graphic* refers to a printing process, engraving and etching. For our purposes we will use the words *graphic arts* to describe art that is reproduced by using printing presses and processes.

The are four general principles in printing designs on fabric, paper and vinyl film.

1. *Relief printing* is like a rubber stamp in that the print surface is *raised* and ink is applied to the lettering or motif with an ink pad. Wood block printing is an ancient and slow process still used for very special printing on fabric. The only color limitation is the number of blocks used to create the pattern. Needless to say it is extremely expensive since it entails much hand-work by highly skilled craftsmen. *Flexography* is a commercially adapted variation using the principle of relief printing but it is not used in the textile design field.

2. *Intaglio printing* is well known as etching and engraving. The surface of a copper plate is eaten into (etched) or scratched (engraved) creating a tiny "ink well" *below* the surface. Ink is applied to the copper plate, filling the tiny holes, then the surface is wiped clean. Paper (or other receiver material) is pressed onto the copper and the ink is transferred to the material. In industry, cylinders of steel with a copper surface are used and the pattern is etched into the roller which is then coated with .005 of an inch of chrome to harden the surface. This is called *direct printing* or *roller printing*. The intaglio process is *below* the surface while relief printing is raised or *above* the surface.

3. In *lithography* the printing area is neither raised above nor etched below the surface, but remains on a single plane only. The principle is based on the physical properties of oil, grease and water. The image is drawn on the granular surface, originally a slab of stone, with a grease medium. The surface is flooded with water and an oil-based ink is rolled onto the stone.

Art is 90 percent perspiration, 10 percent inspiration.

Rotary screen printing is used extensively for apparel and home fashion products. A separate cylinder is used for each color.

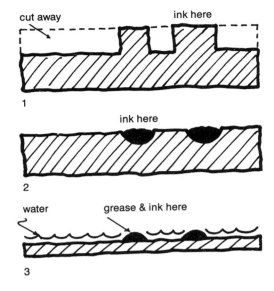

1

2

water   grease & ink here

3

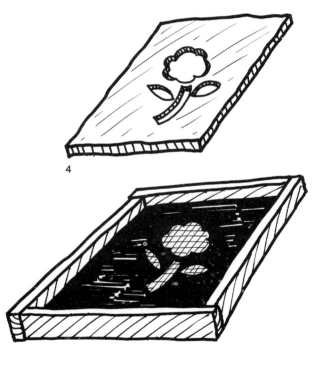

4

The water repels the ink while the greased image attracts the ink. Paper is pressed to the surface for printing.

In early times this method was called *planeography*. The industrial variation of this is *offset lithography* and is commonly seen in the color photographs of magazines and books. It is *not* used in the textile design field.

4. Another method used in creating patterns is the *stencil*. The design to be reproduced is cut from a coated paper and the ink prints in the open areas. This principle is the basis for silk-screen printing used extensively in industry. In screen printing, silk, nylon or Dacron® fabric is stretched on a wooden or aluminum frame. A resistant coating, such as enamel or tusche, blocks the dyestuff from penetrating the mesh in the desired areas. A squeegee forces a paste-like color through the screen onto the surface to be printed. One frame is used for each color. The screen is lifted and re-positioned as the work progresses. The entire process may be by hand or fully automated.

A more recent development commercially of this method is the *rotary screen* which uses a nickel alloy in place of the Dacron®. The flexible cylinder is hollow permitting the ink to be placed on the interior surface of the cylinder and forced through the roller onto the fabric being printed. *Percentones* are possible because the nickel alloy screen allows for tiny holes that control the printing of lighter values of a color. With a magnifying glass look closely at a newspaper photo. Tiny dots can be seen which create the variations of gray from light to dark. A limited use of *wash* or *photographic* effects is possible. Today rotary screen printing is used extensively on textiles in both the apparel and the home fashions field.

Another variation for printing on fabric is the *heat-transfer process*. Here patterns are engraved onto copper cylinders and printed on a specially treated paper with dispersion inks. Commercially this method is also known as *Sublistatic printing*. The term *Sublistatic* is derived from the *sublimable inks* used in the process which go from a solid to a gas in the transferring step, without becoming a liquid. The inks are transferred from the release paper to the fabric by applying heat and pressure. The Sublistatic Corporation in New York City has been a prime source for heat transfer textiles.

Great accuracy of registration is a special feature of this method. Even though only four or five rollers are engraved, an unlimited number of colors can be printed. This is possible by the intermixture of tiny dots of several colors. The eye *blends the dots* together giving the illusion of *many colors*.

The heat-transfer process was originally used for printing on polyester fibers, but recent development allows printing on cotton blends as well as on vinyl film for upholstery materials.

In the textile design industry the three main tools used for printing on fabric, paper and vinyl film are *engraved cylinders, rotary screens,* and *flat-bed screens*.

When a customer buys a design it is necessary to "put it in repeat" in order that the design will print continuously without gaps and interruptions along the length of the fabric. Any design can be put into repeat, even the most seemingly difficult ones. Before it can be printed a repeat has to be painted by the textile artist. An engraver makes the rollers or a screenmaker produces the rotary screens or the flat-bed screens from the artist's painted repeat.

Often the stylist meets with the engraver and the printer before this procedure begins in order to study the pattern and to anticipate and avoid problems. Color limitations, sequence of rollers, engraving techniques, and printing problems all are discussed and considered in this early planning stage.

In every form of printing it is necessary to make a separate cylinder or screen for each color. The engraver or screenmaker is responsible for the color separation of the repeat. A separate sheet of acetate is painted for each

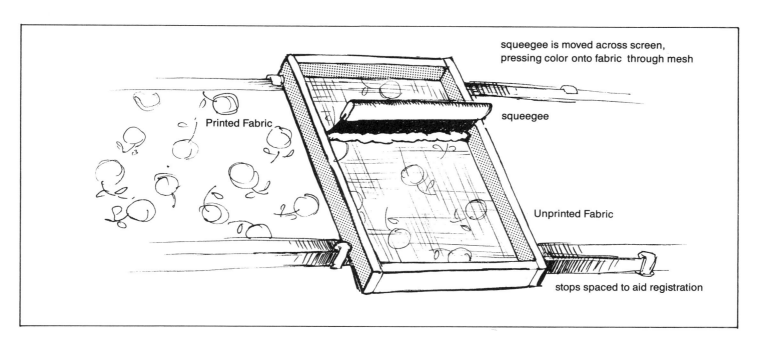

squeegee is moved across screen, pressing color onto fabric through mesh

Printed Fabric

squeegee

Unprinted Fabric

stops spaced to aid registration

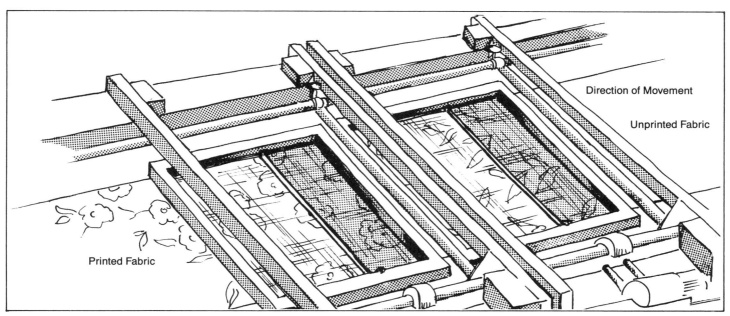

Direction of Movement

Unprinted Fabric

Printed Fabric

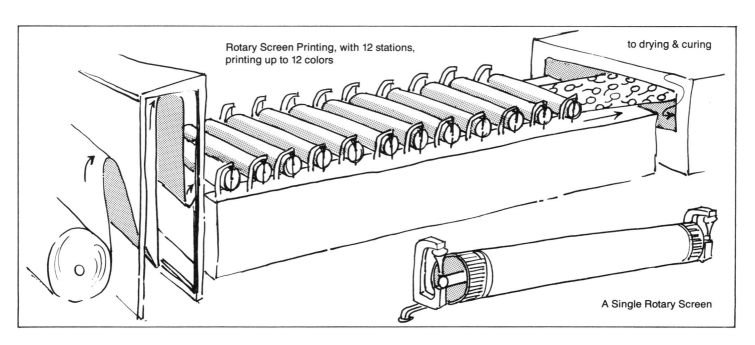

Rotary Screen Printing, with 12 stations, printing up to 12 colors

to drying & curing

A Single Rotary Screen

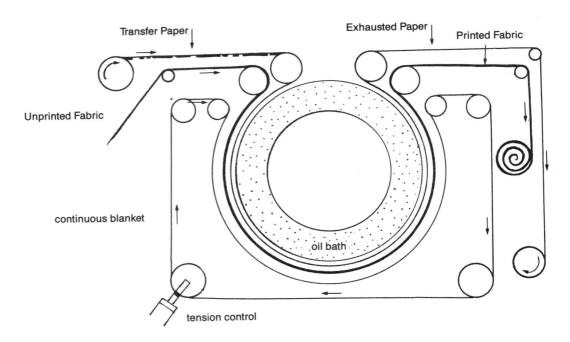

Transfer Paper

Exhausted Paper

Printed Fabric

Unprinted Fabric

continuous blanket

oil bath

tension control

color in the repeat. The cylinders or rollers are then sent to the printer to print the fabric.

At this time a *strike-off* is made. *Strike-off* is the term applied to the first few yards that come off the printing machine. It is used for the purpose of evaluation. The accuracy of interpretation of the design by the engraver and the registration of one color to another are scrutinized, and generally it is necessary to make sure the design prints perfectly and there are no errors. If errors are found, the print rollers are checked and must be re-engraved if the error cannot be readily corrected.

Additional strike-offs are then made to establish a set of *color standards* that are acceptable to the stylist and/or customer.

The original colors of the design as well as color combinations are printed. When they are approved by the stylist, it is the responsibility of the printer to remain faithful to the final choices in production. Stylists and designers often refer to this phase as "mill work."

At this point the stylist's job at the mill is finished. The fabric is printed and then shipped to the customer who proceeds with sales and distribution.

REPEATS

Now for a discussion of the principles and mechanics of *repeats*. For the beginner the idea of *repeats* is often confusing. Frequently we notice a motif used "repetitively" in a pattern. This however is *not* the repeat. *The repeat* is the mechanical adaptation of a design to the printing tools of industry, usually an engraved cylinder or a rotary screen which is also cylindrical. A repeat is also necessary for flat-bed screen printing.

A *croquis* is artwork originated for the purpose of communicating design ideas to a potential buyer. In order to print this design on yards and yards of fabric or on running footage of wallcovering, it must be "put into repeat" so that the original design is not interrupted by a gap as the design repeats itself along the yard goods. The design must be organized so that it will not overlap itself in the printing process. It must flow evenly and consistently as the pattern is printed. Motifs and colors are balanced to assure an even, flowing appearance. When the printing process uses rotary screens, or steel cylinders, the size of the repeat is determined by the *circumference* of the cylinder. Another limitation is the *width* of the printing roller. Therefore the design must repeat *horizontally* (which relates to the width of the roller), as well as *vertically* (which relates to the circumference of the roller). When the printing process uses flat-bed screens, the size of the repeat is determined by the screens.

We refer to *the repeat* as the artwork prepared for the engraver or screenmaker. Repeats are usually painted after the sale of the croquis from which they are derived, or after a decision to use that particular design has been made. Usually it is a newly painted piece separate from the croquis. Often it is painted by the original designer of the croquis. This is perhaps the ideal method since the spirit of the original *must* remain intact. That is what the customer has bought, and the repeat must look like the original croquis.

The repeat may be farmed out to a professional repeat artist who faithfully reproduces the original. Often this professional repeat artist does only repeats. Occasionally, some engravers or screen-print companies execute the repeat as part of the service of making the rollers. In addition, converters and manufacturers who have their own studios, often buy only croquis and have their artists put the designs into repeat. This way they have more control of the artwork, especially if changes and variations are required.

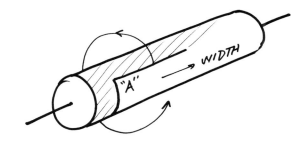

When painting a repeat it is absolutely necessary to reproduce the same colors and techniques of the original as well as the "hand": the gesture of the brush strokes, the total look of the croquis down to the most minute details.

Sometimes a repeat can be *finished off.* This means mounting or splicing the original croquis onto a larger sheet of paper, identical to the paper used in the original. Even the direction of the grain of the paper must be the same. The repeat is then added onto the original artwork which remains intact and is part of the final repeat. Splicing aids the repeat artist, when painting the repeating areas, to maintain the same hand and look of the original.

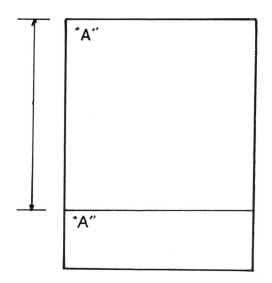

More frequently it is necessary to paint the entire repeat since changes are usually called for and the original must be modified in some way. If minor changes are required, the design is still yours and frequently the changes improve the work. If major changes are required in the design, you will still be paid full price for the design which is the inspiration or springboard for the new work. Repeats often look better since more thought and organization have gone into the final artwork. Also it is larger than a croquis and, for this reason, has more impact. Changes are usually made in light of marketplace requirements. And remember that this art form is a service to industry which means being responsive to industry needs.

A question may arise: why not put all designs in repeat from the start? Repeats are mechanical in essence. The purpose of a repeat is to relate designwork to a cylinder for production. The inspiration and excitement of creating the original artwork may be stifled or cramped if mechanical limitations are also considered at this time. The artist often feels encumbered by the technical and mechanical demands required of repeats. It is necessary to concentrate on the exploration and expression of new design ideas without being pulled in two directions.

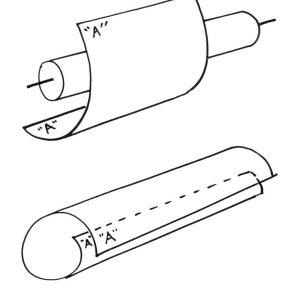

In addition, artists can produce many croquis in the time it takes to do one repeat. It is better to get the design ideas down on paper in order to communicate them to the stylists, and then put them into repeat after the croquis has been sold.

Another reason for not doing repeats initially is that the stylist or buyer may wish to modify the design. Motifs and colors may have to be changed and this is best accomplished in the croquis phase rather than in the repeat phase.

When designing the artist is not always sure on what product his/her design will end up. You may have a bedsheet in mind for the design you are creating and it may well be purchased by a wallcovering manufacturer. The repeat parameters are entirely different and a new repeat would have to be executed anyway.

Now, after all these reasons for not working up new ideas initially in repeat we have to examine the *exceptions.* Sometimes new designs *are* worked up in repeat! A *set layout* requires the designer to consider the possible repeat dimensions. It is wiser, for example, to choose a 2-inch grid system which is a fraction of an 18-inch repeat rather than an arbitrary size which will not fit into any standard repeat dimension. If the pattern itself is

The size of the vertical repeat is determined by the circumference of the roller. The horizontal repeat relates to the width of the cylinder (roller).

a checkerboard, it is logical to work the layout into a standard repeat measurement.

Borders are executed in repeat when the repeat unit is small and if we are to show an adequate amount of the design for selling purposes. Borders are designed to appear along the edge of the fabric (the selvage) and repeat vertically around the circumference of the cylinder. The field beside the border covering the remainder of the fabric is put into the usual type of repeat.

Stripes are usually put into repeat when they are initially designed. Simple bands of color are already repeating vertically. Horizontally the color sequence must begin again for the side repeat. If the stripe is made up of motifs or a combination of bands and motifs, it is quite simple to design the repeat into the original croquis.

Designs for the *home fashions field* are often worked up in repeat since they are large in scale and the repeat influences the design process. However, designs for the apparel market are almost always initiated in croquis form and only seldom in repeat.

If we are working directly with a stylist or manufacturer on a *special order* basis, we may know the exact measurements before we begin. Special order is desirable since all work has a good chance of selling. The ideal arrangement is that the artist is paid for whatever he/she is assigned to do. The designer works closely with the stylist, for instance on a wallcovering or upholstery design. A theme or general direction is outlined, the designer gathers reference material, works up a rough layout (on tracing paper) and executes one or two exploration sketches. With all this material, he/she meets with the stylist again to discuss the ideas. More exploration sketches may be made and when both designer and stylist are satisfied, the final design is executed *in repeat.* There is very little wasted effort along the way and large designs are not painted up on *speculation* only to have them revised to suit the needs of a future buyer.

Engineered designs as discussed in **Chapter 4** are not repeating patterns, but are designs fitted to a specific area such as a pillowcase or a scarf. It is possible to paint only a portion of an engineered design if it repeats again within the designated area. Only one quarter of a scarf, for instance, is painted if each quarter is identical.

Engineered motifs are usually fitted onto a roller or flat-bed screen for continuous printing and later cut into pieces for the final product.

Sizes of Repeats

The sizes of repeats which are dependent on the circumference of the printing roller vary with each manufacturer and with each product. In the apparel area, the most commonly used printing method today is rotary screen printing. 25¼ " (100 centimeters) is the standard *circumference* of the rotary screen. However, designs may be printed first with flat-bed screens for purposes of evaluation and sales and only later transferred to rotary screens. The flat-bed screen sizes are 30", 32" and 36".

The 25¼ " rotary screen is used for home fashion products as well. These repeat sizes are usually used, but the customer will designate the final dimensions required.

The Mechanics of Layout for a Repeat

The following steps can be used for all types of designs on all sizes of repeats, for apparel as well as for home fashions products. They are typical of most repeat work and it is wise to follow them carefully. *Do not* skip any of them. The artist is often pressured to get the work out, and time can be wasted if errors occur. Subsequent steps will also be incorrect and a great deal of work will have to be redone.

You will need the following materials and tools for layout: Roll of tracing paper, 36" wide; metal ruler, 36" long; large triangle; soft pencil, #1 or 1B; 2H pencil; kneaded (rubber) eraser; masking tape; Rapidograph-type pen or a ballpoint pen. When painting a repeat, you will need the same *art medium* and the *paper* used to create the original design.

Borders repeat around the circumference of the cylinder (top). Engineered designs are fitted to a specific area such as a pillowcase (center). There is no repeat factor. The repeat of some scarf designs may require painting only one-quarter of the scarf (bottom). Design can rotate on center front or flop on repeat lines. The half-drop layout is very apparent in "St. Etienne," a design by GREEFF FABRICS (facing page). A detail of this design appears in the color section.

printed fabric to drying chamber

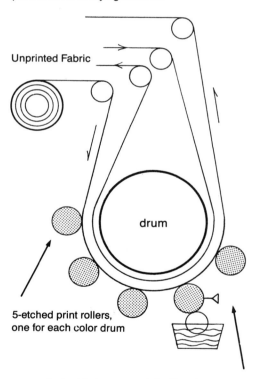

Unprinted Fabric

drum

5-etched print rollers,
one for each color drum

doctor blade scrapes ink off surface of roller

A gravure printing press using engraved cylinders.

A 36-inch roll of tracing paper is necessary for the large repeats of home fashions and wallcovering designs. A medium-weight tracing paper (#80) is better than lightweight tracing paper. *Do not* use heavyweight tracing paper or vellum or any opaque paper. A metal ruler is more accurate than plastic or wooden, and *accuracy is essential.*

Step 1 Tape a sheet of tracing paper over the original design for its protection, indication of instructions, and *squaring off.* Write TOP on the tracing paper at the top of the design. Clear acetate may also be used but is more expensive. Protecting the artwork is especially important for rice paper and other fragile originals.

Step 2 Let us assume we are instructed to put the design into an 18-inch repeat, and that we are working with a layout in which the motifs are tossed. The original croquis must now be carefully studied to determine the best *vertical repeat* size. If the design is intended for apparel and is made up of small motifs, we can use a dimension which is a *fraction* of 18″. Remember that this dimension refers to the circumference of the roller. We could choose to do a 9-inch repeat or any fraction of 18.

If the original croquis is large in scale or intended for drapery or wallcovering, it will be necessary to use the full 18″. Other repeat sizes are also used.

Study the original croquis. Choose a large motif near the upper left-hand corner of the design and place the ruler on the top of the motif. Measure down vertically. Envision this motif recurring again at the 18-inch repeat line. Does the design need the full 18″ or would 9″ work as well? This will help us to determine if a smaller repeat is possible (9″, 6″, or even 3″). Use careful judgment. A small repeat size will save a lot of work but if too small a repeat is attempted, the motifs could be cramped and poorly balanced. The color balance as well may suffer. A good rule to follow when laying out a repeat: if you have any doubts, do a larger rather than small layout. Let's proceed with an 18-inch vertical repeat.

Step 3 On a separate piece of tracing paper from the 36-inch roll, draw four coordinate lines. The purpose of these coordinate lines is to relate the pattern, in a mechanical way to the cylinders. These lines do not appear in the final pattern on the fabric. Start by placing the 90 degree angle of the triangle in the upper left-hand corner of the tracing paper. Do not use the edges of the tracing paper but place the triangle at least 2″ in from the edges. With a Rapidograph™ pen or fine ballpoint pen draw the first two coordinate lines along the top and left side of the triangle.

Carefully extend these lines with the ruler as far as necessary. Now measure down, vertically 9″ and 18″ from the top, and draw the third and fourth coordinate lines. (The line at 9″ is called the *half-drop line*— explained in **Step 7**.)

A more accurate line is drawn by measuring at two different places from the top line to establish the 18-inch repeat line. The same for the 9-inch line. Penlines are more precise than pencil lines and will remain throughout any erasing which will follow. Write TOP as you did on the tracing paper covering the original croquis. Also write "#1" in the margin.

Step 4 Return to the original croquis. Draw two penlines on the tracing paper covering the original artwork—on or close to the upper left-hand corner of the original. Use the 90 degree triangle again. These two lines will be more accurate than the cut edges of the original croquis, which are sometimes used. Now place the coordinate lines in the upper left-hand corner of Tracing #1 carefully over the two lines drawn on the protective tracing paper covering the croquis.

With a soft pencil (a #1 pencil—with an eraser) trace the design onto the large sheet of tracing paper *making no changes at this time.* When motifs are detailed trace only the bold silhouette of the objects and ignore the fine details in this initial outlining step. Also choose only the major or most important motifs to begin with and know that you will trace the secondary motifs later.

Step 5 Now take a second, large sheet of tracing paper, draw four duplicate coordinate lines in pen. Write TOP and #2 in the top margin. These

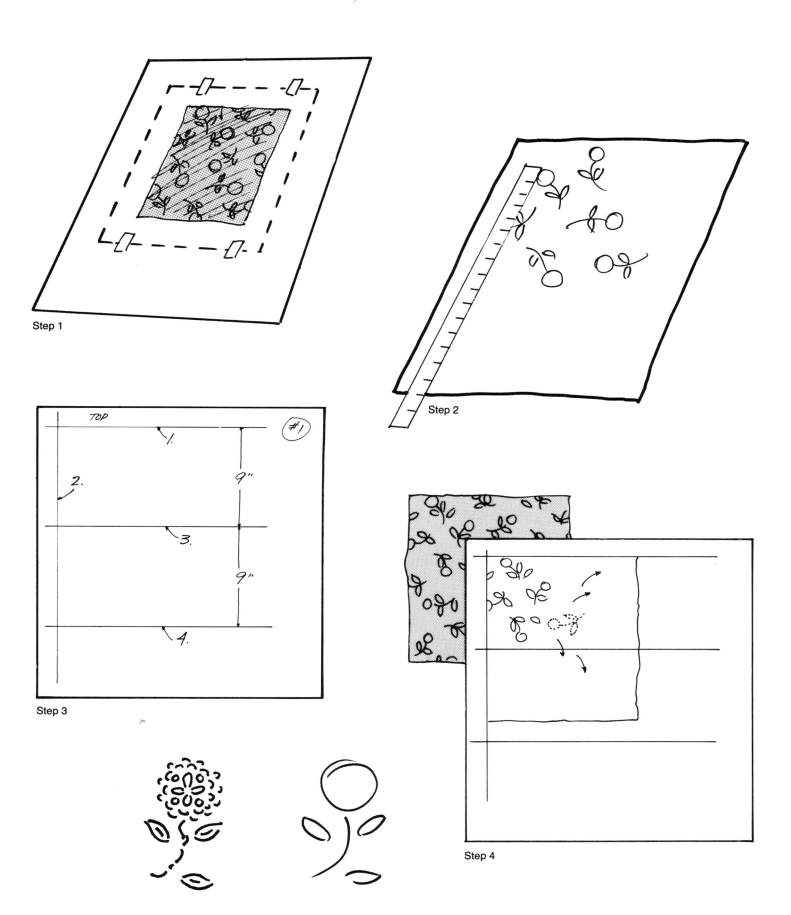

Step 1

Step 2

Step 3

Step 4

First four steps of the repeat process. Loosely trace only the bold silhouettes of the motifs and ignore fine details. (For purposes of illustration motif has been simplified.)

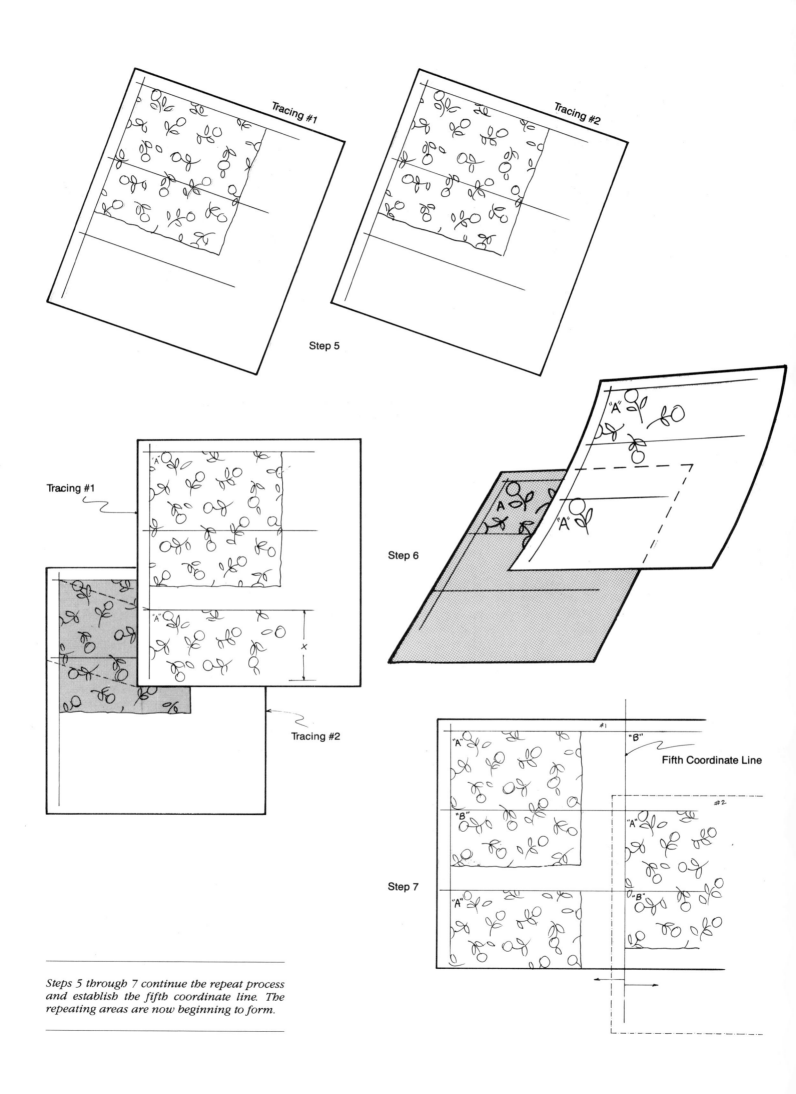

Tracing #1

Tracing #2

Step 5

Tracing #1

Tracing #2

"A"

"A"

x

Step 6

"A"

"A"

"A"

#1

"B"

Fifth Coordinate Line

"B"

"A"

#2

"A"

"B"

Step 7

Steps 5 through 7 continue the repeat process
and establish the fifth coordinate line. The
repeating areas are now beginning to form.

two duplicate tracing paper layouts will aid you in "getting around" the layout. Additions and corrections will be made by slipping them over and under each other as we proceed.

On Tracing #2 draw the pencil-line silhouettes from Tracing #1 so that Tracing #2 is identical to #1. Still *no changes* are made and only the major motifs of the original are drawn in boldly as silhouettes.

Step 6 Now place the 18-inch coordinate repeat line, which is near the bottom of Tracing #1 over the coordinate lines in the upper left-hand corner of #2. Draw in the silhouettes of the motifs again. Include about 6" to 8" of the design below the 18-inch repeat line. These two areas are designated as the "A" corners.

Step 7 You must now determine the *side repeat* which will be placed halfway down the vertical dimension on the right-hand side of the layout. You will see the "A" corner on the right side of the layout is dropped halfway down the 18-inch vertical measurement—to 9". If you move Tracing #2 left or right, always keeping the top coordinate line on the 9-inch half-drop line, you can judge the best distance from the original in order to establish the fifth coordinate line. This determines the width of the side repeat.

Repeat layouts for apparel and some home furnishings designs allow the artist freedom to decide the width of the side repeat. The side repeat usually is determined by the rhythm and balance of motifs across the width of the design. The number of times the pattern is repeated across the width of the fabric (from selvage to selvage) is not crucial. The placement of the side repeat is adjusted to fit the demands of the design and the distance can be wider or narrower to help establish the smooth transition from the original to the repeated areas.

Do not try to save time by compressing motifs into a narrow repeat. Variety of motifs and distribution of color are the guiding factors. Allow enough space so that relationships feel comfortable and not cramped. The most important factor is that the repeat layout looks continuous and flowing without gaps and interruptions, the same necessity required of the vertical repeat.

Some products such as wallcovering and drapery require specific measurements for the side repeat. 27" or 28" is a common side repeat for wallcovering since rolls of wallcovering material are available in this width. Each manufacturer will specify the repeat limitations required.

The fifth coordinate line is now drawn by measuring at two different places from the left vertical line. This line may be drawn in ink if a side repeat limitation has been designated. If you are doing the repeat for the apparel market and *no* side repeat limitation is specified, draw the fifth coordinate line in pencil since you may wish to erase and move it if layout problems develop.

Now in the new repeat areas to the right of the fifth coordinate line, once more draw in the major motifs, simple silhouettes only. The motifs in the third "A" corner are now established and you will see the "B" corner is also beginning to form. Be sure to place the motifs in the "B" corner in the upper right-hand part of the layout as well. Use Tracing #2. Beginners could mark "A" and "B," but this is not usually done.

Step 8 You have now set the limits of the working area which allows you to move ahead more easily. There are now unfinished areas to the right and below the original which is often referred to as the "L" or "no-man's-land." It is usually the most difficult part of the layout. Still using a soft pencil and silhouettes, *flow* the design together from the original to the repeated areas marked "A" and "B."

It is usually necessary to add new motifs and improvise more of the design in order to connect the pattern to itself. It is sometimes helpful to trace individual motifs on separate pieces of tracing paper. Use motifs from the original or possibly variations of these motifs. These individual motifs can be placed and shifted in the "L" area to help visualize the spacing and rhythm from the original to repeat areas. If the new addition does not balance well, shift it, rotate it, flop it (turn the tracing paper face down).

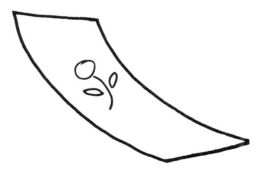

Trace individual motifs on separate pieces of tracing paper.

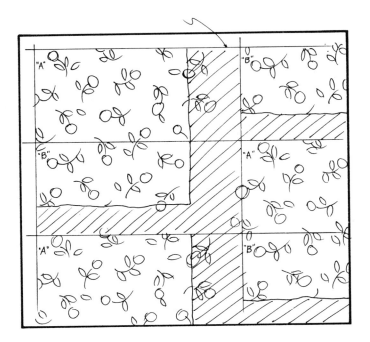

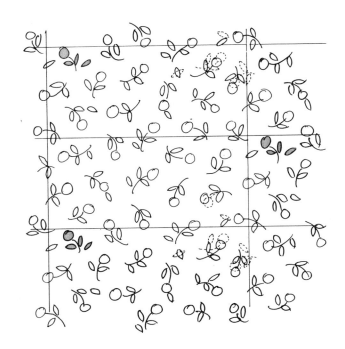

Left: *Extend motifs from the original into the connecting spaces, keeping the same spacing and rhythm. Add motifs into "L" area.* Right: *Shift, change and adjust motifs in "L" area so there is a flow from the original to the repeated areas. Edges of original design disappear. Keep original layouts intact where possible.*

Keep the same feeling and spirit of the original layout. In order to achieve an allover balance of motifs as you fill in the "L" area you may have to change the position of some or even all of the original motifs. Generally it is wiser *not* to change the motifs in the original. Be careful here, since the spirit of the original can be lost completely. If you find you are completely bewildered, it is best to turn back to the original and start again.

With Tracing #2 you can copy the changes and additions that have been newly created on Tracing #1 and duplicate them in the "B" areas and along the repeat lines. You will find there is a lot of back and forth shifting of the two tracing paper layouts in order to finalize the layout so that it flows evenly from the original to its repeated areas. Note how the "B" areas are directly above the "A" areas, both on the left-hand side of the layout as well as along the repeat line on the right. The "B" areas also appear in three different places in the layout.

Check the repeat in a mirror and by turning the tracing upside down. Errors become more apparent using these techniques.

In this phase of the repeat you may encounter several problems: the original croquis may be *smaller* than the 18-inch vertical repeat and only slightly larger than 9 inches. You may be tempted to force it into a 9-inch repeat, but this is usually a mistake. The motifs will be cramped and there will not be enough space for a comfortable balance of primary and secondary motifs. Good color spotting also needs more space rather than less. It often saves time and makes for a better repeat to design larger rather than smaller allowing enough air for all the elements to "breathe."

If the original croquis is *larger* than the 18-inch specified repeat size, you will have to eliminate or combine motifs in the "L" area and along the repeat lines. Motifs that have been eliminated in the vertical direction can often be re-introduced to the right of the original before the side repeat begins. It may be necessary to move the side repeat line further to the right. This will compensate for a lack of space in the vertical repeat.

Keep in mind the *negative spaces* around the motifs. These background areas are as important as the motifs themselves. There must be room for them as well and they must balance in the same way that the motifs balance. Eliminate any obvious holes by moving the surrounding motifs or by adding motifs. Moving one motif can unbalance another area and it will mean shifting other motifs in order to regain the balance of spaces and the continuous flow. (See **Chapter 5** for additional information on balance.)

Avoid channels or alleys of negative spaces. These may appear vertically, horizontally or diagonally in the background. Be aware of the whole layout. Step back and view the entire tracing to see the overall effect. Check for all the factors discussed here.

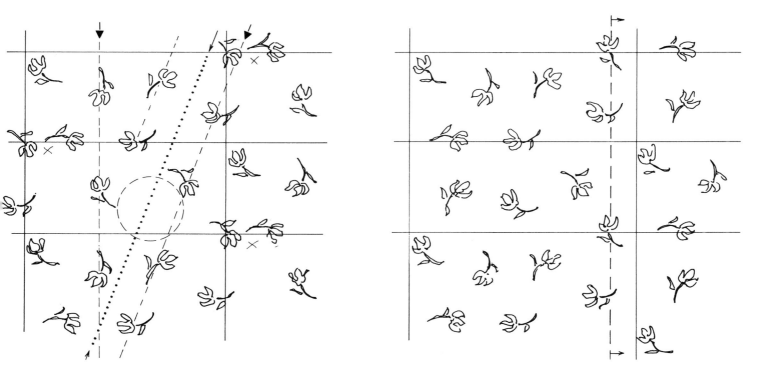

Motifs, like spaces can also *line up* and if this is not a feature of the original croquis (we are working with a tossed layout) then the repeat must not introduce this new aspect. Three or more motifs can create a *line up*. Shift the motifs slightly to break up the line and retain the tossed layout look.

In the "L" or "no-man's-land" area make the necessary changes and adjustments by adding, eliminating, moving or combining motifs to make a smooth flow at the repeat line. *Don't* cram a lot of little motifs together to fill in space. *Don't* squeeze in a motif that is too large for the space.

Whenever an addition or change is made on one tracing, be sure to make the same change on the other tracing so that the two will match as you work back and forth between them.

Don't be afraid to let a motif fall on a coordinate line. If it is incomplete or cut in half on the top coordinate line, it will be completed on the 18-inch repeat line below. The same is true for motifs on the left side coordinate line. They are completed in the half-drop areas to the right. The whole purpose here is to establish a smooth flowing pattern with no hint of the coordinate repeat lines.

Some artists prefer to work with charcoal on the tracing paper to explore layout variations. Since the charcoal is easily rubbed off, changes can be made more readily. However it is messier. For large decorative repeats, charcoal is quite satisfactory. For apparel repeats it may not be necessary.

Step 9 When the "rough" layout is complete, on Tracing #1, retrace the original motifs with a sharp #2 or 2H pencil. Now include all the details. It will be necessary to erase, motif by motif as you work, the simple silhouettes that you used initially to establish your layout. Trace only the motifs in the one total repeat unit that are full and complete. Half-motifs and motifs already carefully traced in one place may be left in the silhouetted state. If Tracing #1 is too messy and wrinkled, use a clean piece of tracing paper for the detailed final layout.

All secondary motifs are now added, and it will be necessary to use Tracing #2 to place them in the repeated areas. Secondary motifs are very helpful to fill empty spaces, to control line-ups of the major motifs as well as alleys of negative spaces that may form (as illustrated). In general, secondary motifs help establish the overall balance of the entire layout. With some designs, secondary motifs are of sufficient importance and must be considered along with the major motifs *from the beginning.*

If a third tracing paper is made, a *single unit* may be traced which includes the complete body of the repeat but none of the repeating areas.

Layout problems that might arise (left): *Channel or "alleys" of negative spaces. Obvious line-ups of motifs (if this is not a feature of the original sketch). "Holes" of negative spaces which are not consistent with the original layout. In this design* (right) *shifting the fifth coordinate line to the right helps solve these problems. Improved layout with more evenly balanced motifs.*

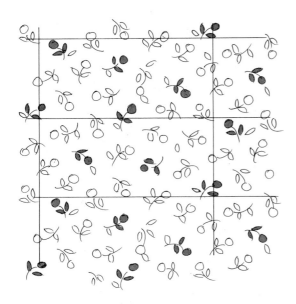

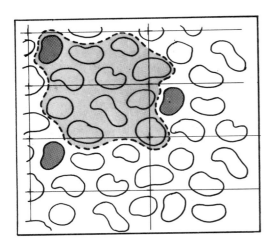

Top: *Final Layout—Color spotting is sometimes worked out as a separate step. The balance of colors must be kept in mind from the beginning.* Bottom: *The engraver needs only one fully painted unit of the repeat.*

Two separate repeat layouts were required for the design on facing page. *(© DOROTHY WOLFTHAL.) The balloons in dotted lines were added in the "L" section to complete the flow of the final repeat layout (top, left). The same was done separately with the clouds (bottom, left). Color balance was carefully studied (top, right). The final repeat layout was fully painted. Motifs in the repeating areas are easily seen. Note one-way layout (bottom, right).*

Trace only the *single unit*. On the tracing paper, ink in registration marks (cross-hair lines) at the intersection of the coordinate lines. This will assure more accuracy when transferring into the repeat areas.

Step 10   The repeat layout (Tracing #1) is now completed. Transfer the layout to the final paper. Draw in the five coordinate lines lightly in pencil on the paper with great accuracy. Cross-hair registration marks in pencil at each corner where the coordinate lines intersect are even better. Be sure the corners are absolutely square and all measurements are identical. The repeat is transferred to the final paper in the same manner we used with the croquis, using a light table or graphite "carbon" paper or rubbing down the backed tracing. Always place the registration marks carefully over those on the final paper and tape the tracing down to avoid errors. Trace lightly so there is a faint line on the final paper and not a heavy black image which will make the painting more difficult.

Step 11   A color spotting is necessary with certain multicolored designs. On Tracing #2 or on a fresh sheet of tracing paper, using markers, crayons or the paint you intend to use for painting the final repeat, spot the outstanding color as it repeats throughout the layout. This may be done loosely as only a general impression is needed. If two or three colors are outstanding, color them in as well. It is necessary to maintain the *color balance* of the original design unless of course the original color balance is obviously at fault. And this balance of color must flow evenly into the repeated areas as well. Adjust the color spotting where necessary.

If it is impossible to create a good balance of color using the existing motifs, it may be necessary to adjust the entire repeat layout. This means going back to the beginning again. A professional repeat artist thinks about color balance when first considering the size of the repeat and the placement of the repeating areas.

Step 12   Complete the final art by repainting it entirely. Remember it is paramount to paint the repeat in the *exact same colors* as the original and to keep *every motif identical,* every gesture, every detail. The final art must be as close as possible to the original croquis in everyway but of course there will be more of it. The exception of course is if the customer has designated otherwise. If the original croquis is usable and the customer's instructions are to repeat it "as is" then finish off the original by splicing on additional paper, if necessary, and painting the repeat.

For the engraver or screenmaker it is necessary to paint only one full unit of the repeat including the motifs that overlap the coordinate repeat lines. However, additional painting helps us to see if the final art is a good repeat. It is wise to paint an additional amount (about 4" to 6") of the repeated areas to be sure the "L" area is well designed. If the repeat is a small size, less repeated area need be painted (average 2" to 3"). If the repeat is large, more of the repeated areas should be painted in (as much as 15").

Save your tracing layouts and store them rolled or flat. Folding tracing paper will cause inaccuracies in the dimensions. When working, beware of humidity and moisture which can distort the images and dimensions of the layout as well.

A word about half-drop repeats: If we extend the grid out to the right twice the width of the layout, you will see that the "A" corner returns to the top of the layout. A kind of *brick/grid* is created by the coordinate lines. (See the A–B–A placement.

Square repeats (sometimes called *straight* or *straight across* repeats) are executed in the same manner as the half-drop outlined above. The only difference is that the "A" corner repeats in the upper right rather than halfway down. The repetition is based on a horizontal and vertical alignment of the four sides of the repeat unit.

A half-drop repeat layout is usually more successful than a simple *square* repeat since the mechanically repeating elements are less obvious, creating a more interesting flow and allover effect of the pattern. Some designs (with a set or grid layout for instance) compose more readily into a *square* repeat layout.

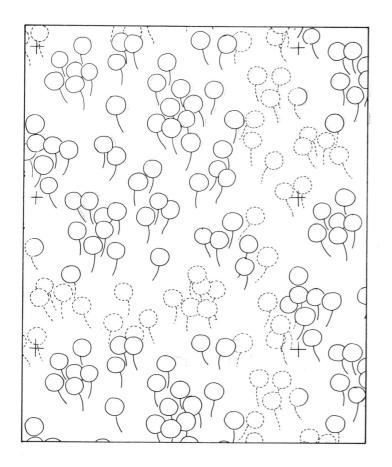

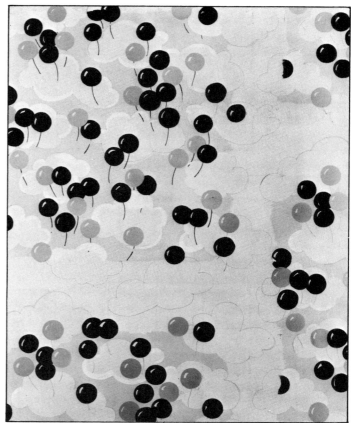

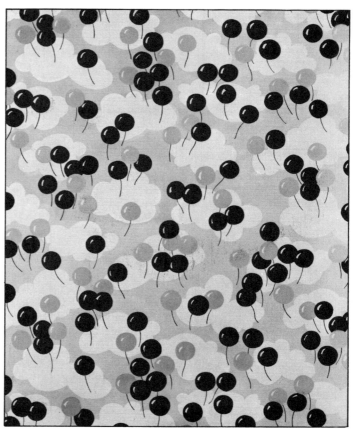

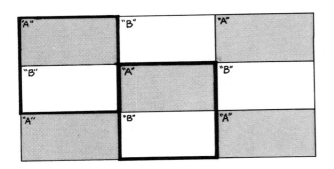

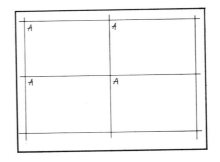

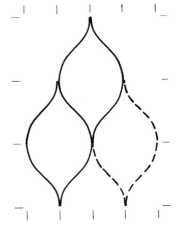

Half-drop repeat when repeat is extended further to the right, "A" corner returns to the top of the layout.

Square repeat (above): *There is no "B" section in this layout. Ogee shapes* (right) *as well as diamond shapes can be used as repeating units.*

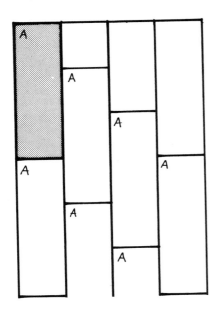

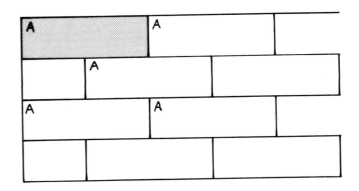

Vertical brick/grid layout (left) *uses a one-third drop rather than a half-drop. Brick/grid layout* (above) *with a strong horizontal effect.*

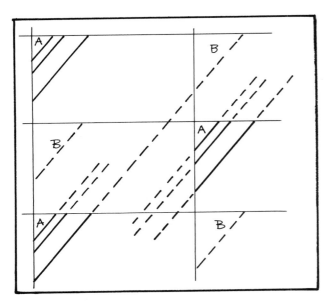

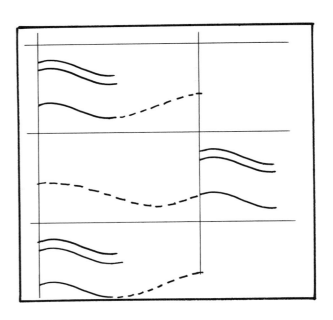

A diagonal layout (left) *in a half-drop repeat. Rhythmic horizontal lines* (right) *can also be repeated as a half-drop.*

Documentary design for apparel based on traditional Japanese art. A diamond grid layout was used. (© DOROTHY WOLFTHAL.)

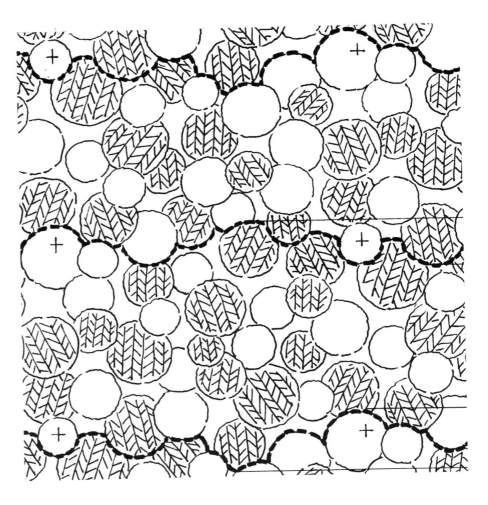

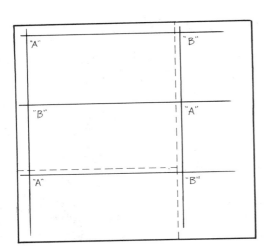

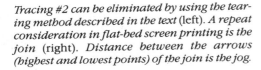

Tracing #2 can be eliminated by using the tearing method described in the text (left). *A repeat consideration in flat-bed screen printing is the join* (right). *Distance between the arrows (highest and lowest points) of the join is the jog.*

Instead of the half-drop in Step 7, try a square repeat. Place the "A" corner of Tracing #2 in the upper right-hand corner of Tracing #1. Align the two top coordinate lines. Do the motifs of the original flow more easily into the repeated area? Does this relationship clarify the placement of the fifth line? If so, consider the possibility of a square repeat.

Other repeating layouts are possible using *diamond* shapes in place of the *brick/grid* as well as *ogee* shapes as repeating units. The *brick/grid* may form into a long and narrow unit and stagger similar to bricks seen on a house or it could be very tall and vertical. The principle of the flow of pattern into the repeating areas still applies. However, the method outlined in **Steps 1** through **12** is a basic one commonly used in the textile design field. There are many variations and with experience you will discover shortcuts and your own way of working.

Special problems will arise and many designs will require unique handling. A design may have a grid background with a floral motif on top. The floral must be put in repeat in the usual manner and, of course, the grid must repeat as well. Both will fall into some fraction of the required repeat dimension.

Half-drop diagonals require special consideration. The key is to establish the three "A" corners and work the diagonals into each other.

If a design has rhythmic flowing abstract lines in an *allover* layout (not separate motifs), the lines must flow into each other at the coordinate lines. Establish the rhythmic lines at the repeat coordinate lines to begin with and then connect them all together.

If the motifs are grouped together in clusters and there is an open-and-closed layout, the clusters are handled like a single motif. Variations within the clusters are possible.

There are other methods of creating repeat layouts. It is possible to establish the repeat lines and then tear the tracing paper ½" away in order to duplicate the repeating areas. This takes the place of Tracing #2. The torn repeat areas are taped back in place after the layout has been finalized. This

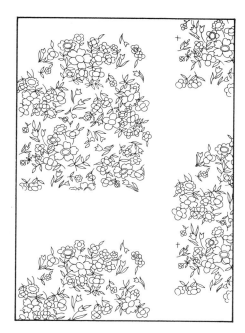

method saves some time by eliminating the Tracing #2.

"Doing repeats" is often the first job that the beginner finds. Repeats are demanding and require concentration and tenacity. Since they are mechanical in nature they differ in spirit from creating original designs. For the beginner a great deal can be learned from doing repeats. Often it takes perhaps five to fifteen repeats before an artist feels comfortable with the procedure. However, it is excellent training in layout and control of media and reinforces the designers' skills in positive ways. There is always a demand for good repeat artists in the industry, and the professional textile designer can find fulfillment in repeats as well as creating original works.

THE JOIN

When screens are prepared for printing, there is a "break" across the top and a corresponding break across the bottom of the screen. This break is known as the *join*. It is rarely a straight line, but rather it follows around the contours of the design. When a repeat is worked in half-drop, as frequently happens, the join is also worked out in half-drop (as illustrated). illustrated).

In many designs there is no need for the repeat artist to be concerned about the join, since plenty of "breaks" occur in the pattern and the engraver or screenmaker can easily discover a logical place to "join" the repeat. This is especially true when the design is on a white background. But sometimes, for example when there is a solid colored blotch, or a broad vertical background stripe, a join may have to be devised. It may be necessary to paint in a leaf or stem or some other design element to provide a place for the join to continue across the entire width of the repeat. When the artist develops and/or indicates a join on a repeat, this is usually done by clearly drawing the join line on a sheet of tracing paper, and placing the tracing paper over the entire repeat. *Do not* mark the "join" on the actual artwork.

The *jog* is the distance from the highest to the lowest point along the join line. In general, the object is to try to keep the join as close as possible to a horizontal line, with not too many ups and downs. The larger the repeat is, the larger is the acceptable jog.

Left: *Start of half-drop repeat layout on tracing paper for "Lancaster."* Right: *Shows portion that was added in "L" section to complete the repeat* (See Step 8, A and B, in repeat series.) *"Lancaster" print is painted in repeat and illustrated in color.* (© *DOROTHY WOLFTHAL.*)

1. *A fresh brush-stroke "hand" gives an airy look to pillowcase and sheet design by* JACK PRINCE.

2. *A scenic print rendered entirely in stipple technique on a black ground.* (DESIGN LAB, FASHION INSTITUTE OF TECHNOLOGY.)

3. *Final rendering of "Lancaster" in repeat. Early exploration sketches appear on page 157.* (© DOROTHY WOLFTHAL.)

4. *"Balloons" design required two separate repeat layouts—clouds and balloons —as shown on page 153.* (© DOROTHY WOLFTHAL.)

5. *An example of a one-color (monochromatic) decorative floral, with a range of values from dark to light.* (DESIGN LAB, FASHION INSTITUTE OF TECHNOLOGY.)

6, 7. *A modern paisley print designed for apparel, with four color variations.* (© FISHER & GENTILE.)

8. *Apparel design inspired by reference material from Metropolitan Museum of Art. Technique is described on pages 84 and 85.* (© RICHARD FISHER.)

9. *"Strawberry Thief"—a classic William Morris original fabric from the* DESIGN LAB *Collection,* FASHION INSTITUTE OF TECHNOLOGY.

10. *A Persian floral executed in dyes; a steel pen pont with bleach was used to create the light background texture and the lines. Repeating areas are outlined only.* (© RICHARD FISHER.)

11–16. *"Party" is fully discussed in Chapter 9. The top color combinations (11, 12, 13) weigh in with each other. The bottom group (14, 15, 16) shows three changes of the color look. Note that the sequence of color tabs remains the same in all six color combinations.* (© DOROTHY WOLFTHAL.)

1

2

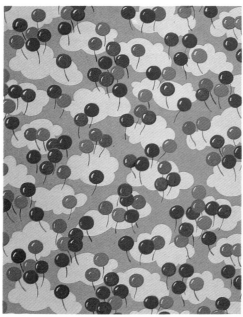

4

5

7

8

9

10

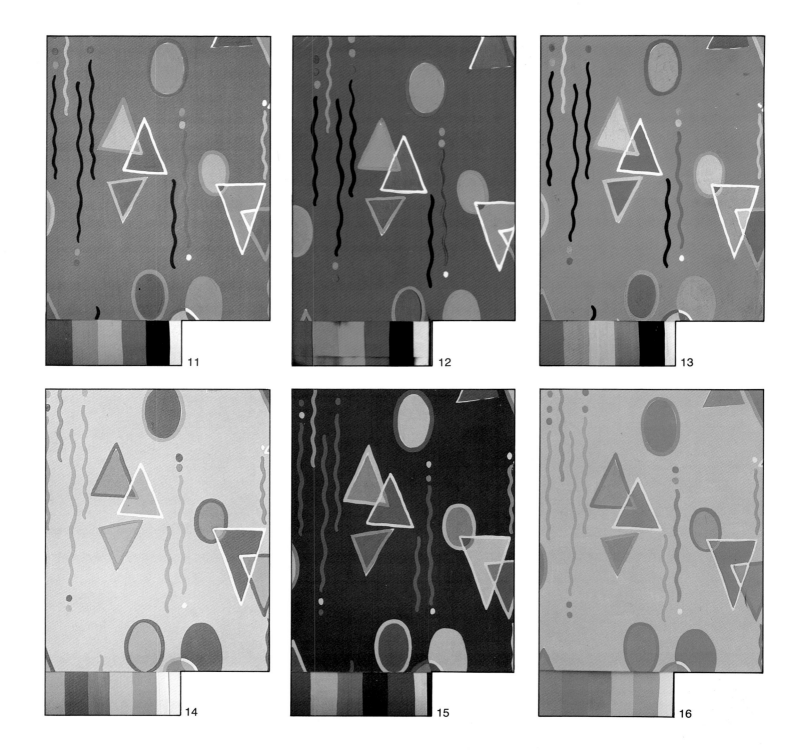

11

12

13

14

15

16

COLOR & COLOR COMBINATIONS

Color is the very heart of textile design, the essential ingredient, the emotional aspect of every pattern. It is the most appealing element. It triggers the first feelings, impressions and responses when we see a design, before the intellect comes into action saying "it's a flower, a red petal, a blue textured background."

The PHYSICIST gives us abstract theories of color and light and sensation; the optical principles involved.

The CHEMIST gives us the pigments and dyes, and the rules for mixing and applying color.

The PSYCHOLGIST names the emotional responses to colors and the effect they have on us.

The ARTIST, consciously or unconsciously, is involved with all of the above, and goes beyond to develop a personal view, creating original variations and combinations, to fulfill an aesthetic purpose. The artist creates new and original relationships and uses of color.

The FASHION STYLIST, for the purposes of excitement and selling, has concocted many provocative and suggestive names which communicate the excitement of current trends of color. Using fancy names helps with promotion and publicity: "in" colors: fire-star burgundy, midnight mystery; ice cream colors: sherbet, peach, chocolate; these and other names are glamorous and market-motivated. It is common practice to have catchy names to sell new colors or trends for the season at hand.

For TEXTILE DESIGNERS the multitude of color names becomes non-communicative and meaningless, and does not help us to match a color in gouache or dyes. The names are vague and it is a matter of opinion what a coral or a salmon color really is.

When mixing colors it is best to use a more simple system of color names: red, orange, yellow, green, blue and purple (three primaries and three secondaries). Each then is combined with its neighboring color giving us yellow-green, blue-purple, etc. We use the names of colors as they appear on the color wheel (red, green, blue) as well as the names on the tubes of paint: Bengal Rose, Indigo, Turquoise, Umber or Yellow Ochre. These names help us to mix and match colors. We can modify them with the values (*light* blue, *dark* blue), and with chromas (*bright* red, or *dull* rose), and describe them in combinations (pale blue-green, dull yellow-green, light blue-gray or reddish-gray). Temperature helps to communicate also, *warm* gray or *cool* gray.

The artist plays in the dark with ultimate things and reaches them.

Paul Klee

"Cinerarias" floral design by GREEFF FABRICS.

But if we say passion blush, flesh, storm black, less is communicated. And then there are the ridiculous extremes like Bizet's carmine, or old Chinese sage, pea green, and heliotrope.

CHARACTERISTICS OF COLOR

Color has three essential characteristics: *hue, value,* and *chroma.*

Hue means color, the name of the color, true, pure, original, not mixed or modified with black or white pigment.

Value The lightness and darkness of a color. The value of a color can be determined by comparing it to a scale of grays ranging from black to white.

Chroma The intensity of a color, dull to bright, low to high. It indicates the saturation level of a color, brilliant or subdued.

A useful *formula* for notating color is found in the Munsell Color Theory: H v/c—each color or hue (H) is modified by its value (v) and its chroma (c). This formula is useful in planning and describing colors. The value is designated by a number on the neutral scale from 10 (white) to 0 (black). Numbers are also used for the chromas. (Refer to *Munsell Color Theory* as listed in **Bibliography**.)

Tint White paint added to any pigment color gives us a lighter value of that color. It also reduces the chroma (color saturation). This applies to gouache and all opaque media. When using dyes, tints are achieved by adding water, allowing more white of the paper to show through.

Shade Adding black to any color gives us a darker value of that color. It also reduces the chroma.

Tone Adding the neutrals of the value scale gives us low chroma variations of each color. Adding grays of the *same* value as the original color will reduce the chroma only. Adding grays, of a darker value will reduce the chroma as well as lower the value of the color (darken it). Adding grays of a lighter value will reduce the chroma and raise the value of the color (lighten it).

Neutral/Gray In color theory, the words *neutral* and *gray* refer to a mixture of black and white only. However, in the textile design field, *neutral* refers to low chroma colors.

Spectrum A band of colors is formed by a prism when a beam of white light passes through it. The colors are *red, orange, yellow, green, blue, indigo* and *violet* (ROY G BIV). This becomes the basis for a color wheel which is a useful tool for designers.

COLOR WHEEL

Using pigments, we can create a series of colors and place them in a circle. The colors are similar but not identical to those in the spectrum:

- Red, Yellow, Blue are the *primary* colors
- Orange, Green, and Purple are the *secondary* colors.
- The combinations Red/Orange, Yellow/Orange, Yellow/Green, Blue/Green, Blue/Violet, Red/Purple are called *tertiaries.*

For practical purposes we use a color wheel which has 12 colors in all.

There are other theories of color and other systems to study if an artist is inclined to delve deeper into this subject (see **Bibliography**). When we use pigments we use a theory which science calls *subtractive* color. When working with light as in computer art, the theory is called *additive* color and the primaries are *red, green* and *blue.* However, the simpler system outlined above is more commonly found in the textile design field. All

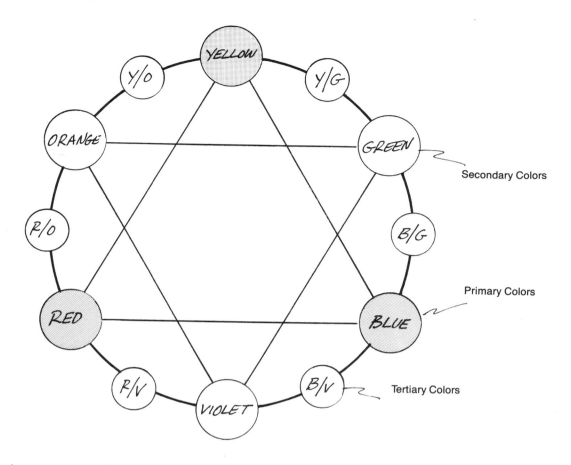

Basic color wheel showing primary, secondary, and tertiary colors.

theories are intellectual and the artist may find them useful as a starting place in the adventure of color. But sooner or later, when he/she gets the *feeling* of color, the theories are left behind.

Relationship of Colors

A very important consideration when mixing and combining colors in a design is their *relationship* to one another. Their influence on each other is very dramatic. A red, for instance, placed on a white ground looks very different from that same red when surrounded by green, or some other color. Each color modifies the other. In relationships lies the mystery and true beauty as well as the challenge of color.

Temperature of Colors

Paint and dye colors can have a *warm* or a *cool* aspect. In general, colors with red, orange and yellow in them are *warm* and those with green, blue and purple are *cool*. This concept is especially helpful when evaluating the vast numbers of grays. Relationship also modifies the *temperature* of a color.

Light

Without light there can be no color. The source of light is very important. In a dim light all colors appear grayish. In very bright sunlight colors look washed-out. This is one reason why very strong colors are used in tropical climates. If you use an incandescent bulb, your colors will look warm. It is disappointing then to see the same colors in fluorescent light or daylight where they look different and all the "warmth" of the colors has disappeared.

Natural light can be *warm* in direct sunlight, and *cool* in a shadow on the north side of a building. North light is always the best for artists as there is little visual temperature variation throughout the day. With artificial light it is necessary to balance this warm/cool aspect.

It is essential to have ample and adequate light in your studio when working. A general overhead light is important as well as a desk lamp to concentrate light on specific areas. All light ideally should be color-corrected and temperature-balanced.

COLOR SCHEMES/COLOR HARMONIES

Monochromatic The same color (mono = one, chroma = color) with value changes from light to dark in a design is called a monochromatic color scheme.

Analogous That which is similar. Colors that are close together on the color wheel, such as blue-green, blue, and blue-purple are *analogous*. If you add white or black to any of them they are still analogous. In a design you can have many colors that have a *common denominator of one color:* pink, peach, maroon, magenta, orange—all have red in them.

Complementary Those colors opposite each other on the color wheel. Red is opposite green and therefore is its *complement*. When complements are mixed they will combine to make a dark gray. This is true of all the opposites on the color wheel. If a red is placed next to a green, strong vibrations occur. In the eye it appears that the touching edges jump and vibrate.

When mixing pigment color it is possible to use the complement of the color to modify it. A *neutralizing* process occurs and the resulting color is chromatically less intense (less loud or noisy). French theories of color in the 19th century likened color to music and described color in musical terms and music in color terms. The word *harmonies* is common to both as well as *chromatic scale* and similar ideas.

COLOR LIMITATIONS

Textile patterns for apparel products in the U.S. mass market have historically been limited to five colors. The number of colors in a design determines the number of rollers engraved or screens used, one for each color. Roller printing presses usually have only five *stations* for the rollers; occasionally six colors are possible. Rotary screen printing is widely used and allows for a maximum of twelve colors to be printed per pattern. However, the cost factor often limits the number of colors used to three, four or five.

An unlimited number of colors is possible with *heat-transfer* printing which is discussed in **Chapter 8.** Hand block prints may use up to twenty and more colors. This approaches the one-of-a-kind, hand-painted, couturier fabrics where the number of colors is unlimited, as with a fine art painting.

Color limitations in the home furnishings field are different from those of apparel. Upholstery and drapery products often use eight to twelve colors per design.

PERCENTONES

When printing on a smooth surface, such as paper and vinyl film (used in wallcovering and upholstery products) it is common practice to use *percentones*. A percentone is a tint or lighter value of color, and is achieved by printing the color in tiny dots rather than a solid covering of ink. The percentone may be any lighter value of the solid color: 80%, 60%, 40%. Very light percentones (10%–20%) are apt to print poorly in production. Too many percentones of any one color in a design becomes too complicated. One or two tones of a color are all that are commonly used.

Although engraved roller printing is the usual method used for printing percentones, they can also be achieved with rotary screen printing since fine holes can be made in the nickel alloy. Look closely at a magazine or newspaper photo with a magnifying glass in order to see the fine dots of ink used to give us the illusion of a continuous tone.

In addition to paper and vinyl film, *halftone* printing (as it is often called by engravers and printers) is used most frequently on silk, polished cotton, chintz, and polyester fabrics, the surfaces of which are smooth and tightly woven. A modified variation of percentone printing is possible on cotton and coarser fabric and is called a *half-etch*. It allows a lighter, somewhat textured variation of a color to be printed.

Traps Using Percentones   When one transparent color overprints on another it produces a third color. The third color is called *a trap*. (See **Chapter 6**—using dyes to create the effect of trapping.)

If percentones are used in a design, it is unwise to use them with this trapping technique. Unexpected complications can occur with other color combinations. However, if carefully thought out, it is *possible* to use a percentone to underprint a color in order to modify it.

COLOR COMBINATIONS *

The designer's work is almost finished when we get to the *color combinations.* When the repeat is completed and accepted by the stylist, it is sent off to the engraver. A *reference piece,* which is a duplication of a section of the final art, is often made by the repeat artist and is retained by the stylist to continue the evaluation of the line or group of designs in progress. It is also frequently used to make color combinations. This is the usual practice in the apparel field. With home fashions the color combinations are often executed at the same time as the repeat.

It may take the engraver from three to six weeks to engrave the rollers. This gives us a period of time to work up the color combinations in anticipation of the *strike-off* when the colors will be finalized in printing inks on cloth.

Three to five color combinations are common with apparel designs. However it varies with each product and each manufacturer.

When the strike-off begins the rollers have been completed and mounted in the printing machine. There is one roller per color in the design. All we can do now is change the colors at each station.

There are artists who work exclusively on color combinations and are called *colorists.* The colorist usually is told how many color combinations to do and whether or not they should *weigh in.* This means that *the values and the chromas remain the same* while the hue (color) changes from combination to combination. If the values and chromas vary from the original, then the color combinations do not *weigh in.* Both types of color combinations are used frequently in the field.

Sometimes the colorist is assigned a general color look—bright, pastel, neutral—usually based on a fashion trend. Possibly a key main color is given to incorporate into the combinations.

There are several ways of choosing colors for a color combination. Perhaps the most commonly used method is called *pitching.* The designer or stylist analyzes the design or swatch of fabric for which a set of color combinations is to be created.

Refer to a design with an abstract pattern of geometric shapes in the following combination (as illustrated here):

1. Yellow-green shapes, lines, and dots
2. Blue-green shapes, lines and dots
3. Red shapes, lines, and dots
4. Black lines
5. Blue-violet blotch

Note: White lines appear here and there but are not counted as a color, since the white is the unprinted part of the fabric.

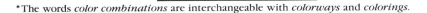

*The words *color combinations* are interchangeable with *colorways* and *colorings.*

Text on "pitching" color combinations refers to this design, "Party." Color combinations of this geometric design are illustrated on page 166. (© DOROTHY WOLFTHAL.)

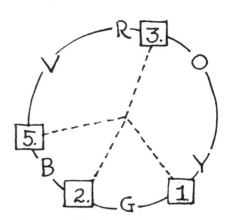

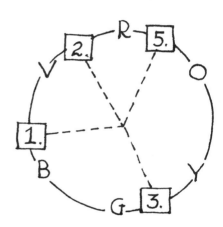

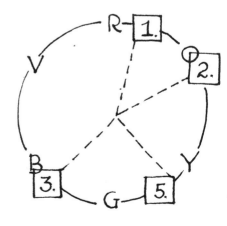

Color wheels showing weigh-in combinations for "Party." Note: "constellations" are similar in shape as they rotate. (Black, color #4, is not indicated.)

We will assume that we're going to make two color combinations to *weigh in* with the original. The first step will be to make a chart similar to the one illustrated.

If one color dominates the original, list this color first on the chart. Since the first three colors appear in approximately equal amounts (no one of them being dominant), list the colors from the lightest to the darkest. This is usually the order in which they will be printed. It is helpful to group together colors that are similar or near one another on the color wheel. For example, the yellow-green and blue-green are listed as colors 1 and 2. The blotch or background color is often listed last.

Now find the first color (yellow-green) on the color wheel. It will be about halfway between yellow and green. Since three colorways will be printed (the original plus two more), for the first new color move about one-third of the way clockwise around the color wheel—two spaces. This brings us to a point between blue and violet. Write "blue-violet" in the first space of line 1.

The next color is blue-green. Find it on the color wheel and again move around two spaces, arriving at red-violet. Write "red-violet" in the second space of line 1.

The third color is red. Moving two spaces around will bring us to yellow and this presents a problem. The red in the original is fairly dark in value, and quite bright (high chroma). Since yellow is a naturally light color which loses its brightness when we darken it, it would be almost impossible to "weigh in" a bright yellow with a bright red. Therefore, we move to a color on either side of yellow on the color wheel. In this case we moved toward the green, which is a color of a naturally darker value, and decided on green-yellow-green. Write this in the third space of line 1.

Next is black, and we will retain black in the fourth space for all three color combinations.

Proceeding in the same manner, always moving two spaces clockwise, color 5, the blue-violet blotch, will be red-orange, keeping in mind that the value and chroma will be as close as possible to the original.

All the color notations for the first new color combination have been entered in the appropriate spaces. To arrive at color combination #2, the same procedure is followed. Starting from the first color in line 1 (blue-violet), again move two spaces clockwise on the color wheel, arriving at red-orange. From color 2 (red-violet) move two spaces around to yellow-orange. (If this seems too pale, let it be more orange than yellow.) Each time you come to a new color, enter it on the chart. This process—writing colors in chart or diagram form—is known as "pitching a set of color combinations." Some studios have pre-printed charts with space for six or more color combinations.

When you are mixing colors for the new combinations, always refer back to the original design, since the *values* and the *chromas* must be the same or at least very close. The combinations will then weigh in if the dark areas are always dark, the brilliant accents remain brilliant, the pale motifs stay pale.

Sometimes it's hard to identify a color. The clear, brilliant colors, the bright pastels (colors high in chroma) are readily understood. More subtle ones such as dusty beige or dark gray must be studied more carefully. Beige may be yellow-orange or orange of a low chroma. A warm gray may be a low chroma yellow-orange or a low chroma red; a cool gray may be a blue or blue-violet, barely discernible because of the low chroma.

You will notice that in the chart some colors are repeated: Yellow-green appears in line 0 (original) and as color 5 in line 2. Blue-violet is in line 0 and again in line 1. Be flexible. Do not use exactly the same color in each case. They must weigh in as closely as possible to *the original,* which *usually* will produce a different value and/or chroma from the new colors already selected. Move a bit further left or right on the color wheel, or in some other way make each new color different (to continue see **Steps 10–12**).

A more visual variation of this procedure of choosing new colors for color combinations that *weigh in* is outlined in the following **steps**:

Step 1   On a small piece of tracing paper, a 5-inch square, in pencil,

	1.	2.	3.	4.	5. (BLOTCH)
ORIGINAL	YELLOW-GREEN	BLUE-GREEN	RED	BLACK	VIOLET-BLUE
1.	LIGHT VIOLET-BLUE	RED-VIOLET	GREEN (G/Y-G)	BLACK	ORANGE-RED
2.	PEACH (R/R-O)	ORANGE	BLUE	BLACK	YELLOW-GREEN

draw a circle and indicate the positions of *yellow, red* and *blue.* They must be equidistant from each other. Be sure the *circle* is close to a perfect *round* and not some oval substitute, and that the three primaries are placed on the circle, each one-third of the way around the circumference.

Step 2 On a second piece of tracing paper, 5-inch square, we will construct a *constellation* of the colors in the original design or reference piece. This analysis of the colors will help us relate them to the color wheel as well as establish a formal relationship of all the colors (the *constellation*). This relationship remains constant from color combination to color combination.

There should be a small dot in the center of the circle and another dot placed in the middle of the second piece of paper, which is placed on top of the first aligning dots.

The dark colors will be placed close to the center, the bright colors on the circle and the light colors will be in the field surrounding the circle. This will account in a general way for most of the colors and their values. Chroma is not indicated in this system yet. If a color is dull or low in chroma, you can still only place it in the constellation according to its hue and value.

A word about *browns* and *tans;* the color wheel seems to have no place for browns and tans. In fact they are low chroma variations of red, orange or yellow. If the *value* of a brown is *dark,* then place it in the *inner* area of the circle. If the *value* is *light,* place it *outside* the circle. And of course if the brown is reddish it is near red on the circle, and the same for orange and yellow.

Let us use a hypothetical design with a dark indigo ground (as illustrated **page 176**). Near the center of the circle and in the direction of blue we would write "GD" for *ground* (as illustrated).

A light blue flower in the pattern is located in the field outside the circle: write "F1" (for flower).

If there is a second flower, this time bright violet, it would be placed in the constellation *on* the circle and indicated as "F2."

Leaves and stems may be a dark grayish-green and would be placed in the inner area of the circle by writing "L" (for leaves and stems). For some designers it might be confusing to indicate the flowers and stems by their color names since we intend to change the colors.

Any other motifs with different colors would have to be added into the constellation until all are accounted for.

Step 3 On the same type of paper used to paint the color combinations, draw a *grid-chart.* This chart will be a slight variation from the one described above. Down the left-hand side of the grid, place an "O" which

The process of writing in colors for "Party" in chart or diagram form is known as "pitching," a set of color combinations. For color combinations to weigh in, values and chromas should be the same vertically in the chart.

A second method of weighing-in color combinations is illustrated on these pages for this floral design. The actual colors are painted in the chart.

	GD GROUND	F¹ FLOWER	F² FLOWER	L LEAVES	OTHER MOTIFS
O					
1					
2					

stands for *original,* "1" for the first color combination, "2" for the second, and so forth. Across the top write *ground, flowers, leaves,* and *other motifs.* On the chart, in row "O" place chips or patches of the colors from the original design or paint in the colors directly so that the color itself is present.

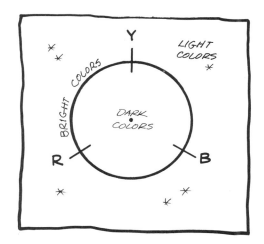

Step 4   Return to the two pieces of tracing paper. Choose the most important color or dominant motif, in this case, F1.

Rotate the *constellation* keeping the center dots on the tracing paper one on top of the other. A push pin is useful when placed through the two center dots. Place flower F1 on a new color (light red—pink). This is a logical choice since we may wish to place flower F1 on three approximately equally distant colors around the wheel. The original was a light blue, the second will be a pink, and the third could be a yellow.

Notice that the *relationship* of the colors remains constant. New colors are suggested for the other motifs in color combination #1 when we see how the constellation relates to the color wheel underneath.

An interesting development occurs. The leaves that were originally green are now a dull violet and in combination #2 they become a dull orange (a muted brown). Colors in textile design are often used "decoratively." The leaves can be any color we choose and are no longer treated naturalistically. This decorative use of color is another element which reinforces the pattern aspect of textile designs.

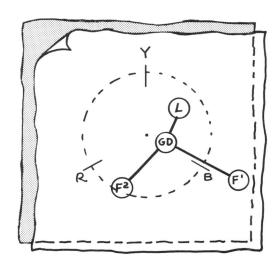

Step 5   Mix the colors suggested by the new position of the constellation. When mixing colors, use a 30-hole palette so that you can quickly create many variations of color. When mixing a color, take the tube of paint closest to the color you want. Adjust the value by adding white and/or black. Then adjust the hue by adding other colors.

It is a good habit to paint a small *dab* of the new color on a strip of paper (the same type of paper used to paint the combination). Paint the dab *off* the edge of the strip of paper so that it can be easily placed next to the reference color for testing purposes; if the dab is painted in the middle of a piece of paper, it is difficult to make an exact comparison. While a dab is drying, another color can be mixed and placed on the strip next to the first one. If the first color is not satisfactory, then the necessary changes can be made and the new color is painted on the strip. Soon there will be many trials as you "fine tune" the colors for the final choice.

Be sure the light source is balanced in temperature. Daylight is the most desirable if it is not actually bright sunshine when mixing colors.

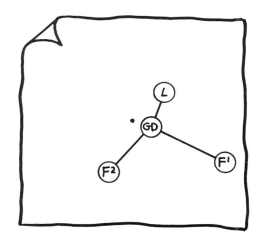

Step 6   Place the new colors on the grid-chart in their proper positions. A visual patch of color communicates more than the written word since we have the exact color as well as its value and chroma. Once all the colors are in the chart we can compare them more readily. We can very quickly *see* and accurately determine if the values and chromas are the *same in each column,* vertically, if the color combinations are to weigh in. We can also spot duplication of colors and modify one of them if it seems desirable.

Step 7   For color combination #2, repeat **Step 3** by rotating the constellation to a second position—flower F1 over the yellow, for instance. If more than two new color combinations are required, flower F1 could be placed at the light orange (peach) position or possibly at the light green position. New colors appear and the *relationships* remain the same.

Step 8   Mix the new colors for color combination #2 suggested by the position of the constellation over the color wheel and place them in the chart.

Continue this process for as many color combinations as required. If only three have been assigned, spread the placement of flower F1 in three positions that *balance* equally around the color wheel. The same balance is possible if four or five color combinations have been assigned.

Flower F1 could, of course, be placed in any position on the wheel. This decision is guided by the number of combinations required as well as by the compatibility of *all* the combinations when viewed as a group. A process of trial and error is usually necessary.

Another method is used in these three illustrations. The 'constellation' is drawn on tracing paper in relation to a color wheel.

	GD GROUND	F1 FLOWER	F2 FLOWER	L LEAVES	
0	(DARK BLUE)	(LIGHT BLUE)	(MAGENTA)	(DULL GREEN)	
1	PAINT A DARK RED	PAINT A PINK	PAINT A YELLOW-ORANGE	PAINT A DULL PURPLE	
2	PAINT A DARK YELLOW	PAINT A GREENISH YELLOW	PAINT A BLUE-GREEN	PAINT A DULL-ORANGE	

Compare vertically

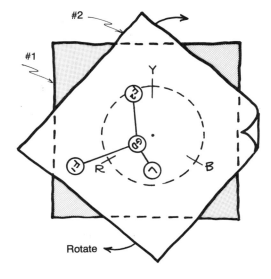

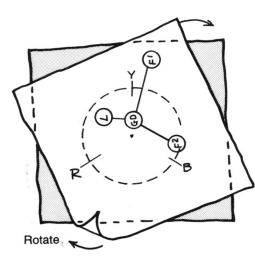

New colors ar determined as the "constellation" on tracing paper is rotated on top of the color wheel. The actual painted colors are shown in this version of the chart. Values and chromas should be the same vertically in the chart.

Step 9 Once again study the chart. Watch out for duplication of colors throughout the chart. Subtle changes and differences are possible by shifting the color slightly *left* or *right* around the wheel or by modifying the chroma slightly.

Duplication of colors is sometimes desirable and intentional. A certain color may be fashionable and the designer may wish to repeat it in more than one color combination. The only consideration is that any two color-ways do not look alike or too similar.

Step 10 Trace the reference piece or a representative section of the design if that is available, and transfer the image to the paper in preparation for painting. The area painted should be *typical* of the design and have all the colors in the design represented at least once in approximately the same proportions.

The actual size of the color combination will vary from approximately 3-inch square (for a small-scale apparel design) to a giant 1' by 3' (for a wallcovering or drapery design). However, the average size for a decorative design is closer to a 12-inch square. The dimensions are largely determined by the layout of the original pattern. An "adequate size" always varies with each design.

Occasionally colorings are painted directly on prepared acetate which is placed on top of the original design. Waxed Masa also can be painted in this direct fashion since it too is transparent.

Step 11 Now paint the color combinations using the new colors from the chart. The new color always replaces *all* of the original color wherever it appears in the color combination. Therefore, the pink replaces the light blue in every motif where light blue was originally.

The only way to make a final judgment of the choice of colors is to see them in context in the painted color combination. In this way you really *see* the proportions of the colors and their relationship to each other.

Be free to change or modify the colors if necessary. Since each textile design will be different, this procedure must remain flexible. Any system is only an approximation, a guide, a springboard to help us get started. Taste and good judgment must take over.

Step 12 Always paint color tabs as you mix and paint the color combinations. For apparel designs tabs should be about 1" x 3". Paint the colors adjacent to one another and trim away excess paper. Mount the resulting card of color tabs underneath the color combinations on mounting paper. Occasionally we are asked to paint larger swatches of color.

Once you have established the order of the color tabs, the sequence must always remain the same. If the first color tab represents the color of the

CHANGING THE LOOK

	1.	2.	3.	4.	5. (BLOTCH)	
LINGERIE (ANALOGOUS PASTELS)	TURQUOISE (GREEN-BLUE)	BLUE	RED-VIOLET	BLUE-GREEN (LOW CHROMA)	PALE BLUE-GREEN	
MENSWEAR (DARK COLORING)	GRAY-PURPLE	LIGHT RED-PURPLE	RED-BROWN (R/R-O)	GRAY-PURPLE (SAME AS COLOR #1)	DARK PURPLE	TINTED GROUND
FALL COLORS	GRAY	RUST (R-O)	KHAKI (Y-O)	GOLD (Y/Y-O)	WARM BEIGE (O/Y-O)	

flowers, the second the leaves, the third the blotch, etc., that sequence must be maintained in the color tabs of all succeeding colorings, no matter what colors are substituted for the original version.

Percentones are indicated by a diagonal division of the color tab, and indicate the full color and the percentone used as well. It is also possible to indicate the percentone in a second box below and adjacent to the color tab indicating the full color. Variations such as these are up to the designer. (Refer to **Chapter 7** for more information on color tabs.)

Color combinations need not always weigh in. We can *change the look*. The reasons vary: a change of season; a different end use (children's wear, women's lingerie, etc.); possibly for another product (a wallcovering or drapery). *To change the look:*

1. Paint a light ground in place of the dark ground of the original. (The *value* is altered.) The same is possible with motifs.

2. Choose a gray or muted look. (The *chroma* of each color is altered.)

3. A monochromatic group of colors could be used.

4. If the original is multicolored (i.e. with colors all over the color wheel) we could try an analogous scheme with possibly a small accent of a complementary color.

5. We might "drop a color" which means to omit a roller during strike-off. Removing a background blotch roller would instantly change the look of the design. The color combination is painted accordingly.

6. We can "double up" or even "triple up" on a color; i.e., flower F1 and flower F2 can both be assigned the same color. The leaves and stems can all be a single color to create a whole new effect—if the design can handle it.

7. During the strike-off at the printing plant, we can print the blotch only. This will depend on the way the design has been engraved.

8. If there is a great deal of line-work, such as a paisley or a Liberty print, try using only the outline and drop all the other colors.

9. Pigment white can be printed on pre-dyed fabric. This too is accomplished on the printing press during the strike-off and the color combinations would be painted in white gouache on colored grounds.

These are a few suggestions for color combinations that do *not* weigh-in. Others are possible. Remember that the print rollers are in the press and the only thing to consider is the change of colors. We cannot alter the layout, add new motifs, or redistribute any other elements within the design.

Color combinations do not always weigh in. The "changing the look" chart refers to "Party." Note: *The men's wear color combination doubles up on colors one and four and is to be printed on a tinted ground*

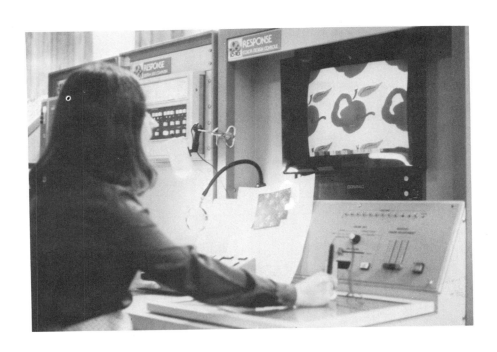

There is another method of creating colorways. The designer or stylist will use pre-painted *chips* of color which are then stapled or taped onto a chart similar to that used above. No color combinations are painted. The chart with all the color chips is sent to the mill; the printing inks are mixed and the colorways are evaluated *after* they are printed on the fabric. Of course production runs of yardage are possible only when the final strike-offs have been approved.

This method is another way of "pitching" colors and is especially valuable if a great many color combinations are necessary and time is short.

If the stylist is present at the strike-off, even the chart may be omitted and the color chips, representing the ground and printing ink, may be clipped together into groups and handed directly to the ink mixer. In the plant during the strike-off, existing mixtures of ink may be tried and experimentation produces unexpected and new combinations. Time limitations create pressure and a good stylist must remain flexible and open to new possibilities.

Color combinations are very satisfying to work with for the designer. If successful, the group will look integrated and the color combinations will be compatible with each other. Designers enjoy color combination assignments for financial reasons as well. And this phase of the work is one more aspect of the whole job of textile designing as a professional service to industry.

Free "blob" technique is also possible using dyes.

BUSINESS PRACTICES

The textile design industry in the U.S. is centered primarily around New York City. There are also several other areas where this type of work is being done. California and Hawaii have their own unique style, and some design work originates there. North Carolina, Massachusetts, Louisiana, New Hampshire, Pennsylvania, and New Jersey, are some other locations where textile designers are employed, usually working in printing plants. Occasionally they do original designing; more frequently their work involves repeats, colorings, and general service work. There are important textile design centers in England, France, and Italy as well as elsewhere in Europe and Asia. However, by far the greatest percentage of textile designing in the U.S. takes place in New York City.

PROFESSIONAL WORK ARRANGEMENTS

Designers work basically in one of two ways
- A *regular employee* (a full-time, salaried job)
- A *free-lance artist* (self-employed).

FULL-TIME EMPLOYEE

For a beginner it is usually wise to work as a full-time employee for a company (a converter or manufacturer), rather than to start off by free-lancing. There are several reasons for choosing this course. First, it is an invaluable learning experience. Inside an active establishment you can begin to sense the rhythm of the profession, get the feel of the marketplace, and how designs are originated and developed. You become familiar with the terminology; you pick up valuable technical skills and crafts.

Second, you begin to acquire the contacts among your colleagues that is the start of "networking"—people helping people. Being right there on the spot provides unexpected opportunities to meet and interact with management, stylists, salespeople, clients, and other artists.

Employed by a Converter

A *converter* is a company that "converts" *untreated* fabric—known as gray goods or greige goods, no matter what color it is—into *finished* fabric.

**The more you know . . .
The more you're worth!**

Ed Neuman

A freely painted abstract apparel design. (© FRESH PAINT STUDIO.)

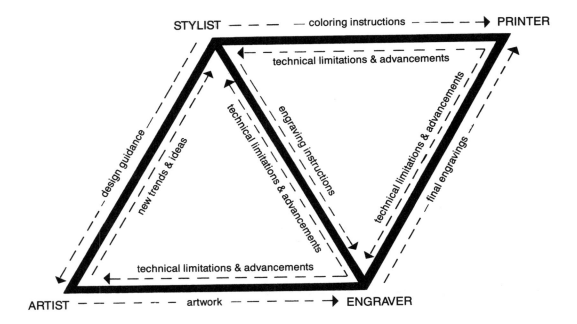

STYLIST — — — — — coloring instructions — — — — → PRINTER

technical limitations & advancements

design guidance

new trends & ideas

engraving instructions

technical limitations & advancements

technical limitations & advancements

technical limitations & advancements

final engravings

technical limitations & advancements

ARTIST — — — — — — artwork — — — — — → ENGRAVER

STYLIST:
Knowledge of Market and Style Trends
Knowledge of Available Production Equipment
Work with Salesmen
Work with Customers

ARTIST:
Creative freedom with constraints
Innovative new designs and trends
Knowledge of Market and Style Trends

ENGRAVER:
Makes print rollers, rotary screen rollers,
    flat bed screens and embossing rollers
Technical constraints of artwork
Knowledge of customer
Limitations of technology, equipment & methods

PRINTER:
Strike-off
Production Runs of Pattern

The interrelationships of artist, stylist, printer and engraver. (Courtesy of M. SHAPIRO of M.S. CHAMBERS & SON INC.)

Finishing includes bleaching, mercerizing, dyeing, and printing. They contract work out to one or several plants with whom they have ongoing working arrangements. Most converting houses will have a studio where some of their print designs originate. They may also buy a good number of their designs from outside sources such as design studios, and agents, as well as from U.S., Europe and the Orient.

Colorist   In a converter's studio, an entry-level position is likely to be that of *colorist*. With considerable direction from the stylist, the colorist develops sets of color combinations on already existing designs—sometimes to weigh in with the original, or sometimes to "change the look" (see **Chapter 9**). As the colorist becomes more proficient he/she will begin to find that color work is fascinating and stimulating and may eventually become a *color stylist* (see below, large converter and/or manufacturer).

Repeat Artist   This person puts into repeat whatever designs the converter is going to produce. The head designer or stylist will most likely oversee the work. The repeat must be correct in all respects, artistic as well as technical, because it is from this that the screens or rollers are made and the fabric is printed (see **Chapter 8**). A good repeat artist who can work with considerable speed is a valuable person in a busy converter's studio.

Designer   The designer is the one who originates the designs, usually after discussion with and direction from the stylist. Designers may be asked to show a few preliminary ideas; they may be given swatches, clippings or other reference material for guidance, or they may be asked to develop a collection independently.

Assistant Stylist   In addition to originating designs, a senior designer is usually responsible for the artistic quality of the work produced in the studio. This person approves the color combinations, checks repeats and layouts before they are put into work, and generally carries out the stylist's requirements. Stylists and senior designers work closely together; one could call this designer the *assistant stylist*.

Stylist   This is the person who determines what designs the converter will print as the "seasons" go by; in the vernacular, he/she "styles the line." It requires an awareness of fashion trends, contact with customers to gain an understanding of their particular needs, an instinct for predicting what will be the right creative direction to go many months in advance. The stylist reads the trade journals, studies the marketplace, meets with clients, attends fashion showings, may travel abroad for inspiration and perhaps to buy designs if necessary. In addition to all this, the stylist works closely with the engravers and tool-makers as well as the printers. The importance of this position is apparent since the stylist coordinates so many services.

Millwork The stylist or assistant stylist is often the person who does the *millwork*. This means traveling to the plant where the designs are to be printed, and approving (or rejecting) the *strike-offs*. A strike-off is a sample piece of yardage of a new design, which is examined to make sure it is correctly printed. The accuracy of the engraving is checked; nothing must have been omitted in the making of the screens or rollers. Any technical problems must be corrected, such as bowing, incorrect register, "bleeding" of colors, etc.

The colors must match the artist's original. A strike-off is made of each color combination. The design is translated from paint on paper to dyes on fabric and both the design and the colors are re-evaluated as they appear on the cloth. Engraving reports must be written. It is sometimes necessary to make many strike-offs before the final *standards* are approved. Only then can the design go into production. It requires a certain amount of experience and know-how to be successful at millwork and beginners should strive to acquire training in this area. Experience can be gained by accompanying the stylist to the mill.

Large converters and/or manufacturers—Burlington, J.P. Stevens, Springs Mills, to mention a few—usually have separate divisions specializing in high fashion and mass-market apparel, children's wear, men's wear, domestics, etc. There usually is an individual stylist for each of these divisions as well as designers, repeat artists, colorists, etc. Often one individual coordinates and directs the entire creative operation. Color stylists study the market and create the color image from season to season. There are obviously many more textile artists employed in such organizations, and proportionately more opportunities for entry level and other positions.

Employed by a Design Studio

Design studios are not connected in any way with the production of fabric, wallcovering or other finished goods. Their only product is the artwork—designs, repeats, colorings, etc. As a rule, textile design studios do not hire many full-time artists. Most of their designers work on a free-lance or commission basis, either from their own studios, or inside the design studio. However, design studios sometimes *do* employ a small number of full-time artists, from two or three to more, depending on how active and well-established they are. Frequently the owner of the studio also acts as stylist; he/she may be the salesperson as well, who communicates the needs of the clients to the artists. The "inside" artists—the ones who are full-time employees—are experienced professionals, capable of doing all phases of the work—color combinations, repeats, adaptations, and original designs. They may even occasionally be called upon to represent or accompany a client to do millwork.

If a designer is a full-time *employee* of a studio, all his/her work belongs to the studio. However, if the designer *free-lances,* even though the work is created solely on studio premises, all his/her work belongs to the designer.

When you are employed by a design studio, it is not considered ethical to free-lance for anyone else, unless there is clearly no conflict. These conditions should be stated clearly and agreed upon at the outset.

When you are employed by a converter, you will often have the opportunity to do additional work *for them* on a free-lance basis. This may happen during a particularly busy period, or when a "rush job" is required. Free-lancing *outside* the office for the same kind of market, when you are *employed* by a converter, is a questionable practice. But if the work for your employer is, let us say, bed-and-bath designing, it should be permissable for you to do free-lance designing for swimwear or other apparel.

In comparing employment in a design studio with employment for a converter or manufacturer: in a studio you are likely to be exposed to a wider artistic experience; you will have contact with more artists and designers from whom you can learn and with whom you can begin to share information and ideas. However, as a beginner you are likely to make less money working for a studio, and generally studios offer fewer fringe benefits, such as paid vacations, medical plans, etc.

Studios occasionally offer the opportunity to do free-lance work for them on your own time, and this can help to increase your income. You will rarely have the opportunity for contact with clients, to do millwork, or anything but artwork. For some artists this is exactly what they would prefer, and in time they may develop into highly skilled professional designers.

Working in the art department of a converter or manufacturer is a somewhat different picture. You would be paid a definite salary, and would qualify for certain benefits such as vacations, medical plans, retirement or profit-sharing. These vary from employer to employer and according to your standing within the company. You might be more likely to have the opportunity to advance within the company, starting as a colorist, moving to repeats and original designing as you acquire greater professionalism.

In time you may have contact with clients and the opportunity to do millwork, thereby broadening your experience and understanding of the industry and strengthening your position within your company. As in a design studio, here too you may have the opportunity to do free-lance work for your employer on your own time, thereby adding considerably to your income.

Against these advantages, you should weigh the likelihood that you would work within a more limited artistic scope, determined to a great extent by the range and variety of your employer's market. If your employer caters to the middle level within the fashion industry, you are hardly likely to design much on the leading edge of textile fashions. If your employer is a converter of apparel fabrics, you will not gain experience in designing wallcoverings.

GETTING FULL-TIME OR FREE-LANCE WORK

You have your portfolio in order; you feel you have the skills and talent; you're ready to set up appointments for interviews to show your work, to get a position or sell your designs. Where do you start? There are a number of resources available to you.

1. *Your school or college* undoubtedly has a placement service. Keep in touch with them. Their counselors are interested in helping you not only upon graduation, but later on, when you may be seeking to change your career direction.

2. *The classified sections of major newspapers,* especially the Sunday edition frequently have notices for textile artists. They are listed under several categories—scan the columns. You will find listings of specific positions as well as employment agencies that specialize in placing artists and designers.

3. The New York Telephone Company's *Business Classified directory* has a listing called "Textile Designers" where you will find the names of textile design studios. The categories "Textile Converting" and "Textile Consultants" also list firms that use the work of textile designers.

4. At most libraries you can find current copies of *professional and trade publications. HFD (Home Furnishings Daily)* and *WWD (Women's Wear Daily)* are the leading trade newspapers of their industries. (See the listing of publications in the **Bibliography**.) These publications periodically announce *trade shows;* it is a good idea to attend these when possible, for purposes of personal contacts as well as to keep current and informed about developments in the field.

5. *Professional organizations.* A very valuable source of help is the Textile Designers Guild, which is one of the disciplines within the Graphic Artists Guild. You will find them listed in the New York phone book. There are several branches in cities throughout the U.S., and a letter of inquiry to the New York office will provide information about this very important organization.

6. *School contacts.* Keep in touch with your fellow graduates who

Three apparel patterns from FISHER AND GENTILE.

may also be entering the textile design field. They can become an important part of the kind of mutual support system that exists within most professions. Your teachers and professors might be sources of help and information as well as people you have met in your explorations and research efforts.

7. *The New York State Employment Service.* The Professional Placement division has an extremely well-informed staff who keep current with prospective employers and can be most helpful. Phone them for an appointment. They will evaluate your portfolio, offer constructive suggestions and make recommendations and contacts for you. (Consult the phone book.)

Interviews

You have researched the many sources suggested and have worked up a list of names, addresses and phone numbers. What do you do next? An unbreakable rule is: *don't go there without an appointment.* Phone for an appointment being sure to get the name of the person to see, usually the stylist, assistant stylist or studio head. If you live some distance away, plan a day or a few days' visit, and telephone or write and arrange for several appointments and interviews during your stay. Again, make sure to see the right person within the organization.

If you are writing, send a copy of your resumé along with your letter. If you do not receive a reply within a reasonable time, it is usually worthwhile to follow up with a phone call.

Before the Interview   Check your portfolio to make sure the zipper, buckles or other mechanisms are working smoothly, so that you don't find yourself struggling awkwardly while your interviewer waits.

Prepare a mental list of questions that you may want to ask. These questions might be about the nature of the work you would do, who are the company's customers, where is the plant, working hours, future opportunities or possibilities for free-lance work. If the interview is for a position in a design studio, you may want to determine what materials are provided. (In some cases, the studio pays for all supplies; in others, they may provide paper and paints, while the artists bring their own brushes or certain other materials. This can be an important financial consideration.)

If your appointment was made by phone, have a fresh copy of your resumé available to leave with your interviewer. If you have business cards, make sure to take a few with you.

The Interview   Arrive on time, or better still a little early, but don't be surprised if you find that you have to wait. In a busy working day, unexpected contingencies can arise, and they may be "running late."

Neatness counts—in the portfolio and in the person. You are presenting yourself as well as your portfolio. Be friendly but business-like; don't feel that you must explain a great deal about your work. If the portfolio is neatly presented and in proper sequence, with only your very best work, it will speak for itself.

Interviewers' styles vary. One person may take considerable time leafing through your work. Others may go so fast that it may seem that they're not really looking at all. (Actually, with a practiced eye, an experienced person can evaluate a portfolio very quickly.) You might find that you are meeting with two or more people.

If you can sense a favorable reaction, ask to see the studio, the type of work you will be doing. The studio is the place where you would be spending a good portion of your time, and this might be one of the determining factors in your decision. Ask about financial and other benefits.

Situations that Might Arise   You may be asked to make your decision during the interview. Do not let yourself be pressured if you have any doubts about the position. You can indicate that this is an important decision for you, that you must consider all possibilities, and would like a little time. This is not an unreasonable request, and most potential employers will grant it. This would give you time to make inquires about the company, to follow through on other interviews you might have, and to think it out in an unhurried manner.

If you are a beginner or have limited experience, the interviewer might ask you to do a sample coloring, a set of colorings, a repeat layout, an adaptation or even a design to determine your ability for the position. This happens only occasionally. If you decide to do this, it should be understood beforehand that you are to be paid for your work at prevailing rates; if you are not paid, the work will remain your property, or it will be destroyed. Obviously you must protect yourself. This knowledge will come with experience.

You may be asked to leave your portfolio with your interviewer so that it can be shown to someone else. *Don't!* If it is at all possible, avoid this. Suggest that you would be happy to bring your portfolio back at a later time that would be convenient.

Another likelihood is that you may be asked to leave one or more of your designs for possible sale. Now you are functioning as a free-lance designer—selling your own work. If you decide to do this, get a signed receipt and include a brief description of the design(s) and the number assigned to each design. Set a limit on the time the design(s) should be held—preferably no longer than five days.

The interview may have gone well, you felt that the interviewer was favorably impressed with your work, and yet there may have been no job offer. It could be that there was no opening at that time; perhaps they had considered someone else to be more qualified. Take a few minutes to ask for suggestions as to how you might improve your portfolio, or whom you might see who could be helpful to you. Ask if you may contact the interviewer in the future or for possible free-lance work. Leave your resumé and/or card. It's possible that at some later time they will call upon you on the basis of your favorable interview.

For the beginner and the recent graduate of an art school, the best course to take is "get a job." That is, work for a company or a studio as a full-time employee and gain the necessary experience in industry to help you become fully professional. For the beginner to start off *free-lancing,* and on-your-own is more difficult. Your experience is more limited and your growth is slower. Working for a company is a good way to start.

FREE-LANCE DESIGNER

Free-lance means that you are self-employed. You are paid on an hourly rate, per diem rate, for each repeat and/or color combination you execute or for each design you sell.

Free-lance with a Design Studio

Design studios explore the trends and fashions in the marketplace, and suggest what types of designs they feel are needed by their clientele. They make the contacts with clients and present your designs along with those of other artists. Frequently the studio provides free working space for a number of their "regular" free-lancers in exchange for the opportunity to handle the artists' work. Others work in their own work places and come into the studio on a more or less regular basis. Design studios generally have flexible arrangements. You may find some artists working on a part-time basis; partly salaried and partly free-lance. An artist may start out with a tentative free-lance arrangement, soon find that the studio "feeds" enough work to make it full-time, and may eventually become one of the salaried artists.

If you're going to free-lance, there are some definite advantages for a beginner working in an active design studio. You are exposed to wider experience and more varied types of work. One week you may be doing juvenile patterns for infant's wear; next week it might be some traditional florals for upholstery, or a group of dramatic abstract patterns inspired by an Italian collection. You have contact in the studio with experienced designers; you receive close guidance in your designing efforts.

For their service, the studio gets a commission—a percentage of the

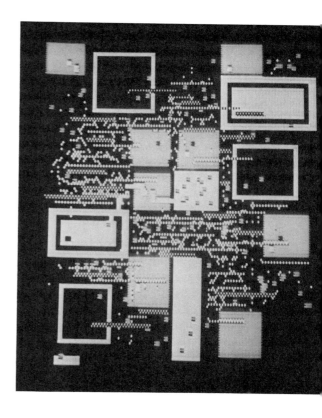

Computer-generated designs are increasingly being used in industry. (© RICHARD FISHER.)

amount of the sale if your design sells. Current practice is 35 to 40 percent to the studio, 65 to 60 percent to the artist. If you free-lance for a design studio, the studio acts as your agent.

Free-lance with an Agent

Another free-lance possibility is to work with an agent—an artists' representative who maintains a business office, *but not a studio.* Your work, along with that of other artists represented by the agent, is shown to prospective customers. A knowledgeable agent will be able to give you directions as to what types of designs may be required at any particular time, and will maintain active contact with the marketplace. You, as the designer will work in your own studio—which means providing your own equipment and materials. Agents may work with designers in other cities, sending clippings and ideas by mail, communicating by phone and occasionally meeting with the designer when necessary. The financial arrangements when working through an agent are just about the same as when free-lancing for a design studio.

Independent Free-lance Designer

If you do not want to work with a design studio, you may work entirely on your own, selling directly to the converter and bypass the services of a studio or an agent. What the designer would be doing then is trading time and energy for the agent's commission. It would require making the phone calls, setting up appointments to show your work, picking up and delivering, conferring with clients, studying the marketplace. It's interesting and stimulating but takes away from the time available for designing. This is usually not feasible for the beginner who may not have many contacts in the industry and has not yet had the opportunity to establish the above-mentioned "networking" contacts. However for an experienced professional, it can work—especially if a small number of clients can offer fairly continuous work.

FREE-LANCE VERSUS FULL-TIME EMPLOYMENT

In comparing free-lancing with full-time employment, we see a different set of pluses and minuses. As a free-lancer, one of the main advantages is that you are your own boss. You can set your own schedule, work at unorthodox hours, dress as you like in your own work space, etc. This sounds very appealing, and it can be a very satisfying way to work. But this is only successful for the designer who can be self-disciplined, can set a realistic schedule and stick to it—in other words, one who has a thoroughly professional attitude to his/her work.

However, the free-lancer's main disadvantage is the unpredictable income. Even highly experienced designers have to learn to handle rejection, because it is going to happen. Your work may be beautiful, but not suitable to the client's needs or it may not conform to a current "look." These experiences are not necessarily a reflection on the quality of your work, but rather the result of the vicissitudes of the marketplace.

You may have many weeks when your work is selling very well, followed by a few slow weeks. Some designers take up the slack during the lean periods by doing repeats and colorings.

As a free-lancer you will usually have to pay all your own expenses if you work in your own studio. This includes art supplies, rent and utilities, stationery, etc.; you will handle your own business and financial affairs, billing, recordkeeping, etc.

By comparison, as a full-time employee you have the security of a regular income, plus fringe benefits. You also have the opportunity to "see it from the inside." You can observe the hierarchy within the company, and how the people at various levels and in various functions interact with one another. You have a broader overview of the field.

A drawback in working with a company is the possibility of being

"type-cast." If you do a particular thing very well—if you have a good "tight hand," or are quick at matching colors, or have a knack for repeats—you may find that you are acquiring only limited experience, doing less designing or less varied designing than you wish.

Frequently a beginner's first job is not the ideal one. If you have stayed with a company for a certain period and sense that you have gone as far as you can, it may be time to consider your options. Sometimes a conference with your employer may open doors for further opportunities within the company. You may, on the other hand, feel that you'd like to try another area, perhaps in the decorative field rather than apparel, and broaden your experience.

For whatever reason, when you move from one employer to another you are increasing your knowledge of the field, learning more, and enlarging your circle of professional acquaintances. Job changes are extremely important. You can increase your income more rapidly and the more experience you gain, the more rewarding your work can be. Take your time, weigh and consider carefully and then make your career decisions.

Pricing Your Free-Lance Work

As a free-lance designer, you are always involved with selling your work, whether it is time and labor or an actual piece of artwork. Current practice is to sell each design work outright to a converter or customer. In the studio the owner usually sets the price in line with the going rates in the industry. If you are working as an independent designer, you can *ask* anything you wish, but most likely you too will establish prices that are in line with the going rates.

Pricing is a complex question since there are many variables:

• *Usage and re-usage* can influence the price in some graphic design areas such as packaging and photography, and should also apply to textile designs.

• *Per diem* rates can vary depending on the individual designer's experience.

• *Royalties* are perhaps the most just way of being paid for your design work, but this is still very rare in the textile design field.

• Special *time demands* (a rush order or work requested over a weekend) should increase the fee.

• A *unique style* or a high *reputation* commands a larger fee.

• The overall *size* of the artwork often commands a higher fee.

Scenic mural—marine life fantasy for panel wallcovering, 60" × 135". (© LINDA BUCHMAN.)

- Special *service* (working closely with a stylist, for instance, developing a line or a group of designs) can command top prices.
- *Research* and *other expenses* incurred on an assignment should be remunerated.
- The *type* of work and the *complexity* of the artwork (some techniques require considerable time), increase the price.
- The company's budget for the current line can limit the price.

Obviously prices can vary a great deal. The final prices must be negotiated between the designer and the buyer. A good way to learn the going rates is to refer to the current *Textile Designers Guild Handbook,* which contains a pricing guide for the graphic arts industries.

Special Order versus Speculation Work

Many free-lancers try to establish the practice of doing *special-order* work. This is work that has been specifically requested (a sure sale), and is contrasted to *working on speculation.* Working closely with a stylist or a manufacturer, the artist develops designs for a specific product. Usually there are clear directions from the stylist, or a mutual searching for new design possibilities.

Among the services that are always special-order are *repeats* and *color combinations.* These are usually executed after the design has sold. Occasionally, the originator of a design will also do the repeat; more frequently it is done by a repeat artist—someone who specializes in this work. When the original design is to be "put into repeat *as is,*" that is with no changes except those necessary to accommodate to the needs of the repeat, this is considered a *regular* repeat. When substantial changes are required—creating new motifs, changing the coverage or technique, or in other ways really altering the nature of the design—this becomes a *re-designing* project. The original designer should be called upon first, to make the changes, and be paid accordingly. If the original designer is not available, as in the case of designs obtained in Europe or elsewhere, or if the designer chooses not to do this, and prefers to delegate it to another artist, probably the repeat artist, this additional work should be reflected in the payment for the final repeat.

In the case of free-lance color combinations, the requirements should be made very clear at the time the work is assigned. If color chips or swatches are provided that are to be matched exactly, this usually requires more time and the fee should reflect this. Often the colorist is given the entire "pitch" for the set of colorings—usually worked out or approved by the stylist. When the colorist has acquired experience and a good working relationship with the studio/agent, this may not be necessary, and the artist is given more leeway. Still it should be made clear whether the combinations are to weigh in and if so, how closely; if not, just what color look the client requires—and any other necessary instructions.

It is common practice, when working on "spec," for free-lance designers to present designs that they originate on their own. But designers should not agree to work on specific projects unless they have an agreement that they will be paid for this work.

Special-order work is preferred by some artists, since all design efforts are paid for. Working closely with a stylist on specific projects assures a flow of designs that will be used by the manufacturer. However, some artists prefer to innovate their own ideas and develop their own collections and feel it is a truer expression of their creative thinking. It depends on priorities and individual preferences.

Free-lancing Ethics

We have discussed working on a free-lance basis when employed by a studio or a converter. Usually it is permissable for you to do free-lance work on your own time for someone else, as long as it does not conflict with your job commitment. You could not help but be influenced by the styling and ideas that are rightfully your employer's.

If you are a free-lancer with one studio, the same principle applies. The studio gives you directions and suggestions, which they have arrived at after research and study of their market. If they are providing you with the major part of your work, it is expected that you will not design for anyone else who serves the same segment of the market. However, a non-competitive area should be open to you. These conditions should be discussed and clarified as part of your working relations with the studio.

Knock-offs/Adaptations   A *knock-off* is a *copy* of someone else's already existing design. The practice is unethical and illegal. Regrettably, knock-offs (sometimes called bump-offs) are still done in the industry from time to time. If you are asked to do one, suggest instead that you do an adaptation, "like it, but different." If your employer insists on a knock-off, you should have a clear understanding that the employer will accept responsibility if legal problems arise.

Creating adaptations is an acceptable practice in industry. An *adaptation* is a design *similar* to an already existing design, frequently used to avoid making a knock-off or to substitute for a design already produced. Adaptations are more acceptable and are essentially a variation on a theme. It may be that a customer has a drapery in his line which is a good selling item. He now wishes to extend his line and asks you to do an adaptation of his own drapery, reducing the number of colors and the scale of the layout and motifs. Obviously there can be no objection to an adaptation of this type. And it is a challenge to a designer to create an exciting, new design that meets these parameters.

A variation of someone else's design is acceptable. Often studios will create a whole line or collection of designs inspired by a marketing direction or new look. This new look could have begun with one designer's work and a trend has begun. The only requirement is that each design be different enough and not look like a copy.

If you have created two or more designs which look very much alike and one of them sells, the others should *not* be shown to the competition. An artist has a responsibility to practice with high ethical standards. Building a relationship with clients in an atmosphere of trust, is a professional necessity.

Keeping Records as a Free-lancer or Consultant

An assignment usually starts with a discussion with your client. You will most likely be working with a stylist or a studio head—someone in a position to authorize this assignment. Now is the time for clear and full communication. Ask questions so that all details are covered; any instructions regarding color, changes, size or other special requirements. Write these instructions down or have the stylist write them. "Get it in writing" is a basic rule for successful business dealings, especially in free-lancing, and cannot be over-emphasized. Include the date of your meeting and the deadline for delivery of the finished work, and mutually agree that the details are correctly stated. We want to avoid the "telephone whispering game" syndrome where a word or sentence is whispered to a person next to you who, in turn, whispers it to the person next to him, and so on—until it comes out at the end—totally distorted.

When initially accepting an assignment, make sure your client understands and agrees that you want the original artwork returned to you since you are still the owner of that physical piece of design and its originality, and that you are selling only the *right to copy* it for his/her particular product. This is still a difficult aspect in your dealings with many companies today, since it is still common practice for the client to buy the design outright (all rights), and all future uses of it. Legally, you are *limiting the use* of your design. This means you are selling only certain *rights*. This should be followed up, when you bill the client. On your invoice you must state what the *limits of use* for your design are to be.

The importance of your own recordkeeping is discussed in **Chapter 7.** Keep a record of every design you produce. Work out a code or system to indicate repeats, colorings, etc., as well names of clients, date of delivery, payment, and any other data you wish to include.

A classic toile de Jouy look, rendered in one color.

Meeting Deadlines

Try to set realistic deadlines. This becomes easier as you become more experienced. At first give yourself more time than you think you'll need. A helpful guide is to estimate how long you need for this assignment and then *double it*. Often this is close to the realistic time it takes. But be flexible and willing to negotiate the time.

Now keep your side of the bargain. Follow instructions meticulously. Check to make sure you haven't overlooked anything. Keep in touch with your client if any questions arise during the execution of the work.

Meet the deadline. As a free-lancer, you are responsible for setting your own schedule. This can give you a feeling of freedom and independence. But it also requires a disciplined, mature approach to yourself and your work. Otherwise you will find that you are unable to complete the work as promised, asking for an extension of time, and generally functioning in an unprofessional manner. Perhaps one of the most difficult challenges a person can meet is to learn to be *self*-disciplined.

Your Client's Responsibility

Changes You have clarified all requirements during your discussion, and are working on the assignment. It may be that the client has second thoughts, or the client's customer has had a change of mind. Changes that are requested in such cases should be reflected in the fee for the work, and you should be allowed additional time to execute these changes.

Cancellation This can happen, too, through no fault of your own or of your client's. If you have met all the requirements stated when you accepted the assignment, or if the deadline date has not been reached and the work is unfinished when a project is cancelled, you should be paid proportionally for the amount of time and effort you have spent. An original design, even if unfinished, remains your property.

Payment Upon acceptance of the assignment, come to an agreement with your client as to the amount and time of payment. You can then expect that your client will keep her/his part of the bargain.

Business Forms

Many courses and seminars are offered in professional business practices. These are especially beneficial to self-employed people and free-lancers

These forms were reprinted from the Graphic Artists Guild Handbook: Pricing & Ethical Guidelines. *The forms may not be reproduced or copied without written permission by the Graphic Artists Guild.*

who may not have much business experience. The *Graphic Artists Guilds Handbook* is a valuable aid. It includes copies of suggested contracts, artist-agent agreements, confirmation forms, invoices, and more. Periodically new editions are published which include trade practices. The business forms printed here are self explanatory.

General Recommendations

1. When leaving designs with a customer, a studio or agent, keep careful records and get a receipt. This could be a *holding form,* or again one of your own devising. It should include your design number or code system, the code or number assigned by the studio, description, dates, etc.

2. Read any contract very carefully and watch out for arrangements that imply *work for hire.* This deprives you of any additional rights to your work, and is being opposed by the Guild as well as other artists' groups.

3. According to the Copyright Law (enacted in 1978) you automatically have a *copyright* on your work from the time you have created it. To protect this right, mark the work with the word "copyright" or the symbol ©, plus your name and the year. This can be placed on the back of the work, or on the front edge where it does not interfere with the design. Some designers have a rubber stamp made up with the © plus name and/or logo, and space for the year—for example: "© Dana Davis Designs, 1986".

4. *Billing*—at the time an assignment is accepted, the amount to be paid will have been agreed upon and recorded, along with other details about the work. You should present your invoice along with the finished work; common practice is to indicate that the bill is payable within a month.

5. As previously stated, it is becoming more accepted that the designer requests return of the original artwork. This is appropriate, since what the artist has sold is *use* of the design for a particular purpose. When first accepting any assignment, discuss with the customer the *limits* that the design will be used for, and then state the limits when you submit your invoice. The artist should have the right to retain the original artwork for display, use in a portfolio when job-seeking, for a non-competitive product such as a poster, or any other legitimate purpose.

6. Request production samples of your work (fabrics, wallcovering, etc.) for future use in your portfolio, for display purposes and general recordkeeping.

7. When working with *quantity orders;* do *not* reduce fees for large orders. Each design is unique and should not be undervalued.

When You Need Help

The above general recommendations are suggested as points to be worked out with your client. A good relationship with your client, agent or studio is necessary if you are to maintain continuous satisfactory business dealings. This is of mutual advantage to both parties: you need a steady market for your work, your client needs the kind of work that you produce, and with good will on both sides, most details can be worked out acceptably. This may require negotiation, which could mean that some compromises are made by both parties. Much has been written about the art of negotiation, and it would be wise to fortify yourself with some information in this regard.

- If you are not being paid for your work within a reasonable time.
- If your work had been lost or damaged by a client.
- If you are unsure about tax matters—income, sales or other.
- If your free-lance business is thriving and the paper work is growing.
- If you are planning to rent or lease studio space, sign a contract, become incorporated.

These are examples of cases when you probably need legal and/or financial advice. Avail yourself of the best you can get. Inquire among colleagues and friends; get in touch with the Graphic Artists Guild (or other professional societies); your local branch of the American Bar Association might put you in touch with groups of lawyers especially geared to the needs of artists. Some of these groups may have fees on a sliding scale, according to income.

CONSULTING

After considerable experience when you have acquired a high degree of professionalism, you may consider working as a consultant. You would function as a stylist or possibly as a combination of stylist and designer. For a small converter or a manufacturer who does not maintain an art staff, you would "style the line." You would become familiar with the needs of your client, do the necessary market research, determine the spectrum of colors to show for the season and market in question, and select the appropriate designs from studios and agents. In addition you would work with the engravers and be responsible for the final strike-offs at the print plant.

A variation of this is to work solely as a *color consultant.* This is sometimes done in conjunction with a fashion or interior designer; more often independently for converting houses.

This type of independent consulting service requires a background of solid experience in the industry, an ability to sense the trends and winds of change. You need a lot of energy, self-discipline and hard work, a certain amount of salesmanship, and the courage of your convictions.

Financial arrangements for consulting services may be based on a specific job or for a specified period of time (possibly on an hourly basis, for the season or for a year). Experience will teach you which is preferable in each case.

WORKING WITH A GROUP

Another option for an experienced, energetic designer is to work with a group on a cooperative basis. After a period of time—it could be a year, it might be a few years—you may have formed a circle of professional colleagues with whom you know you can work well. It might be that their various skills balance one another—one is a first rate colorist, another has an excellent tight hand, or is an outstanding floral designer; all should have, in addition to their special skills, good all-around designing ability and a practical understanding of the market.

The group could be comprised of as few as two or three people, or more. They must all be compatible, and willing to abide by the decisions of the group. A number of successful design studios that have been in existence for years have started in this way.

To ensure the success of such an enterprise, it must be handled in a straightforward businesslike way. Legal help is required to draw up the necessary documents for such a partnership or incorporation which would define the separate individuals' rights and responsibilities, protect the group in its dealings with clients, maintain proper accounting as well as all other business practices.

"WEAR 4 HATS"

Success comes for many reasons. An individual is more valuable and more able to do a total job if he/she is knowledgeable in various disciplines. If you combine skills in *art* with an expertise in business management, you immediately become more unique and more valuable in the job market. And if you add the understanding of the marketplace *and* technology your strength is even greater.

A stylist can wear the hat of a salesperson, but a salesperson, without training in design, could not be a stylist. It is more difficult for the salesperson to set a trend since he/she is not aware in a total sense, that is artistically aware.

Combine any two disparate disciplines and you are stronger and have a much greater chance of success.

DOCUMENT EXPERT

Documents from past periods and other cultures have already been discussed in **Chapter 4.** This type of reference material often is freely adapted and reinterpreted by the designer to give it a contemporary look or to fit a current market. For example, the "Art Deco" in the 1980s captures the flavor of the 1920s spirit, but with contemporary variations.

However there is a big demand for *true document work* which is *authentic* and *faithful* to the look of the original. It is important to work from the actual fabric or material rather than a photographic print of it. The new designs are as close as possible to the original and faithful in every detail. There may be fewer printing rollers and the use of traps might be necessary. The original may have 36 colors, the modern printing press is limited to 12 rollers and the final may have as many as 20 traps to be worked out. Technical know-how is necessary. The expert designer must know the periods of textile history as well and be able to re-create the missing portions of the document authentically. It is very demanding work and the designer must have a love and a sense for these treasures in order to re-create a *true* document for reproduction.

Document work and designers are desperately needed. A single design can take as long as four weeks to study and execute. Clients can wait six months or more for this service and prices go up because of the demand for this expertise.

DESIDERATA

Royalties

A much-desired arrangement although still hard to achieve is to be paid on a royalty basis. This means receiving a percentage of the profits earned by your designs and the designer's share can be from 1.5 to 5 percent. The designer should try to negotiate an advance on future sales at the outset

Kitchen wallcovering design of realistically painted vegetables. (© SUSAN LUTSKY.)

(payment "up front"). Royalties are very advantageous, especially when the designs are exceptionally successful and/or long-running. It requires a certain amount of trust and confidence between client and designer; this is arrived at with time and experience and a proven track record. A royalty arrangement is more likely in home fashions and other product areas than in apparel textiles.

Leading designers have long been fighting for royalties and equitable financial arrangements as well as greater recognition for designers. It is the responsibility of every designer to continue this fight so that royalties become a common practice in the textile design field.

Recognition

There is great satisfaction in making your living with your talent and skills, doing the work you enjoy. When you see your designs in use in a room, being worn, featured in a store display, a catalogue or a magazine, you feel a fine sense of accomplishment and professionalism.

However, these are your own personal, private feelings. After many years of successful designing, you become known within the industry, and your reputation can enhance your earning capacity. But it is all too rare that the *designer's* name appears on the selvage, has been mentioned for advertising or publicity purposes, or is in some way made known to the buying public. The person buying a dress or wallcovering almost never has any awareness that a designer created the design. In the apparel industry, the names of fashion designers are given great importance. But the artists who designed the prints remain unknown, even though they have helped to make fortunes for their companies. Textile designers need and deserve public credit and recognition, for personal as well as professional advancement, and this is an objective to be worked for. People should be aware that a human being created that design!

When you get started in the textile print design field, you begin to see how much more there is to learn. As in other industries, the textile industry is also undergoing change. Automation, computerization, new developments are constantly taking place. Business becomes more and more international, with worldwide competition for trade. As the industry changes, artists too, must change. It becomes more important to be informed and involved in politics, economics, technology, literature, the arts—all are important influences. Become a member of the world and what is happening, in New York, San Francisco, Dallas, Memphis, Paris, London, Milan, and Tokyo. Be totally aware of the present moment and never stop training, learning and growing.

Suggested Projects

*Textile print design products to experiment with have been outlined at the end of **Chapter 5**, pages 96 and 97. Do these first. Below are additional suggestions which can be used for building individual portfolios or for classroom projects.*

1.   Start a sketchbook
Get into the sketchbook habit. Make it an on-going effort. Record everything you see from cityscapes to household objects. Nature is especially important: wildflowers and garden flowers, leaves, textures of bark and wood grain, clouds, colors in nature, and light. Go to a museum of natural history or use books and magazines, study and sketch bird feathers, minerals and gems, seashells (shapes as well as patterns) and marine life, animal skins and reptile skins. Use pencils, markers, color pencils, pen and ink (black and colors) and paints (a small portable paint box with cakes of opaque and/or transparent watercolor paints is handy to carry).

"Never let the day go by without drawing or sketching."   Al Strausman, artist, designer, teacher

2.   Patterns from nature
Using the studies from your sketchbook and reference books as well, create a group of designs based on motifs found in nature. More subjects include wood grains, water, clouds, rock formations and plant life. With a microscope or a magnifying glass, study textures and patterns for design ideas.

3.   Documentary floral rendered in dyes
If there is a particular country in the political or cultural limelight (China for instance), research some documents of this country and design a floral croquis combining various motifs from different reference sources. Repeat the motifs with variations, use color either from the documents or update it with a more contemporary color look. Have a particular product in mind, perhaps bedsheets and pillowcases.

4.   "Window" Idea
Using a "window" or small square mask (see **Chapter 2, page 32**) and reference from a magazine or book, look for abstract layout ideas and motifs. Trace and repeat the image, rotate it, place it next to itself and extend the layout to full croquis size. Grid layouts based on a single square design can then be painted in any of the color schemes previously suggested in text. Rectangle and triangle masks can also be used.

5.   Designing with Lines
Create a collection with a printed-woven look. Using lines made with ruling pen (on prepared acetate) or markers and brushes (on paper) and using woven fabrics and photos of various weaves for reference, interpret these textures, simplifying them, enlarging them in scale, making them *graphic* (flat and printable). Use one to three colors.

6.   Quickies
Time yourself allowing only 1 ½ to 2 hours for a croquis. This will challenge you to be spontaneous and to work without reference or preconceived ideas. Try a black and white geometric or abstract design, 30 to 50 percent coverage.

7.   Change the technique of an existing design
A croquis painted flatly, in gouache could be repainted in a stipple dot simulating pointillism. Flower petals could be treated as a wash instead of flatly. A colored line could outline the motifs, a sponge texture could be introduced. Hard edges could be made soft and dry-brushed. Invent your own technique and experiment.

8.   For color practice:
Paint a color wheel, paint a value scale in black and white, paint a tint, tone and shade chart.

From a magazine photo, match the colors and paint stripes in approximately the same proportions of colors as the original photo. Use from five to ten of the dominant colors. Select a photo that has a strong color appeal to you.

9. Color combinations

Make a set of color combinations of one of your designs. Refer to **Chapter 9.** Try weigh-ins as well as "changing the look." A bright combination may be done in neutrals or an analogous color scheme and so forth.

10. Coordinates

Design some coordinates to your already existing patterns. Color ties them together. Try a simple linear stripe; try a variation of scale using only one motif of the original, try a new layout such as a border or a stripe made up of one of the motifs; explore a positive/negative (reverse) variation of the design or paint only a blotch of the original.

11. Do a repeat of your own design
See **Chapter 8.**

12. Design for other products

Work with products other than textiles. Surface designs can be created for *china, pottery, pots and pans, and pantryware.* Work on Plasti-vel or Denril which can be cut and mounted on the product with spray adhesive. Also work up ideas for *drinking glasses and plastic tumblers.* Paint in gouache on clear prepared acetate and slip it into a clear tumbler.

Paper products napkins, cups and plates, tablecloths and party favors can all be coordinated with color and design. The field of packaging also uses many surface design patterns.

Greeting cards are another important area for the artist.

Always research the market before you design.

Glossary

A

abstract Non-recognizable forms and layouts, as contrasted to floral and conversational motifs and designs. Examples: non-representational and geometric motifs, rhythmic and flowing lines, zigzags and angular shapes.

accessories Products worn as part of an ensemble, such as shoes, hats, handbags, jewelry, and scarves.

acetate A clear plastic film used with gouache. Caution: it must be *prepared* acetate which has a coating to inhibit beading and chipping of the paint.

achromatic See NEUTRALS.

Acrylic Artists' Colors Pigments suspended in acrylic polymer latex emulsion. Not commonly used in textile designing.

adaptation A design based on another design but sufficiently modified and altered to be considered new and different.

air-brush (ing) A technique for applying paint in a fine mist, using an air-gun to blow the paint onto a surface.

allover A layout in which motifs are fairly close and evenly distributed as opposed to stripes, borders, plaids, and engineered designs. Another term is *overall*.

analogous colors Colors that are close together on the color wheel.

apparel print design Textile designs created for men's, women's and children's clothing.

application printing See DIRECT PRINTING.

art deco A style of design popular in the 1920s with a strong geometric flavor.

art nouveau A style of design of the Victorian period (1890-1910) known for its flowing vine-like motifs and natural forms.

automatic screen printing A machine variation of hand screen printing. Also see FLAT-BED PRINTING. Fabric moves along under a series of screen printing frames. Dyestuff is pushed through the screen which has been partially blocked where the design does not print like a stencil. All operations are fully automatic.

B

backing Re-tracing on the reverse side of a design on tracing paper with graphite or chalk for the purpose of transferring the images to final paper.

batik A resist technique using hot wax to prevent dye from coloring the surface of fabric or rice paper in the areas where the wax is applied.

bayadere A design that is laid out in a horizontal direction.

beach sheets Towels that are larger than bath size and used as beach towels.

bleeding Color running or seeping beyond its intended edges, or migrating onto neighboring fabric. Not desirable, except in certain madras fabrics. When painting, certain gouache colors or dyes seeping through layers of overpainted gouache.

blends Fabrics woven with a combination of yarns having two or more types of fibers, *e.g.,* wool and cotton, cotton and polyester.

block printing The oldest form of printing known; a type of RELIEF PRINTING; motifs are printed with wooden, linoleum or copper blocks; a hand operation which is slow and produces small production runs.

blotch The ground color painted or printed around the motifs of a design. On paper it is painted, on fabric it is printed.

border print A pattern designed to run lengthwise along the edge of the fabric. A double border may have the same or different designs along both edges. A border print may appear by itself, or, more frequently, combined with other design material on the rest of the fabric (which is called the FIELD).

botanical Motifs which are realistic representations of herbs, garden plants, etc.; also designs based on these illustrations.

bowing The pulling of the filling, or weft threads during the printing process which can result in distorted, or "bowed" horizontal elements of the design.

bump-off Synonym: KNOCK-OFF. A copy of an already existing design with little or no changes; generally considered an unethical practice.

C

calico Small allover floral designs in bright colors originally from India and later associated with American country-style.

challis A fabric with a soft "hand", combining cotton and wool, wool-rayon-polyester or similar blends. Typically printed in florals, Persians, or foulards and used mainly for apparel.

check A pattern of squares which may be printed or woven.

chevron A traditional, woven design of zigzags in a stripe layout, also called *herringbone*. Printed variations are possible.

chintz Glazed fabric, usually cotton or cotton-blend typically printed in bright florals and stripes; most frequently used for drapery and upholstery, but also for apparel.

chroma One of the properties of color: its relative brilliance or dullness.

collection A group of designs that relate to each other by having a common theme. Each design is a separate and independent work but a unifying concept ties them together.

color combinations Painted color variations of a design, used as a guide when matching inks during the strike-off of a pattern; can also refer to the printed fabric. (In apparel, also called COLORINGS, in home fashions, COLORWAYS.)

colorings Another term used in apparel industry for COLOR COMBINATIONS.

color separation A process in which each color in the finished repeat is transferred photographically or by hand-painting onto individual sheets of acetate for the purpose of making print rollers or screens.

color spotting A step in determining the color balance within a design or repeat layout.

color tabs Blocks or strips of color painted on or next to a design or color combination, to indicate every color used for printing purposes. Color tabs are always shown in the same sequence, no matter how different the color combinations may be.

colorways Similar to COLOR COMBINATIONS but term is used primarily in home fashion field.

complementary colors Two colors that are opposite each other on the color wheel.

confined A pattern sold exclusively to one client for a specified length of time; a practice used mainly by converters.

conversationals Designs using recognizable motifs such as cups or toys, or combinations of motifs, including themes such as boating, circus, sports, etc. *Scenics* and *figuratives* are special categories of conversationals.

converter A company which purchases gray goods and contracts for the printing and finishing of the fabric. Being style- and market-oriented, the converter must respond quickly to the demands of fashion; also a person who monitors production steps.

coordinate designs Two or more designs that relate to each other in color, subject matter and/or technique and which are intended to be used together.

coordinate lines The guidelines which relate a repeating design to a printing cylinder or screen.

country look French, American or similar provincial style of design.

coverage The amount of area taken up by the design in relation to the negative space, *e.g.* dense, crowded or open, widely spaced.

croquis A French word for sketch; used to designate a fully painted design that is not in repeat. See SKETCH.

crow quill pen A very fine-line flexible pen nib used with various inks.

cruisewear Clothing used in the winter months and associated with vacation garments.

D

damask A jacquard woven fabric similar to brocade. The fabric is reversible and can be printed; used for drapery, upholstery, and evening wear.

decorative design Artwork created for bed-and-bath products, kitchen and dining room products, wallcoverings, drapery, rugs and upholstery, almost everything but apparel.

direct printing Also known as APPLICATION or GRAVURE PRINTING. Colors are printed directly onto fabric, paper or vinyl film. The design is etched into the copper surface, one roller is required for each color.

discharge printing A method of "printing" with a bleaching agent on pre-dyed fabric (usually medium to dark colors). The discharged areas may be left white and/or simultaneously printed with other colors. Also called *dye-and-discharge*.

documentary design A type of design based on visual material and documents from other cultures and past periods usually found in museums, libraries, and books; can be authentically reproduced or loosely interpreted.

domestics Products such as sheets, pillowcases, bedspreads, and towels.

dry-brush A technique of painting with only a small amount of paint in the brush; it produces a feathered, textured effect.

duplex printing Printing on both sides of the fabric with the same or different designs.

dyes For the artist, a concentrated watercolor medium; for the textile technologist, a specially formulated dyestuff used in printing fabric.

E

embossing A process creating a three-dimensional texture or design on fabric and other surfaces, usually with steel cylinders, heat and pressure.

engineered design A motif or group of motifs that are designed to fit a specific shape such as a pillowcase or placemat. In apparel, the layout of the design relates to the clothing pattern to be cut. These designs are non-repeating and are self-contained.

engraving The process of transferring a design to the surface of a printing plate using a sharp tool (burin or graver). In the textile industry it usually refers to the etching of the design into the surface of a print roller. The term has also come to be used when referring to flat-bed and rotary screens. See INTAGLIO.

ethnic Designs based on folk art or art typical of a specific nationality.

extract printing See DISCHARGE PRINTING.

F

fall-on See TRAPPING.

fashion In the world of clothing design and merchandising, this term implies the leading edge of innovation; in a larger sense, the term includes taste, trends, and customs within a culture as well as the style and look of various products.

figurative A type of conversational design using human figures.

field The area of a design that is *not* the border. See BORDER PRINT.

filling The horizontal threads or yarn in woven

fabric, running from selvage to selvage, as contrasted with the warp threads which are vertical. Another less frequently used word for filling is *weft*.

finishing Treatment of gray goods to produce certain results such as bleaching, washing, dyeing, embossing, glazing, waterproofing, or otherwise influencing the "hand," serviceability or appearance. Also see GRAY GOODS.

flat-bed screen printing An automatic printing method which uses a screen mesh to print designs; the fabric is moved while the screens remain stationary. Also see HAND-SCREEN PRINTING and ROTARY-SCREEN PRINTING.

flocking Fibrous material is applied to a surface electrostatically or by means of adhesive. Flocking produces a raised, velvety design, and may be used on fabric, as well as on wallcoverings.

florals Designs using flowers and can include nature motifs such as leaves, seed pods, and marine plants.

folkloric See ETHNIC.

foulard A silky fabric with a twill weave, typically printed in small traditional designs, popular for neckties, robes, and other men's wear as well as women's tailored clothing.

free-lance Working independently as a self-employed designer, as contrasted to working in a salaried position.

frisket A liquid masking material used as a resist. *Frisket paper* is a thin sheet of film used as a resist.

G

galvano screens Printing screens capable of producing tonal and photographic effects.

geometric Motifs and designs based on squares, circles, triangles, zigzags, etc.

gesso modeling paste An acrylic polymer latex emulsion and titanium white pigment, which when applied to art paper, produces a three-dimensional surface that can be textured while wet and carved when dry.

gingham Fabrics woven in a block or check effect.

gouache Opaque water-soluble paint most frequently used in textile design.

graphic Printable; for the purposes of printing. Graphic arts are those which are intended to be printed by one process or another. *Graphic* can also refer to a design with a bold look.

gravure An intaglio process of etching with acid into a copper surface of a printing roller; great detail and half-tone effects are possible.

gray goods Also called *greige goods*. Newly woven or knitted fabric in an unfinished state, ready to be *finished* by the converter; does not refer to its color. See FINISHING.

greige goods See GRAY GOODS.

ground brush A large, flat brush to paint backgrounds for designs.

H

half-drop The most frequently used layout for repeating a design in which the entire side repeat unit is repeated halfway down the side of the vertical measurement, in a brick-like formation.

half-etch A term used in apparel printing to refer to a half-tone effect.

half-tone A general term in textile print design referring to a lighter value of a color achieved by an etching process. *Percentone* is a more accurate term. The designer simulates half-tones by painting lighter values of the same color. See PERCENTONE.

hand **1.** An artist's individual style; the look of the design that is unique to the individual designer. **2.** The feel of a fabric.

hand-screen printing A printing method using a fabric screen mesh to print designs. The surface to be printed remains stationary and the screen is lifted and repositioned as the work progresses. Sometimes called silk-screen printing. Also see FLAT-BED PRINTING and ROTARY SCREEN PRINTING.

heat-transfer printing A method of printing with gravure rollers onto a coated paper with sublimable dyes. The dyes are later transferred to fabrics using heat and pressure. *Sublimable* means going directly from a solid to a gas (no liquid state).

herringbone See CHEVRON.

holiday A period in the fashion-apparel year after the fall-winter designing season, but before spring. Also see CRUISEWEAR and TRANSITIONAL.

home fashion The field of design which includes products such as draperies, upholstery, wallcoverings, rugs and carpets, sheets, pillowcases, bath towels, and bedspreads. Interchangeable with HOME FURNISHINGS.

home furnishings Interchangeable with HOME FASHION, dealing with products such as draperies, upholstery, rugs, used in interior design and decoration.

hound's tooth A two-color check produced by weaving in such a way as to form a kind of four-pointed star. Variations of the hound's tooth check are often imitated in printed patterns.

hue The outstanding trait of a color, referring to its place in the spectrum, *e.g.*, red, blue, purple.

I

ikat An ancient technique in which threads are dyed before the fabric is woven (a look similar to warp printing). Designers can paint a simulated ikat-effect.

intaglio A general term for the method of printmaking in which ink is transferred to paper from cut or etched marks in a smooth-surfaced plate. These "ink wells" are created *below* the surface with a gouging tool (engraving) or with acid (etching). See GRAVURE.

J

jacquard A method of weaving which permits great detail of design by individual control of each warp thread (or end).

K

knock-off   A direct copy or steal of another design (generally considered an unethical practice). Also see BUMP-OFF.

L

lamé   Any fabric in which metallic threads are interspersed.

laminate   **1.** (verb) To bond fabrics and other materials (foam, vinyl and paper). **2.** (noun) *Laminates* are materials that are bonded together.

liberty print   A particular type of small floral print, often using detailed line-work to delineate the motifs; originating with Liberty Ltd. of London.

line-up   Three or more motifs forming a straight line, horizontally, vertically, diagonally; not desirable in tossed layouts.

lucy   A projector which reduces and enlarges images; useful in creating designs and layouts.

M

madras   A plaid originating in India. Modified variations are created for today's market.

metallic   A property of paint with the look of gold, silver or copper; dyestuffs with the same properties.

monochromatic   One color but with many values and chromas.

monotone   A design using only one color.

motif   A single element or design unit which can be used again with variations within a croquis. For example: a flower, a cluster of flowers, an object, a shape.

N

negative spaces   The areas between motifs in a layout.

neutrals   In color theory, a term applied to gray without any color in it. Synonym: *achromatic.* In the fashion world of textile design, the term *neutral* usually refers to low chroma colors, muted colors or grays with a hint of color.

non-crawl   A liquid added to dyes, gouache, inks and clear water to make them adhere to water-repelling surfaces such as waxed Masa. (The same as *Wax-grip*.)

O

ombré   A shaded effect with gradual changes from dark to light in value, open to closed in coverage; also a transition in colors, lines or motifs.

over-all pattern   See ALLOVER.

overprint   Printing on top of already existing colors or designs.

P

packed   A layout in which the motifs are placed close together. Also see COVERAGE.

paisley   A stylized teardrop-shaped design originally on shawls from Kashmir and mass-produced in Paisley, Scotland.

pastel color   A color that is lighter than its strongest chroma.

pastels   An artist's medium similar to color chalks, occasionally used in designing.

patchwork   Originally pieces of fabric sewn together to make a quilt or pillow; a pattern simulating a pieced-together effect of different design elements.

pattern   The continuous repetition of a design as it prints along the length of a bolt of fabric, wallcovering material or other surfaces. (Not to be confused with dressmaker's *pattern*.)

percentones   A lighter value of a color made by engraving and printing a dot pattern instead of the solid color. On surfaces such as paper and vinyl film, tones can range from 10–90 percent, but 60 percent is the most commonly used. See HALF-TONE.

Persian design   A type of design using stylized floral shapes with complex detail and color, closely associated with the paisley-type; traditionally characterized by intricate detail.

photographic effect   A wash rendering in a design with tones from dark to light of a color. Also called WASH EFFECT or *watercolor technique.*

piece goods   Fabrics sold by the yard in retail stores. Also called *yard goods.*

pigment white   Opaque white paint applied onto a croquis; opaque white dyestuff printed on fabric.

pitching   Selection of colors for color combinations using a chart and writing in the names of colors desired. A variation of pitching uses actual chips of colors; also a term used when registering rollers in the printing process.

plaid   A woven or printed pattern of crossing bands or stripes of color. In woven plaids the colored threads are always vertical and horizontal, crossing at right angles. Plaids may also be printed, allowing for much freedom in interpreting the criss-crossing effect.

polyester   A man-made fiber or fabric. Also see SYNTHETICS.

polymer acrylic   A clear plastic latex emulsion. It may be added to gouache to make it more flexible and durable. Matte and glossy are available for special effects.

portfolio   A carrying case for designs; a collection of designs.

preppy look   A conservative style of clothing or design.

primary colors   Red, yellow and blue on the color wheel.

printing   The application of colors to various surfaces such as fabric, vinyl and paper. There are many methods of printing, for example: roller printing, direct printing, flat-bed screen printing, automatic screen printing, rotary screen printing, block printing, warp printing, discharge or extract printing, heat transfer printing, relief printing, resist printing.

R

recall The repetitive use of the same or similar motifs within a croquis or sketch. Variations in the motifs can include color, shape, weight, scale.

reference materials Any visual matter used as inspiration in the design process. Documents of other periods and other times as well as images of present cultures can be found in museums, libraries, books and magazines.

reference piece A duplicate segment of a design retained for various purposes: to be used by sales personnel and stylists while the repeat is being engraved; to make color combinations; and to have a record of the design.

regimental stripes Stripes of colors originally from British regiments and used primarily for neckwear.

register marks Cross-hairs or other guide marks used to align images or colors on two or more layers of tracing paper or acetate.

registration The alignment of colors to each other on the fabric during the printing process.

relief printing A method of printing in which the high parts of a stamp, linoleum block or other raised surfaces are inked and printed. In designing, the use of Artgum® eraser-stamps is a relief-printing technique (see BLOCK PRINTING).

rendering Another term for a finished croquis. See SKETCH.

repeat The technical layout of a design measured so that it joins to itself for the purpose of printing without interruption. Note: *repeat* is not to be confused with *recall* which is the use of the same or a similar motif within a sketch or croquis.

resist technique A method which uses a substance to block certain areas on paper or fabric that are designed not to receive dyes or paints. Wax, rubber cement and frisket are a few of the resist materials used.

roller printing A method of printing directly on fabric or other surfaces using a separate steel cylinder with an outer layer of copper in which the design has been etched, one for each color. Also known as DIRECT PRINTING.

roman stripe Bright, multicolored vertical stripes.

rotary screen printing A form of printing using nickel alloy screens formed into cylinders; dyestuff inside each cylinder is pressed out onto the fabric through the holes of the screen; a frequently used method of printing in the textile industry.

rubbing down A process of transferring an image from tracing paper to final art paper. The image on the tracing paper is retraced on the back and then rubbed down with the edge of a teaspoon or dull knife or other instrument.

ruling pen A drafting tool used with gouache, inks and dyes; can be used with a freehand technique or with a straight edge such as a T-square and triangle.

S

Saral® paper A transfer paper available in several colors, that works like carbon paper. See TRANSFER PAPER.

scale The relative size of a motif or layout.

scenic A type of conversational design of landscapes, cityscapes and various outdoor settings.

screen printing All printing using a mesh through which dyestuff is pressed onto a surface. Also see HAND-SCREEN PRINTING, AUTOMATIC SCREEN PRINTING, and ROTARY SCREEN PRINTING.

secondary colors Orange, green and violet on the color wheel.

selvage Closely woven edges along either side of fabric which prevents unravelling and keeps the cloth even.

separation See COLOR SEPARATION.

set layout The composition of a design in which the motifs are arranged as if on a hidden grid.

shades (as in tints, tones and shades) Colors to which black has been added.

sketch A formal rendering, usually in color, of a design idea. Also called a CROQUIS.

spatter A fine cloud-like spray of paint or dye usually applied with a toothbrush and scraper.

spectrum The band of colors produced when white light passes through a prism. For the purposes of textile design, the spectrum refers to the sequence of colors on the color wheel: red, orange, yellow, green, blue and violet.

square repeat See STRAIGHT-ACROSS REPEAT.

squeegee A rubber-edged tool used in screen printing for pressing the paste-ink across a screen.

standards The combinations of colors of a pattern that are authorized to be printed in production.

stencil A shield of paper or other material with cut-out shapes through which paint is applied to a surface.

stipple Dots placed closely together, applied with a pen, marker, brush or other suitable tool, creating a textured or shaded effect.

straight-across repeat A layout for repeating a design in which the entire side-repeat unit appears on a line directly horizontal to the left or right of the original design unit (as differing from the more frequently used half-drop). Also called a *straight repeat* and *square repeat*.

straight repeat See STRAIGHT-ACROSS REPEAT.

strike-off The initial printed samples of material used to check the accuracy of the engraving and to establish the standards of colors before going into production.

stylist The person who coordinates the work of designers, engravers, production personnel, and sales personnel and who is ultimately responsible for the selection and look of the line of products of a company.

stylized The modification or abstraction of a motif or design to give it a more decorative look.

swatch A small piece of cloth used as a sample.

synthetics Man-made fibers or fabrics made from these fibers, including nylon, dacron, polyester.

T

tartan Plaids originally woven for Scottish Clans but now any plaid with a similar look.

tattersall A simple open check or plaid.

tertiary colors Yellow-orange, red-orange, red-violet, blue-violet, blue-green, yellow-green on the color wheel.

themes Subject matter for designs or collections.

thumbnail sketch A small, usually rough drawing of motifs or layout ideas, used for quick visualization of a concept. Scale is usually smaller than the final rendering.

ticking A closely woven fabric frequently used for covering box springs, mattresses and pillows, typically in a simple white and dark blue stripe.

tinted ground A light color on paper on which the design is painted; a light color that is pre-dyed onto fabric on which a design is to be printed.

tints (as in tints, tones and shades) Colors to which white has been added.

tjanting pen A tool used in the batik process for drawing with hot wax. Also spelled *janting, djanting.*

toile (Toile de Jouy) Fabrics originally printed in Jouy, France, in the 18th c.—now generally associated with scenic picture designs, usually one color with the look of copper plate engraving.

tones (as in tints, tones and shades) Colors to which black and white have been added. Refers to the *chroma* of colors.

transfer paper A chalky-coated paper used like carbon paper to transfer images from tracing paper to final art paper. The most commonly used brand is Saral™ which is available in graphite and assorted colors.

transitional Mid-winter period when winter fashions and colors begin to be more colorful as they look toward spring; colors of this period.

trapping One transparent color falling on another producing a third color; the term is used in printing as well as designing with dyes. (Also called *fall-on.*)

V

value The lightness or darkness of a color.

vinyl film *Polyvinyl chloride* or *PVC,* a plastic film commonly used in wallcoverings and children's upholstery as well as automobile interiors. Other products include rainwear, placemats, shower curtains, and tablecloths.

W

wallcovering Any material used to cover walls; paper, fabric and vinyl film backed with paper or fabric are most common.

warp The vertical yarns in woven fabrics, running parallel to the SELVAGE.

warp print Printing on the warp threads of a fabric before it is woven. A simulation of this effect can be designed by using vertical lines. Also see IKAT.

wash effect A technique of applying paint and dyes while, at the same time, adding water, creating tones from dark to light of a color. Also called *watercolor technique or* PHOTOGRAPHIC EFFECT.

waxed rice paper Masa or other rice papers which are impregnated with paraffin.

Wax-grip™ See NON CRAWL.

weft See FILLING.

weigh-in A characteristic of a set of color combinations in which values and chromas are similar to the original. Only the hues change from combination to combination.

wet-in-wet A painting technique applying wet paint to an already wet surface creating a subtle blending of colors and tones. See PHOTOGRAPHIC EFFECT.

Y

yard goods See PIECE GOODS.

yarn dye Dyeing the yarn before the fabric is woven. Woven stripes and plaids are produced from yarn-dyed fibers.

Bibliography

The bookshops found in every museum in the country are an excellent source for reference books. Also public and private libraries are recommended.

BOOKS

Abell, Walter. *The Collective Dream in Art: A Psycho-Historical Theory of Culture.* New York: Schocken Publishing Co., 1966.

Albers, Josef. *Interaction of Color.* New Haven: Yale University Press, 1971.

Anderson, Donald. *Elements of Design.* New York: Holt, Rinehart & Winston Co., 1961.

Audsley, W. G. *Designs and Patterns from Historic Ornament.* New York: Dover Publications Inc., 1968.

Austin, Robert and Koichiro, Veda. *Bamboo.* New York: John Weatherhill Inc., 1972.

Ballinger, Louis B., and Thomas F. Vroman. *Design Sources and Resources.* New York: Van Nostrand Reinhold Company, 1965.

Bancroft, Peter. *The World's Finest Minerals and Crystals.* New York: Viking Press, 1973.

Bergher, Klaus. *Odilon Redon: Fantasy and Color.* New York: McGraw-Hill Book Co. (no date).

Bevlin, Marjorie Elliott. *Design Through Discovery,* 2nd edition. New York: Holt, Rinehart and Winston Co., 1977.

Bianchini, F., and F. Corbella. *The Complete Book of Fruits and Vegetables.* New York: Crown Publishers Inc., 1976.

Biegeleisen, Jacob I. *Screen Printing.* New York: Watson-Guptill Publishers, Inc., 1971.

Birren, Faber. *Principles of Color.* New York: Van Nostrand Reinhold Company, 1969.

Bossert, Helmuth Th. *Farbige Dekorationen: Beispiele dekorativer Wandmalerei vom Altertum bis zur Mitte des 19. Jahrhunderts.* Berlin: Wasmuth, 1928.

——————. *Folk Art of Asia, Africa and the Americas.* N.Y.: Hasting House, 1975.

——————. *Folk Art of Europe.* N.Y.: Hastings House, 1975.

——————. *Peasant Art.* New York: Hastings House, 1975.

Boucher, François. *20,000 Years of Fashion.* New York: Harry N. Abrams Inc., 1967.

British Textile Design in the Victoria and Albert Museum, London. 3 volumes. Tokyo: Gakken, 1980.

Brodatz, Phil. *Textures: A Photographic Album for Artists and Designers.* New York: Dover Publications Inc., 1966.

——————. *Wood and Wood Grains: A Photographic Album for Artists and Designers.* New York: Dover Publications Inc., 1974.

Bruandet, Pierre. *Painting on Silk.* (Available through Ivy Crafts or Sureway Trading Enterprises.)

Chaet, Bernard. *The Art of Drawing,* 3rd edition. New York: Holt, Rinehart and Winston Co., 1983.

Christensen, Edwin O. *The Index of American Design.* New York: MacMillan Publishing Company, 1950.

Christie, Archibald H. *Pattern Design: An Introduction to the Study of Formal Ornament.* N.Y.: Dover Publications Inc., 1969.

Clark, Fiona. *William Morris: Wallpapers and Chintzes.* New York: St. Martin's Press, 1973.

Clark, W. *An Introduction to Textile Printing,* 4th edition. New York: Halsted Press, 1974.

Cohen, Arthur A. *Sonia Delaunay.* N.Y.: Harry N. Abrams Inc., 1975.

Comini, Alessandra. *Gustav Klimt.* New York: Braziller, 1975.

Crawford, Tad. *Legal Guide for the Visual Artist.* New York: Hawthorn Books Inc., 1977.

——————. *The Visual Artist's Guide to the New Copyright Law.* New York: Graphic Artists Guild, 1978.

Crawford, Tad and Arie Kopelman. *Selling Your Graphic Design and Illustration: the complete marketing, business, and legal guide.* New York: St. Martin's Press, 1981.

Curtis, Seng-gye Tombs, and Christopher Hunt. *The Airbrush Book.* New York: Van Nostrand Reinhold Company, 1980.

Damase, Jacques. *Sonia Delaunay, Rhythms & Colours.* Greenwich, Connecticut: New York Graphic Society Ltd., 1972.

Day, Lewis. *Pattern Design.* N.Y.: Dover Publications Inc., 1979.

Doczi, Gyorgy. *The Power of Limits, Proportional Harmonies in Nature, Art & Architecture.* Boulder, Colorado: Shambhala Publications Inc., 1981.

Durart, Stuart. *Victorian Ornamental Design.* N.Y.: St. Martin's Press, 1972.

Enciso, Jorge. *Design Motifs of Ancient Mexico.* New York: Dover Publications Inc., 1953.

Encyclopedia of Textiles. by the Editors of *American Fabrics and Fashion Magazine.* Englewood Cliffs, N.J.: Prentice-Hall Inc., 1980.

Erdmann, Kurt. *Oriental Carpets.* N.Y.: Universal Books Inc., 1960.

Ernst, Bruno. *The Magic Mirror of M.C. Escher.* New York: Ballantine Books, 1976.

Escher, M.C. *The World of M.C. Escher.* New York: Harry N. Abrams Inc., 1971.

Evans, Joan. *Pattern, A Study of Ornament in Western Europe from 1180 to 1900.*

Fifty Masterpieces of Textiles. London: Victoria and Albert Museum, South Kensington, HMSO, 1951.

Franck, Frederick. *The Zen of Seeing, Seeing/Drawing as Meditation.* New York: Vintage Book, Random House Inc., 1973.

Froncek, Thomas, Managing Editor. *Arts of China.* By the Editors of *Horizon Magazine.* N.Y.: American Heritage Publishing Co., 1969.

Fry, Charles Rahn. *Art Deco Designs in Color.* New York: Dover Publications Inc., 1975.

Gibbs, Joanifer. *Batik Unlimited.* New York: Watson-Guptill Publishers, 1974.

Gleason, Kay. *Stamp It!* New York: Van Nostrand Reinhold Company, 1969.

Graphic Artists Guild Handbook, Pricing and Ethical Guidelines, 5th edition. New York: Robert Silver Associates, 1984.

Grohmann, Will. *Paul Klee.* N.Y.: Harry N. Abrams Inc., 1967.

Haeckel, Ernst. *Art Forms in Nature.* New York: Dover Publications Inc., 1974.

Haftmann, Werner. *Emil Nolde.* N.Y.: Harry N. Abrams Inc., 1959.

Harlow, William M. *Art Forms from Plant Life.* New York: Dover Publications Inc., 1976.

Hatton, Richard G. *Handbook of Plant and Floral Ornament.* New York: Dover Publications Inc., 1960.

Hartung, Rolf. *More Creative Textile Design: Color and Texture.* New York: Van Nostrand Reinhold Company, 1965.

Hicks, David. *Wallpaper, a History.* New York: Rizzoli International Publications Inc., 1982.

A History of Printed Textiles. Cambridge, Mass: M.I.T. Press, 1969.

Hofman, Armin. *Graphic Design Manual.* New York: Van Nostrand Reinhold Company, 1965.

Hornung, Clarence P. *Treasury of American Design.* 2 volumes. New York: Harry N. Abrams Inc., 1976.

Itten, Johannes. *The Art of Color: The Subjective Experience and Objective Rationale of Color.* New York: Reinhold Book Corporation, 1961.

Irwin, John. *Origins of the "Oriental Style" in English Decorative Art.* London: The *Burlington* Magazine, April 1955.

Irwin, John and Katharine Brett. *Origins of Chintz.* London: Her Majesty's Stationery Office, 1970.

Jacques, Renata and Ernst Fleming. *Encyclopedia of Textiles.* New York: Praeger Publishers, 1985.

Jaffee, Hans L. *Klee.* N.Y. & London: Paul Hamlyn Ltd., 1972.

Janson, H.W. *History of Art.* New York: Harry N. Abrams Inc.
Volume I: *Free-style Designs*
Volume II: *Geometric Designs*
Volume III: *Okinawan, Ainu, and Foreign Designs*

Jayakar, Pupil and John Irwin. *Textiles and Ornaments of India.* New York: The Museum of Modern Art, 1956.

Johnes, Raymond. *Japanese Art.* London: Spring Books, Paul Hamlyn Ltd., 1961.

Johnston, Meda Parker and Glen Kaufman, *Design on Fabrics.* New York: Van Nostrand Reinhold Company, 1981.

Jones, Owen. *A Grammar of Ornament.* New York: Van Nostrand Reinhold Company, 1972.

Joyce, Carol. *Designing for Printed Textiles*. Englewood Cliffs, N.J.: Prentice-Hall Inc., 1982.

Jung, Carl. *Man and His Symbols*. N.Y.: Doubleday & Co., 1964.

Justema, William. *Pattern, A Historical Panorama*. Boston: New York Graphic Society, Little, Brown & Co. Inc., 1976.

——————. *The Pleasures of Pattern*. New York: Van Nostrand Reinhold Company, 1968.

Kaswell, Ernest R. *Handbook of Industrial Textiles*. New York: Wellington Sears Company Inc. (West Point Pepperell), 1963.

Katzenbach, Lois and William Katzenbach. *The Practical Book of American Wallpaper*. Philadelphia: J.B. Lippincott Co., 1951.

Kemper, Rachael. *Historical Handbook*. New York: Fashion Institute of Technology, 1967.

——————. *A Short History of the Western World, Part 1 and Part 2*. New York: Kendall-Hunt, 1976.

Kepes, Gyorgy. *Education of Vision*. Vision Value Series. New York: George Braziller Inc., 1965.

Kleeburg, Irene C. *The Butterick Fabric Book*. N.Y.: Butterick, 1975.

Koestler, Arthur. *The Act of Creation, A Study of the Conscious and Unconscious in Science and Art*. N.Y.: Dell Publishing Co., 1964.

Kosloff, Albert. *Screen Printing Techniques*. Cincinnati, Ohio: Signs of the Times Publishing Company, 1966.

Larsen, Jack Lenor. *The Dyer's Art: Ikat, Batik, Plangi*. New York: Van Nostrand Reinhold Company, 1976.

Larsen, Jack Lenor and Jeanne Weeks. *Fabrics for Interiors*. New York: Van Nostrand Reinhold Company, 1975.

Lee, Sherman E. *A History of Far Eastern Art*. New York: Harry N. Abrams Inc., 1964.

Lewis, H.L. *Butterflies of the World*. Chicago, Follett Publishing Co., 1973.

The Liberty Style (All Colour Paperback). Introduction by Victor Arwas. New York: Rizzoli International Publications Inc., 1979.

Lipman, Jean and Alice Winchester. *The Flowering of American Folk Art*. New York: Penguin Books, 1977.

Loeb, Marcia. *Art Deco Designs and Motifs*. New York: Dover Publications Inc., 1972.

Lubell, Cecil. *Textile Collections of the World*.
Volume 1: United States and Canada. New York: Van Nostrand Reinhold Company, 1976.
Volume 2: United Kingdom and Ireland. New York: Van Nostrand Reinhold Company, 1976.
Volume 3: France. New York: Van Nostrand Reinhold, 1977.

Maier, Manfred. *Basic Principles of Design*. 4 Volumes. New York: Van Nostrand Reinhold Company, 1977.

Maurello, Ralph S. *The Complete Air Brush Book*. New York: W. Penn Publishing Corp., 1955.

McClelland, Nancy. *Historic Wallpapers*. Philadelphia: J.B. Lippincott Co., 1924.

Meilach, Dona Z. *Contemporary Batik & Tie-Dye (for cotton)*. New York: Crown Publishers, 1975.

Meilach, Dona Z., Jay Hinz and Bill Hinz. *How to Create Your Own Designs: An Introduction to Color, Form and Composition*. Garden City, N.Y.: Doubleday & Co. Inc., 1975.

Menten, Theodore. *Japanese Border Designs*. New York: Dover Publications, Inc., 1975.

Meyer, Franz Sales. *Handbook of Ornament*. New York: Dover Publications Inc., 1957.

Michele, Vincengo. *Minerals: Their Beauty and Structure*. London: Orbis Publishing, 1972.

Mitchell, Peter. *Great Flower Painters. Four Centuries of Floral Art*. Woodstock, New York: Overlook Press, 1973.

Mirow, Gregory. *A Treasury of Design for Artists and Craftsmen: 725 Paisleys, Florals, Geometrics, Folk and Primitive Motifs*. New York: Dover Publications Inc., 1969.

Morris, William. *William Morris: Wallpapers and Chintzes*. New York: St. Martin's Press, 1973.

Munsell, Albert. *A Grammar of Color*. New York: Van Nostrand Reinhold Company, 1973.

Nicolaides, Kimon. *The Natural Way to Draw*. Boston: Houghton, Mifflin Co., 1941.

Nihon Sen'i Isho Senta, Osaka. *Textile Designs of Japan*. 3 Volumes. Osaka: Japan Textile Color Design Center, 1965.

Nylander, Richard C. *Wallpapers for Historic Buildings, A Guide to Selecting Reproduction Wallpapers*. Washington, D.C. The Preservations Press, 1983.

O'Brien, James F. *Design by Accident*. New York: Dover Publications Inc., 1968.

Ostwald, Wilhelm. *The Color Primer*. New York: Van Nostrand Reinhold Company, 1969.

Parry, Linda. *William Morris Textiles*. N.Y.: Viking Press, 1983.

Perry, Frances. *Flowers of the World*. N.Y.: Galahad Books, 1972.

Pope, Arthur Upton. *Masterpieces of Persian Art*. New York: Dryden Press, 1945.

Proctor, Richard M. *The Principles of Pattern*. New York: Van Nostrand Reinhold Company, 1969.

Prueitt, Melvin L. *Computer Graphics: 118 Computer-Generated Designs*. New York: Dover Publications Inc., 1975.

Racinet, A.C. *Handbook of Ornament in Color*. 4 Volumes. New York: Van Nostrand Reinhold Company, 1978.

Reichman, Charles, ed. *Textile Printing Manual*. New York: National Knitted Outerwear Association, 1976.

Reid, Mehry Motamen. *Persian Textile Designs*. Owings Mills, Maryland: Stemmer House Publishers Inc., 1984.

Rewald, John. *Post Impressionism, Van Gogh to Gauguin*. New York: The Museum of Modern Art, 1956.

Rheims, Maurice. *The Flowering of Art Nouveau*. New York: Harry N. Abrams Inc., 1966.

Robinson, Stuart. *A History of Printed Textiles*. Cambridge, Mass.: M.I.T. Press, 1969.

Rossbach, Ed. *The Art of Paisley*. New York: Van Nostrand Reinhold Company, 1980.

Rottger, Ernst and Dieter Klante. *Creative Drawing, Point and Line*. New York: Van Nostrand Reinhold Company, 1964.

Rubin, William. *Dada and Surrealistic Art*. New York: Harry N. Abrams Inc., (no date).

Safford, Carleton L. and Robert Bishop. *America's Quilts and Coverlets*. New York: Weathervane Books, 1974.

Santangelo, Antonino. *A Treasury of Great Italian Textiles*. New York: Harry N. Abrams Inc., (no date).

Schindler, Maria. *Goethe's Theory of Colour*. Rev. ed. Sussex, England: New Knowledge Books, 1964.

Schwalbach, Mathilda V., and James A. Schwalbach. *Screen-Process Printing for the Serigrapher and Textile Designer*. New York: Van Nostrand Reinhold Company, 1970.

Seguy, E.A. *Exotic Floral Patterns in Color*. New York: Dover Publications Inc., 1974.

Shattuck, Joseph. *The Banquet Years*. New York: Random House Inc., 1968.

Speltz, Alexander. *The Styles of Ornament*. New York: Dover Publications Inc., 1959.

Spiller, Jung (ed.). *Paul Klee Notebooks, Volume 1, The Thinking Eye*. London: Lund Humphries, 1969.

Stix, Hugh, Marguerite Stix and R. Tucker Abbott. *The Shell, Five Hundred Million Years of Inspired Design*. New York: Harry N. Abrams Inc., (no date).

Strache, Wolf. *Forms and Patterns in Nature*. New York: Pantheon Books, a division of Random House Inc., 1973.

Sugden, Alan Victor and John Ludlam Edmondson. *A History of English Wallpaper, 1509–1914*. London: B.T. Batsford Ltd, 1925.

Teplitz, Irving. *Principles of Textile Converting*. New York: Textile Book Publishing Inc., 1947.

Tuer, Andrew W. *Japanese Stencil Designs*. New York: Dover Publications Inc., 1967.

Vasarely, Victor. *Planetary Folklore*. Greenwich, Conn.: New York Graphic Society, 1973.

——————. *Vasarely*. Neuchatel, Switzerland: Editions du Griffon, 1965.

Vedlick, Joseph. *The Ten Bamboo Studio, A Chinese Masterpiece*. N.Y.: Crescent Books, a division of Crown Publishers Inc., 1979.

Waterman, V. Ann. *Surface Pattern Design*. New York: Hastings House Publishers, 1984.

Wheeler, Alwyne. *Fishes of the World, An Illustrated Dictionary*. New York: MacMillan Publishing Company, 1975.

Whitford, Frank. *Kandinsky*. London: Paul Hamlyn Ltd., 1967.

Wingate, Isabel B. *Fairchild's Dictionary of Textiles, 6th edition*. New York: Fairchild Publications, 1979.

Wolberg, Lewis R. *Art Forms from Photomicrography*. New York: Dover Publications Inc., 1974.

Yasinskaya, I. *Revolutionary Textile Design, Russia in the 1920's and 1930's*. New York: Viking Press, 1983.

Trade Associations & Professional Organizations

American Printed Fabric Council, Inc. 1440 Broadway, New York 10018

American Society of Industrial Designers, 60 West 55th Street, New York 10019

American Society of Interior Designers, 1430 Broadway, New York 10018

American Textile Manufacturers Institute, 1501 Johnston Building, Charlotte, North Carolina 28202

American Wool Council, 570 Seventh Avenue, New York 10018

Color Association of the U.S., Inc., The, 200 Madison Avenue, New York 10016

Cotton Importers Association, Inc., 37 Wall Street, New York 10005

Cotton, Inc., 350 Fifth Avenue, New York 10016

International Silk Association of U.S. Inc., 299 Madison Avenue, New York 10016

Japan Silk Association, Inc., 385 Fifth Avenue, New York 10016

Linen Trade Association, 111 Fifth Avenue, New York 10003

National Association of Textile and Apparel Wholesalers, 350 Fifth Avenue, New York 10016

Society of Industrial Artists and Designers, Carlton House Terrace SW 1Y 6AB, London, England

Surface Design Association (Surface Design Journal), 311 E. Washington Street, Fayetteville, Tennessee 37334

The Textile Color Card Association of the U.S., Inc., 200 Madison Avenue, New York 10016

Textile Designers Guild, 30 East 20th Street, New York 10003

Textile Distributors Association, Inc., 1040 Avenue of the Americas, New York 10020

Vinyl Fabrics Institute, 60 East 42nd Street, New York 10017

Wallpaper Institute, 969 Third Avenue, New York 10017

Forcasting Services

These services predict trends in the fashion and textile industries (colors, fabrics, silhouettes and design), one to three seasons ahead. It is possible to subscribe to these services. They can also be found in some libraries.

FASHION FOLIO INTERNATIONAL • *Women's wear and men's wear* • *London*
Issued four times a year; predicts trends one year ahead; Covers all apparel, day, outerwear, sportswear, children's wear, evening wear, etc.

HERE AND THERE • *Women's wear* • *New York, Los Angeles*
U.S. ready-to-wear coverage; couture collection coverage; Japanese Prêt-à-Porter collections; Knitwear (Italian and French fairs); Fabric fairs: Interstoff-Ideacomo-Premier Vision-Prato fairs.

IM INTERNATIONAL • *Women's wear* • *New York*
Covers New York ready-to-wear and Milan/Paris designer collections (monthly). Issues color predictions for fabric and yarn 18 months ahead (semiannually).

KARTEN FOR KIDS (BETH KARTEN) • *Children's wear* • *New York*
Emphasis on looks for American mass market.

NIGEL FRENCH • *Women's wear* • *London*
Styling Issue; Fabric Issues; Interstoff Report; Knitwear; Prêt-à-Porter (Ready-to-wear). New York Designer Collections, European Designer Collections and Color Predictions.

PROMOSTYL REPORT • *Women's wear, men's wear and children's wear* • *Paris*

SEVENTEEN MAGAZINE FORECAST • *Juniorwear* • *New York*
Issued twice a year, Springcast and Fallcast.

SPORTSWEAR AND CLOTHES FOR LEISURE • *Women's wear, men's wear* • *London*
Issued twice a year; predicts trends one year ahead.

TOBE REPORT • *New York*
Weekly report. Covers New York market trends in apparel and accessories.

Papers Commonly Used in Textile Design

Name & Description	Sizes	Prime Media
Georgian inexpensive watercolor paper	35″ x 46″	Gouache
Bee #1120 watercolor paper similar to Georgian	10 yd rolls 30″, 36″, 42″ wide	Gouache
Seminole acceptable watercolor paper	18″ x 24″	Gouache
Carousel more porous than Georgian, softer	35″ x 45″	Gouache
D'arches (Arches) best quality 100% rag content—very durable surface cold press, rough texture hot press, smooth texture	29″ x 41″ Also in rolls #140 only)	All media: dyes, washes, gouache, pen & ink
Pastelle hard surface	26″ x 40″	Gouache
Strathmore #814 Watercolor paper for home fashion field	18″ x 24″ Also in rolls 36″, 42″, 48″ wide 10, 42, 48 yds long	Gouache, Pen & ink, Dyes
Coquille a distinctive pebble texture	18″ x 24″	Pencil, Dyes, Pen & ink
Waxed Masa a rice paper coated with paraffin wax	18″ x 24″	Dyes
Canson charcoal paper in different colors: white available in rolls as well	Sheets 19″ x 22″ Rolls 59″ wide	Pastels, Charcoal, Gouache
Coverstock two-ply, different colors	20″ x 26″	Gouache, Mounting designs

Beau Brilliant inexpensive watercolor paper	26″ x 40″	Dyes, Gouache
Fairfield Bristol two-ply, smooth surface	22″ x 28″	Pen & ink, Mounting designs
Becket Board smooth surface	20″ x 26″	Mounting designs, Gouache, Pen & ink
Oatmeal Paper unusual texture, but fragile	18″ x 24″	Gouache, Pencil, Watercolor, Dyes
Grandee strong textured surface in different colors	20″ x 26″ 26″ x 40″	Gouache
Flint Paper a high gloss surface, many colors	20″ x 26″	Gouache (add Sobo™ glue)
Morilla Board yellowish, with mottled surface	15″ x 20″ 19″ x 24″	Gouache, Pen & ink
Prepared Acetate clear transparent film	Pads (various sizes), Sheets 20″ x 25″ Rolls 40″ x 12 Ft.	Gouache, Pen & ink
Strathmore 1, 2 & 3 ply bristol—hot press smooth texture	22″ x 28″	Gouache, Pen & ink, Dyes
Strathmore cold press, rough texture	22″ x 28″	Gouache
Tracing Paper medium weight	Pads & Rolls	Pencil, Charcoal
Reeves Copperplate printmakers' paper	22″ x 30″	Gouache
Newsprint	Pads	Charcoal, Pencil, Markers, India ink
Strathmore Grande in colors	25″ x 38″	Gouache
Rice Paper very absorbant, sold under various names	25″ x 36″	Dyes
Vellum similar to heavyweight tracing paper	Pads & Rolls	Pencil, Pen & ink, Most media
Denril a plastic material smooth surface, translucent	Pads	Gouache, Pen & ink
Plastic-Vel vellum similar to Denril™	Sheets (various sizes)	Gouache, Pen & ink
Star White similar to Georgian	35″ x 46″	Gouache
Stonehenge printmakers' paper	22″ x 30″	Gouache
PMS colored papers	22″ x 30″	Gouache
Coloraid a chalky surface, rich colors	18″ x 24″	Gouache

Sources for Art Supplies, NYC

Most suppliers have a mail-order service. Write or telephone for catalogue.

A.I. Friedman Inc., 25 West 45th Street, New York 10036

Art Brown & Bros. Inc., 2 West 46th Street, New York 10036

Camco Art Materials, 165 Lexington Avenue, New York 10016

David Davis, 539 La Guardia Place, New York 10012

Eastern Artists Materials Inc., 352 Park Avenue South, New York 10010

Pearl Paint, 308 Canal Street, New York 10013

Plaza Artists Materials, Inc., 173 Madison Avenue, New York 10036

Sam Flax Inc., 25 East 28th Street, New York 10016

Utrecht Art & Drafting Supplies, 111 4th Avenue, New York 10003

Consult the Yellow Pages in other areas for other suppliers.

Sources for Painting on Fabric

Horikoski, 55 West 39th Street, New York 10018

Ivy Crafts Imports, 6806 Trexler Road, Lanham, Maryland 20801

Cerulean Blue, Ltd., P.O. Box 5126, Seattle, Washington 98105

Createx Colors Colorcraft Ltd., P.O. Box 936, Avon, Conn. 06001

Index